100 BULLETS: THE HARD WAY

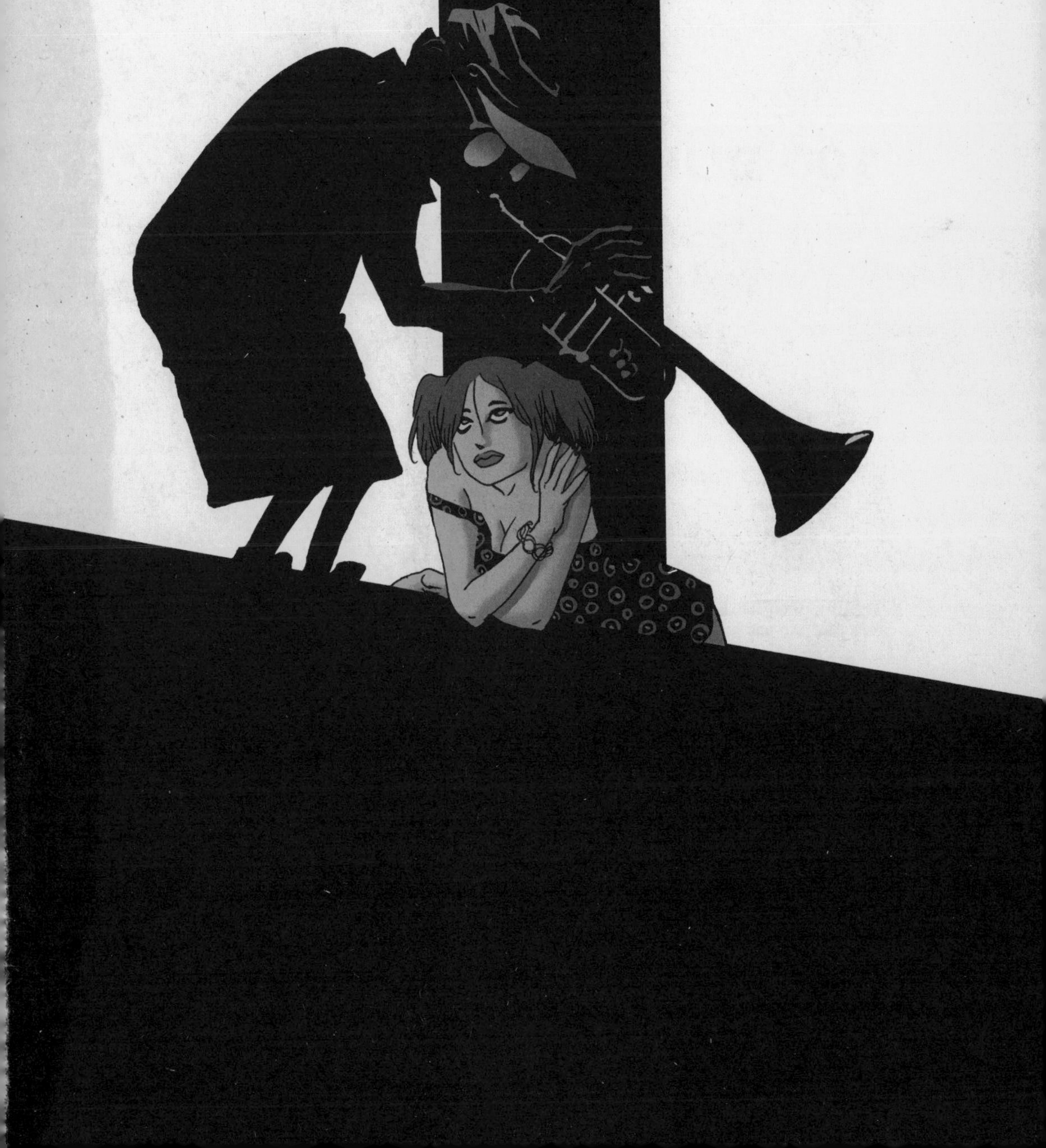

100 BULLETS: THE HARD WAY

Brian Azzarello Writer

Eduardo Risso Artist

Patricia Mulvihill Colorist

Clem Robins Letterer

Dave Johnson Original Series Covers

100 BULLETS **created by**
Brian Azzarello **and** Eduardo Risso

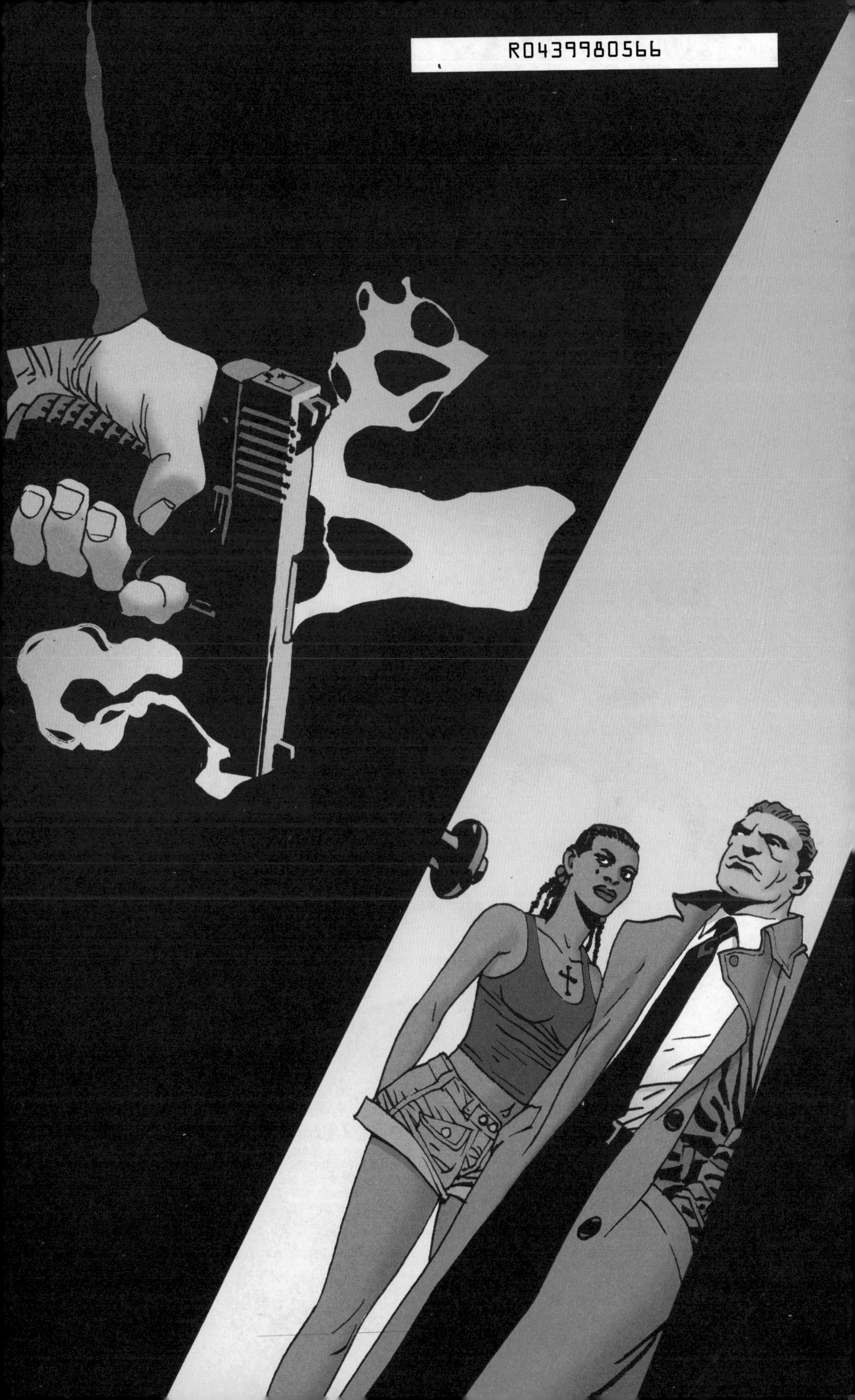

100 BULLETS: THE HARD WAY.
Published by DC Comics. Cover, introduction and
compilation Copyright © 2005 DC Comics. All Rights Reserved.
Originally published in single magazine form as 100 BULLETS
50-58. Copyright © 2004, 2005 Brian Azzarello, Eduardo Risso
and DC Comics. All Rights Reserved. All characters, their
distinctive likenesses and related elements featured in this
publication are trademarks of DC Comics. The stories,
characters and incidents featured in this publication are
entirely fictional. DC Comics does not read or accept
unsolicited submissions of ideas, stories or artwork.
DC Comics, 1700 Broadway, New York, NY 10019.
A Warner Bros. Entertainment Company.
Printed in Canada. Second Printing.
ISBN: 978-1-4012-0490-7.
Cover illustration by Dave Johnson.
Publication design by John J. Hill.
Special thanks to Eduardo A. Santillan Marcus
for his translating assistance.

INTRODUCTION BY JASON STARR

The best fiction — and art in general — stretches the constraints of its genre to such a degree that contemporary critics are unsure of how to characterize it. From the paintings of Vincent van Gogh to the writings of F. Scott Fitzgerald and Jim Thompson, history has been littered with the work of great artists that was disregarded or misunderstood at the time of its creation, only to be recognized later as truly groundbreaking.

In some ways, it's easy to dismiss 100 BULLETS as merely a series of comic books. It has all of the sensational artwork, hip dialogue and pure escapism that we expect from a great comic. But just because a work of fiction is entertaining, and reading it doesn't feel like homework, doesn't mean it can't be literary — and, while 100 BULLETS functions on one level as pure fun, it also happens to be some of the greatest neo-*noir* of our time.

It's unfortunate that *noir* has become such a murky word. Many books, films, and even albums are sloppily advertised today as *noir*. The entertainment industry, when at a loss for how to describe its products, uses *noir* as a synonym for "dark" or "dangerous" or "scary." In recent years, a broad range of fiction from mysteries to chick lit has been promoted as *noir*, and the Irish crime writer Ken Bruen has described this sort of proliferation as "*noir* light." This is no knock against the authors of these works, who often have no control over how their products are marketed, but there's no arguing that the clutter of *noir*-advertised material makes it harder for the public to recognize the real thing.

The term "*noir*," in respect to fiction, is derived from the term *film noir*, coined by French film critics to describe a certain style of American movies from the 1940s and '50s. Further exploring this newly defined genre, the French began to look at the works of such writers as Dashiell Hammett, Raymond Chandler,

James M. Cain and David Goodis — whose novels provided the foundations for many *films noirs* — and classifying them under the new category of *roman noir*. In France today, *noir* is still used to characterize a broad range of dark literature. In the United States, however, *noir* took on a much narrower definition during the late 1980s when Barry Gifford's Black Lizard Press began publishing writers such as Cain, Goodis and, most notably, Jim Thompson. The *noir* novels in most of Gifford's line had protagonists that weren't cops or detectives — at least not good ones. The plots focused on non-professional criminals, average Joes and/or losers who'd suffered bad breaks and were forever doomed and screwed.

Another term which gets misused as often as *noir* is "neo-*noir*." It seems like any book that is set in the present day and has any darkness in it at all is called neo-*noir*. But true neo-*noir* pays homage to the style and themes of previous *noir* works, occasionally taking on an in-the-know, tongue-in-cheek quality, while stretching the limits of the genre. Neo-*noir* is often lumped with other *noir* or crime fiction because, by definition, it doesn't fit neatly into the category. It's beyond the genre — something we haven't seen before. One of the first neo-*noir* writers was Charles Willeford. In his 1960 classic *The Woman Chaser*, Willeford took the familiar theme of a little man's quest for the American dream and spun it into a scalding sendup of the film industry.

100 BULLETS is true neo-*noir* in the Willeford tradition. The series is based on a simple revenge concept — a "little guy" is approached by the mysterious agent Graves and offered a once-in-a-lifetime chance to right all wrongs with a gun containing untraceable bullets. The person has a choice — to control his own fate or to let fate control him — and the decision he makes is inevitably the wrong one. It's a

fascinating premise in itself, but Brian Azzarello and Eduardo Risso use this payback device as a springboard to explore a broad range of issues and ideas which extend far beyond the usual constraints of the genre. The series has dealt with everything from drug warfare to a Hall of Fame baseball player, from Kennedy assassination theories to a warped history of the United States — not the usual themes that come up in most comics.

Like all neo-*noir*ists, Azzarello and Risso are very aware of past masters. For example, Wylie Times, the hapless gas station attendant at the center of this volume, is a tribute to Frank Chambers in Cain's *The Postman Always Rings Twice*. Milo Garret, the P.I. with the bandaged face in THE COUNTERFIFTH DETECTIVE, is an homage to Chandler and Hammett and to Vince Parry, the protagonist of Goodis's *Dark Passage*. There are many other references to Goodis's novels throughout the series, and to the work of such writers as Thompson and Willeford. Similar to how neo-*noir* filmmakers Quentin Tarantino and Robert Rodriguez occasionally take on the styles of classic *film noir*, '70s blacksploitation films and classic kung fu cinema, Azzarello's dialogue often contains "shout-outs" to past classics, and Risso's artwork revels in the shadowed images and dark urban settings often associated with *noir*. But while there are many homages to the past in 100 BULLETS, the series never approaches the level of parody — an important distinction. In the same way that hip-hop artists "sample" the works of past rappers, Azzarello and Risso take aspects of previous *noir* and mix them together with up-to-the-second lingo and modern imagery to create something entirely their own.

In this latest volume of their singular creation, an already white-hot series gets even hotter. Azzarello's dialogue has never been sharper or funnier than it is here, and his ungodly synergy with Risso continues to amaze. The main storyline approaches a climax as two of the comic's best characters — Wylie and Dizzy — get plenty of page time: Wylie is put in the very *noir* predicament of trying to determine who is responsible for his actions — himself for using the gun, or Graves for giving it to him — and we learn more about Dizzy's mysterious relationship with Shepherd. The back-and-forth between Wylie and Dizzy, two truly lost souls, is hilarious and heartbreaking, and Risso creates a bleak, despairing New Orleans landscape with no Mardi Gras in sight. This volume also gives us one of the series' most moving characters in Gabe, a trumpet player who is living in a hell of ugliness, with music as his lone salvation.

100 BULLETS has a resonance that few comics — or novels, for that matter — can match. Its desperate, fateful characters linger with us for days and haunt us at night. This is, without a doubt, the crack cocaine of crime fiction — exhilarating, dangerous, and painfully addictive. It also may be an early glimpse into the future of *noir*.

— Jason Starr

JASON STARR is the author of six crime novels which have been published in nine languages. His novel **Tough Luck** *won the 2004 Barry Award for Best Paperback Original and was nominated for the 2004 Anthony Award for Best Paperback Original. His latest novel,* **Twisted City**, *is available from Vintage Crime/Black Lizard.*

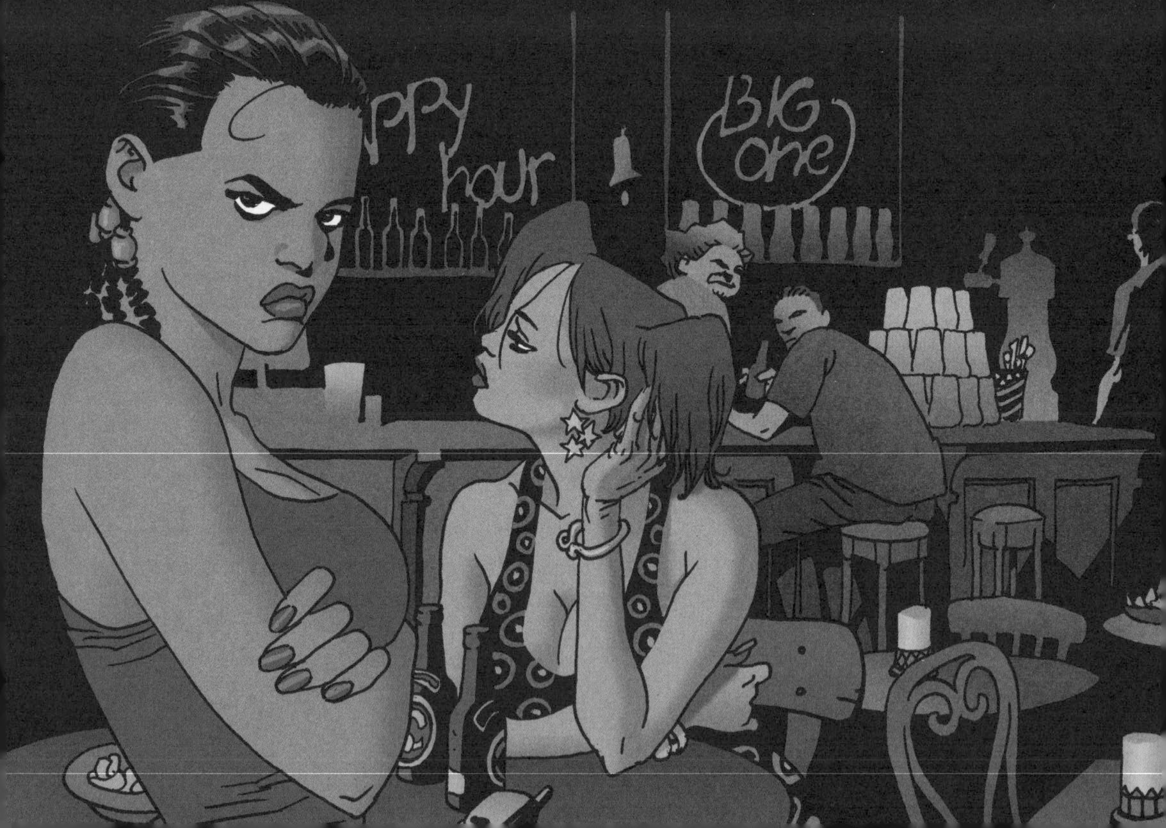
hour
BIG one

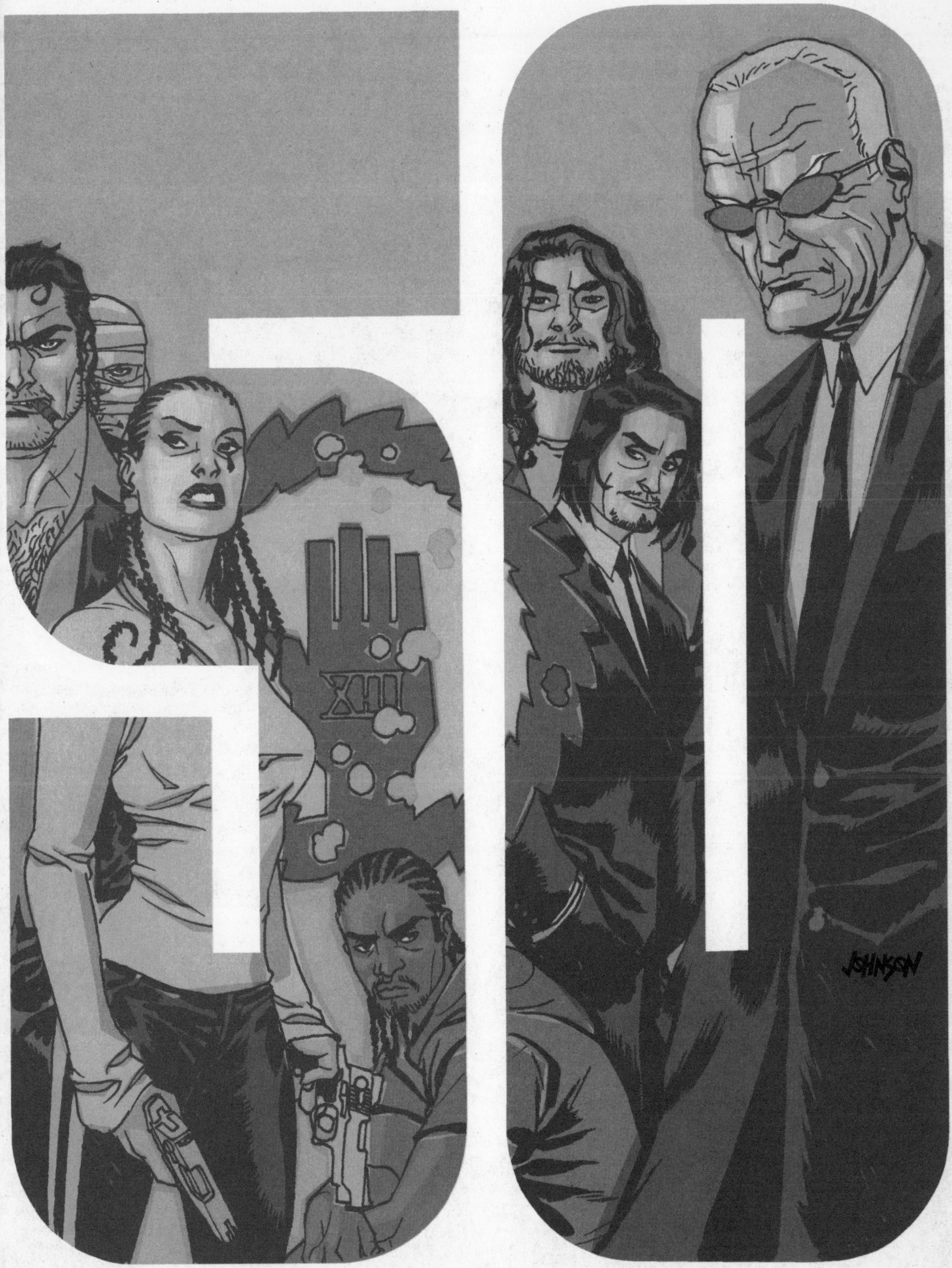
XIII
JOHNSON

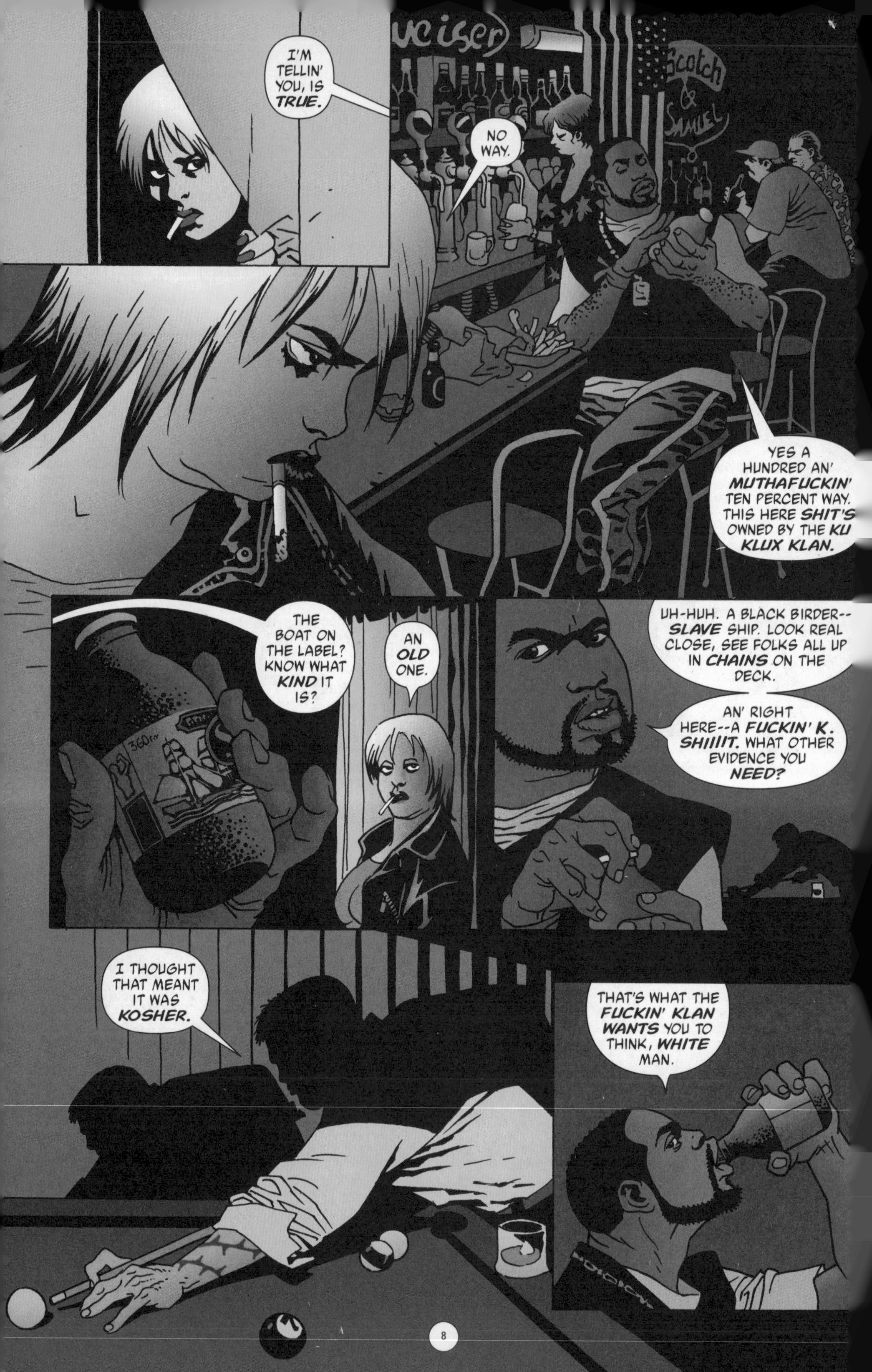
I'M TELLIN' YOU, IS TRUE.
NO WAY.
YES A HUNDRED AN' MUTHAFUCKIN' TEN PERCENT WAY. THIS HERE SHIT'S OWNED BY THE KU KLUX KLAN.
THE BOAT ON THE LABEL? KNOW WHAT KIND IT IS?
AN OLD ONE.
UH-HUH. A BLACK BIRDER--SLAVE SHIP. LOOK REAL CLOSE, SEE FOLKS ALL UP IN CHAINS ON THE DECK.
AN' RIGHT HERE--A FUCKIN' K. SHIIIIT. WHAT OTHER EVIDENCE YOU NEED?
I THOUGHT THAT MEANT IT WAS KOSHER.
THAT'S WHAT THE FUCKIN' KLAN WANTS YOU TO THINK, WHITE MAN.

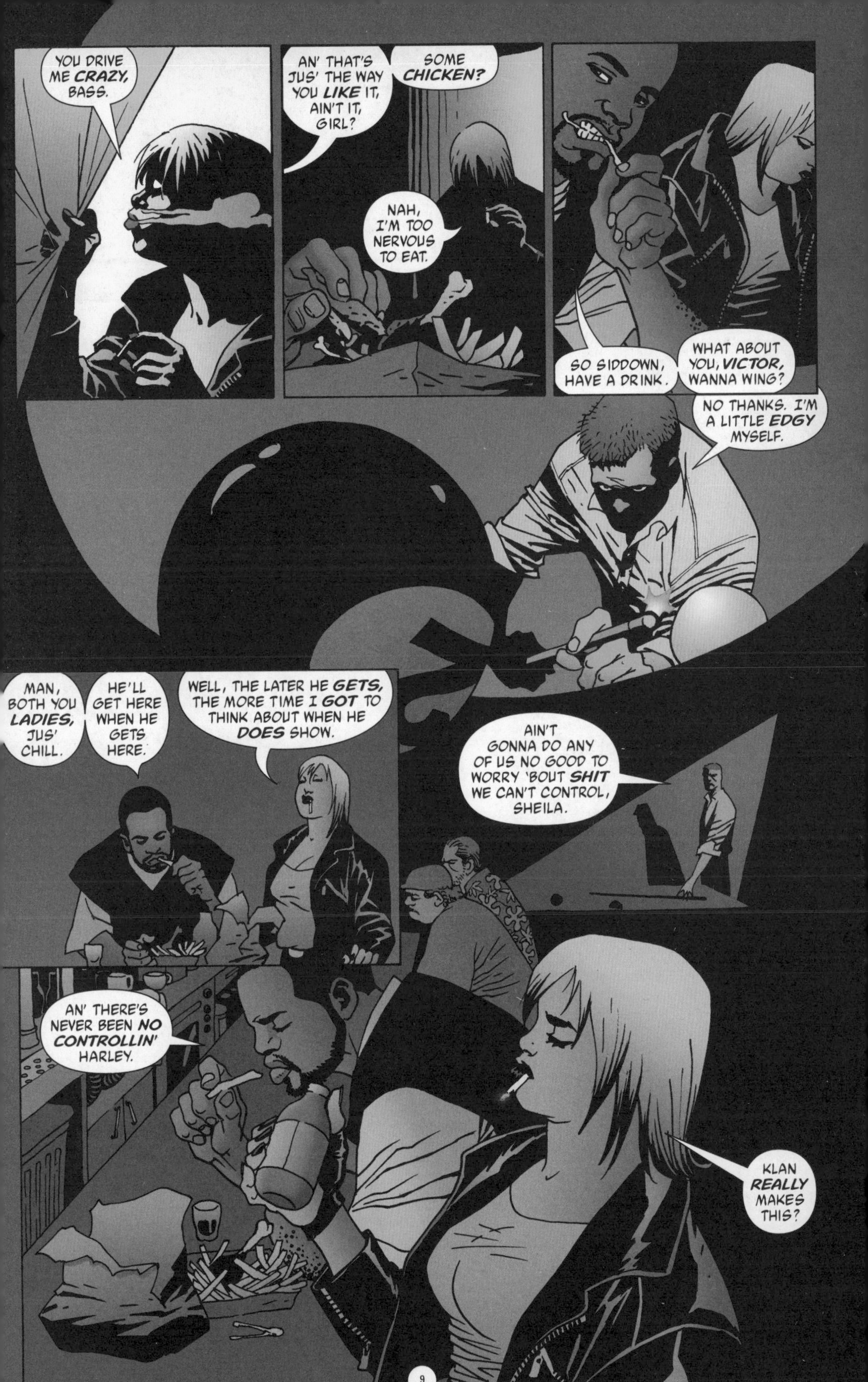

YOU DRIVE ME **CRAZY,** BASS.
AN' THAT'S JUS' THE WAY YOU **LIKE** IT, AIN'T IT, GIRL?
SOME **CHICKEN?**
NAH, I'M TOO NERVOUS TO EAT.
SO SIDDOWN, HAVE A DRINK.
WHAT ABOUT YOU, **VICTOR,** WANNA WING?
NO THANKS. I'M A LITTLE **EDGY** MYSELF.
MAN, BOTH YOU **LADIES,** JUS' CHILL.
HE'LL GET HERE WHEN HE GETS HERE.
WELL, THE LATER HE **GETS,** THE MORE TIME **I GOT** TO THINK ABOUT WHEN HE **DOES** SHOW.
AIN'T GONNA DO ANY OF US NO GOOD TO WORRY 'BOUT **SHIT** WE CAN'T CONTROL, SHEILA.
AN' THERE'S NEVER BEEN **NO CONTROLLIN'** HARLEY.
KLAN **REALLY** MAKES THIS?

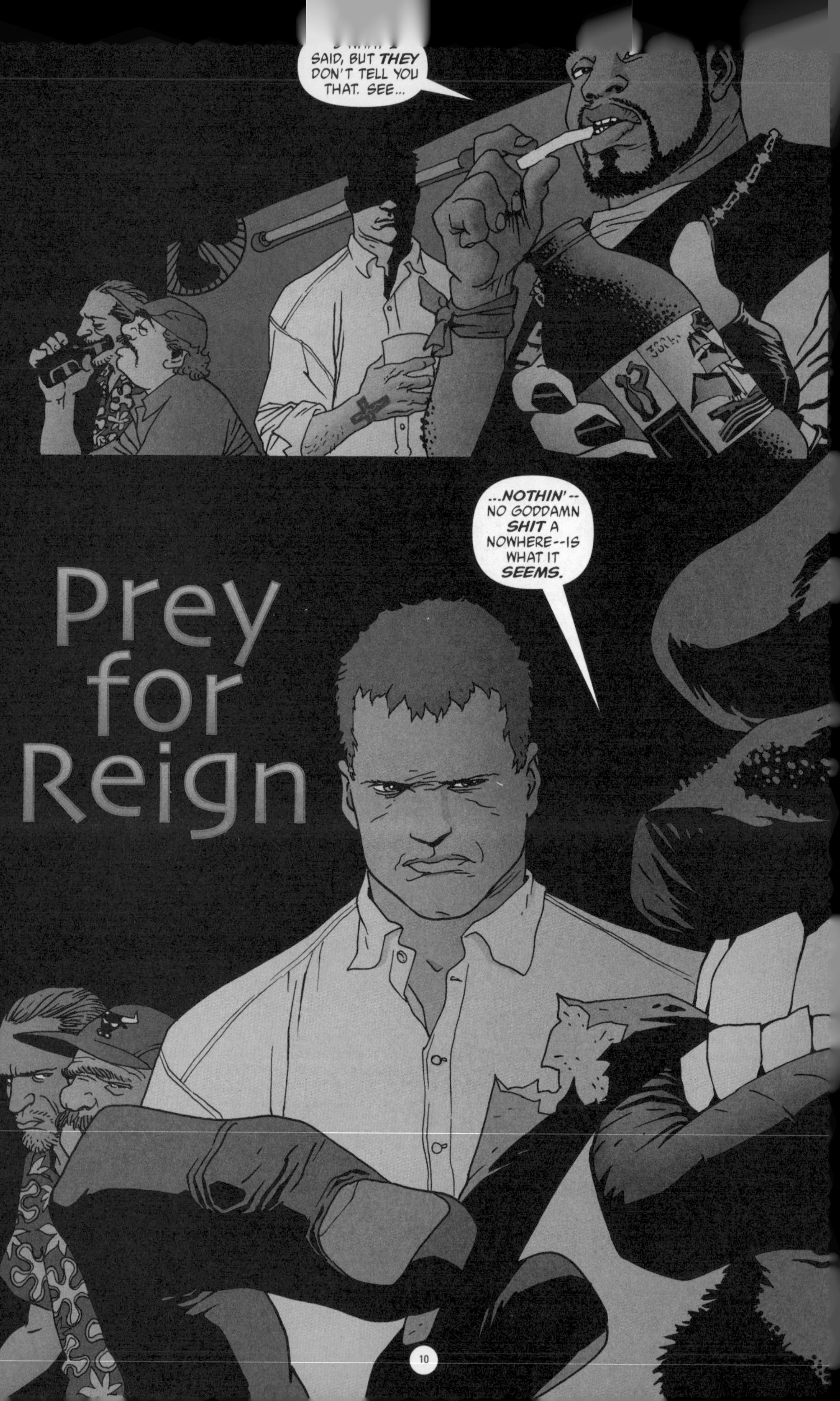
SAID, BUT **THEY** DON'T TELL YOU THAT. SEE...
...**NOTHIN'**-- NO GODDAMN **SHIT** A NOWHERE--IS WHAT IT **SEEMS.**
Prey for Reign

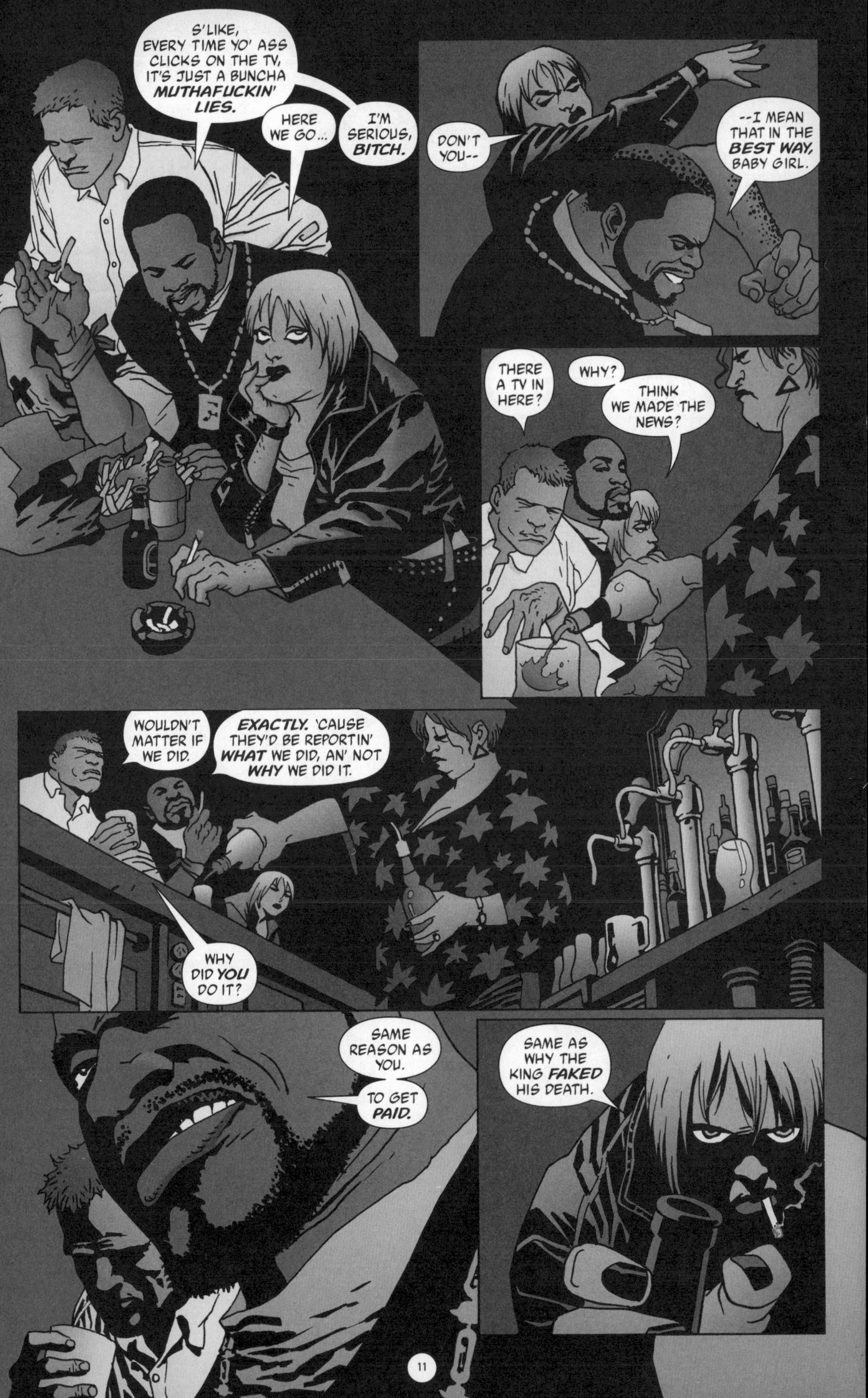
S'LIKE, EVERY TIME YO' ASS CLICKS ON THE TV, IT'S JUST A BUNCHA **MUTHAFUCKIN'** **LIES.**
HERE WE GO...
I'M SERIOUS, **BITCH.**
DON'T YOU--
--I MEAN THAT IN THE **BEST WAY,** BABY GIRL.
THERE A TV IN HERE?
WHY?
THINK WE MADE THE NEWS?
WOULDN'T MATTER IF WE DID.
EXACTLY. 'CAUSE THEY'D BE REPORTIN' **WHAT** WE DID, AN' NOT **WHY** WE DID IT.
WHY DID **YOU** DO IT?
SAME REASON AS YOU.
TO GET **PAID.**
SAME AS WHY THE KING **FAKED** HIS DEATH.

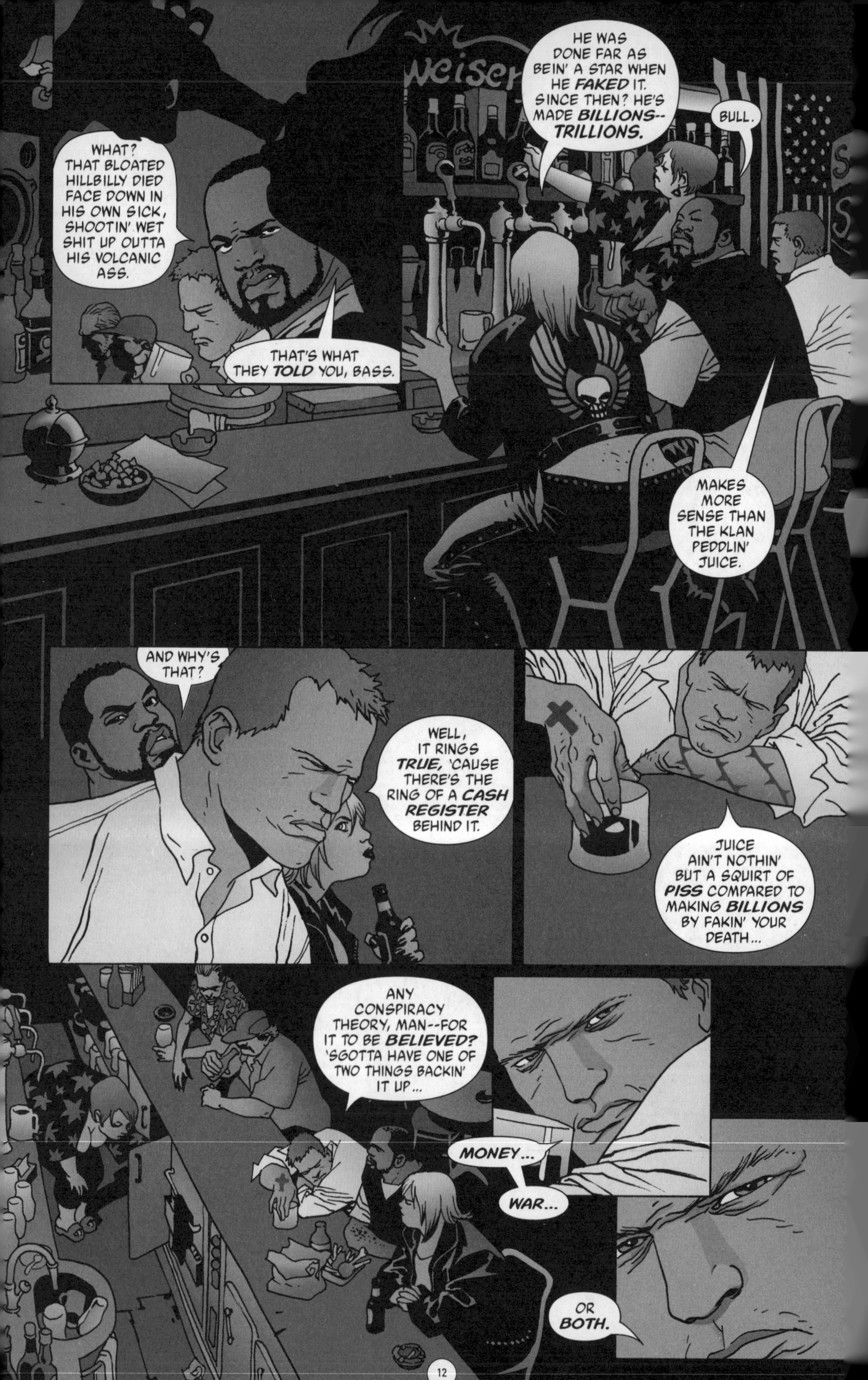
WHAT? THAT BLOATED HILLBILLY DIED FACE DOWN IN HIS OWN SICK, SHOOTIN' WET SHIT UP OUTTA HIS VOLCANIC ASS.
THAT'S WHAT THEY TOLD YOU, BASS.
HE WAS DONE FAR AS BEIN' A STAR WHEN HE FAKED IT. SINCE THEN? HE'S MADE BILLIONS-- TRILLIONS.
BULL.
MAKES MORE SENSE THAN THE KLAN PEDDLIN' JUICE.
AND WHY'S THAT?
WELL, IT RINGS TRUE, 'CAUSE THERE'S THE RING OF A CASH REGISTER BEHIND IT.
JUICE AIN'T NOTHIN' BUT A SQUIRT OF PISS COMPARED TO MAKING BILLIONS BY FAKIN' YOUR DEATH...
ANY CONSPIRACY THEORY, MAN--FOR IT TO BE BELIEVED? 'SGOTTA HAVE ONE OF TWO THINGS BACKIN' IT UP...
MONEY...
WAR...
OR BOTH.

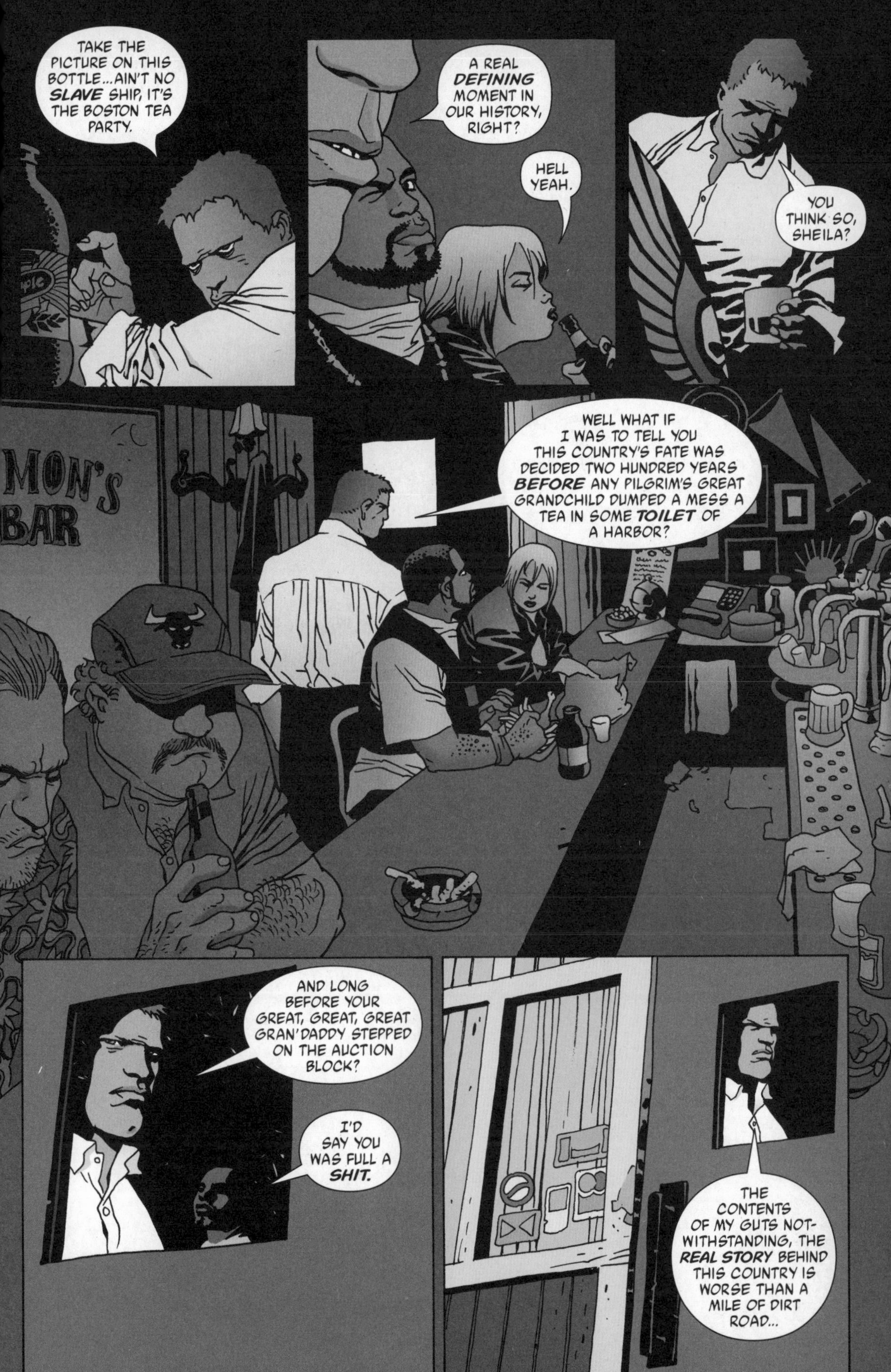
TAKE THE PICTURE ON THIS BOTTLE...AIN'T NO SLAVE SHIP, IT'S THE BOSTON TEA PARTY.
A REAL DEFINING MOMENT IN OUR HISTORY, RIGHT?
HELL YEAH.
YOU THINK SO, SHEILA?
MON'S BAR
WELL WHAT IF I WAS TO TELL YOU THIS COUNTRY'S FATE WAS DECIDED TWO HUNDRED YEARS BEFORE ANY PILGRIM'S GREAT GRANDCHILD DUMPED A MESS A TEA IN SOME TOILET OF A HARBOR?
AND LONG BEFORE YOUR GREAT, GREAT, GREAT GRAN'DADDY STEPPED ON THE AUCTION BLOCK?
I'D SAY YOU WAS FULL A SHIT.
THE CONTENTS OF MY GUTS NOT-WITHSTANDING, THE REAL STORY BEHIND THIS COUNTRY IS WORSE THAN A MILE OF DIRT ROAD...

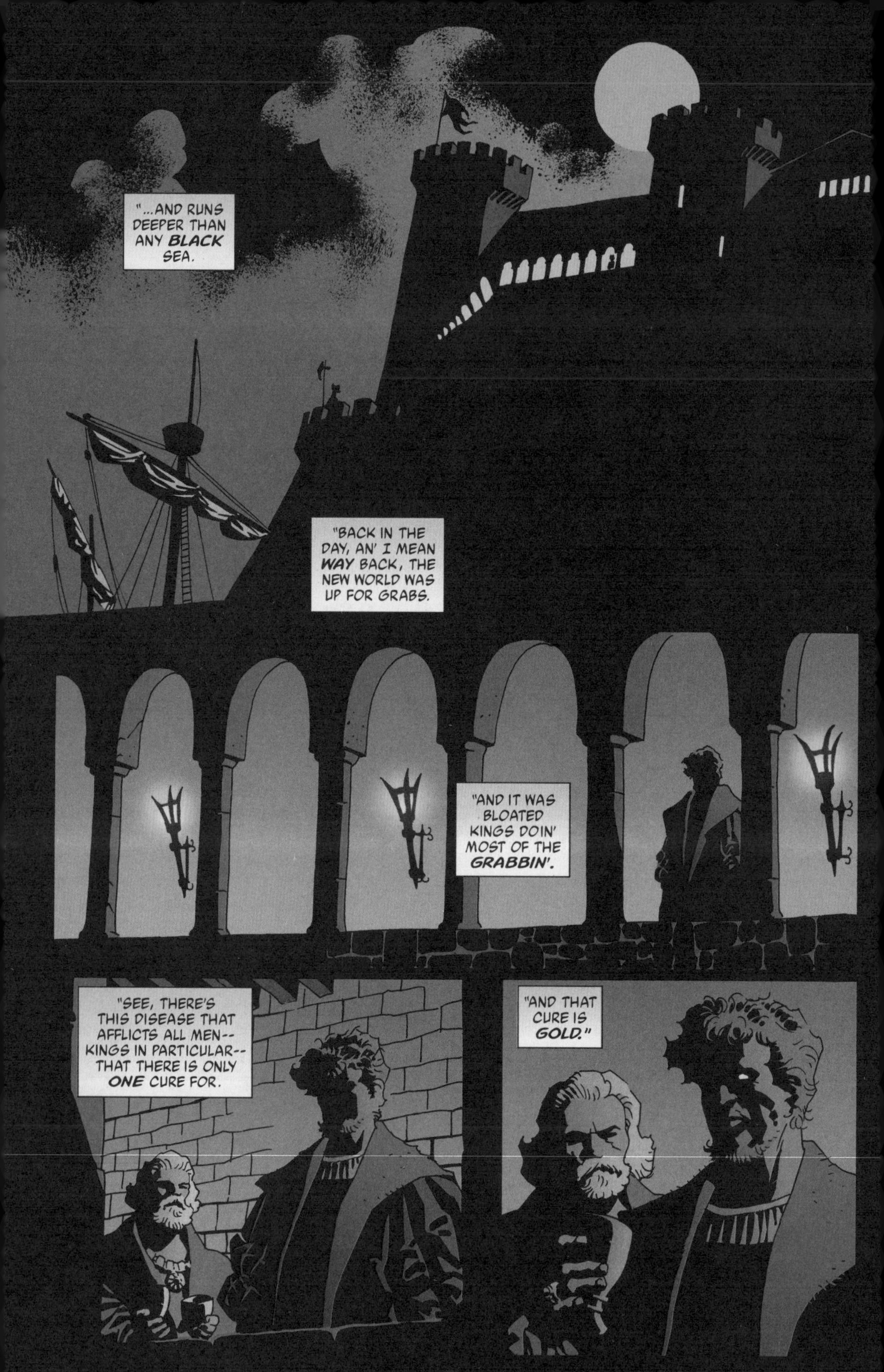
"...AND RUNS DEEPER THAN ANY BLACK SEA.
"BACK IN THE DAY, AN' I MEAN WAY BACK, THE NEW WORLD WAS UP FOR GRABS.
"AND IT WAS BLOATED KINGS DOIN' MOST OF THE GRABBIN'.
"SEE, THERE'S THIS DISEASE THAT AFFLICTS ALL MEN--KINGS IN PARTICULAR--THAT THERE IS ONLY ONE CURE FOR.
"AND THAT CURE IS GOLD."

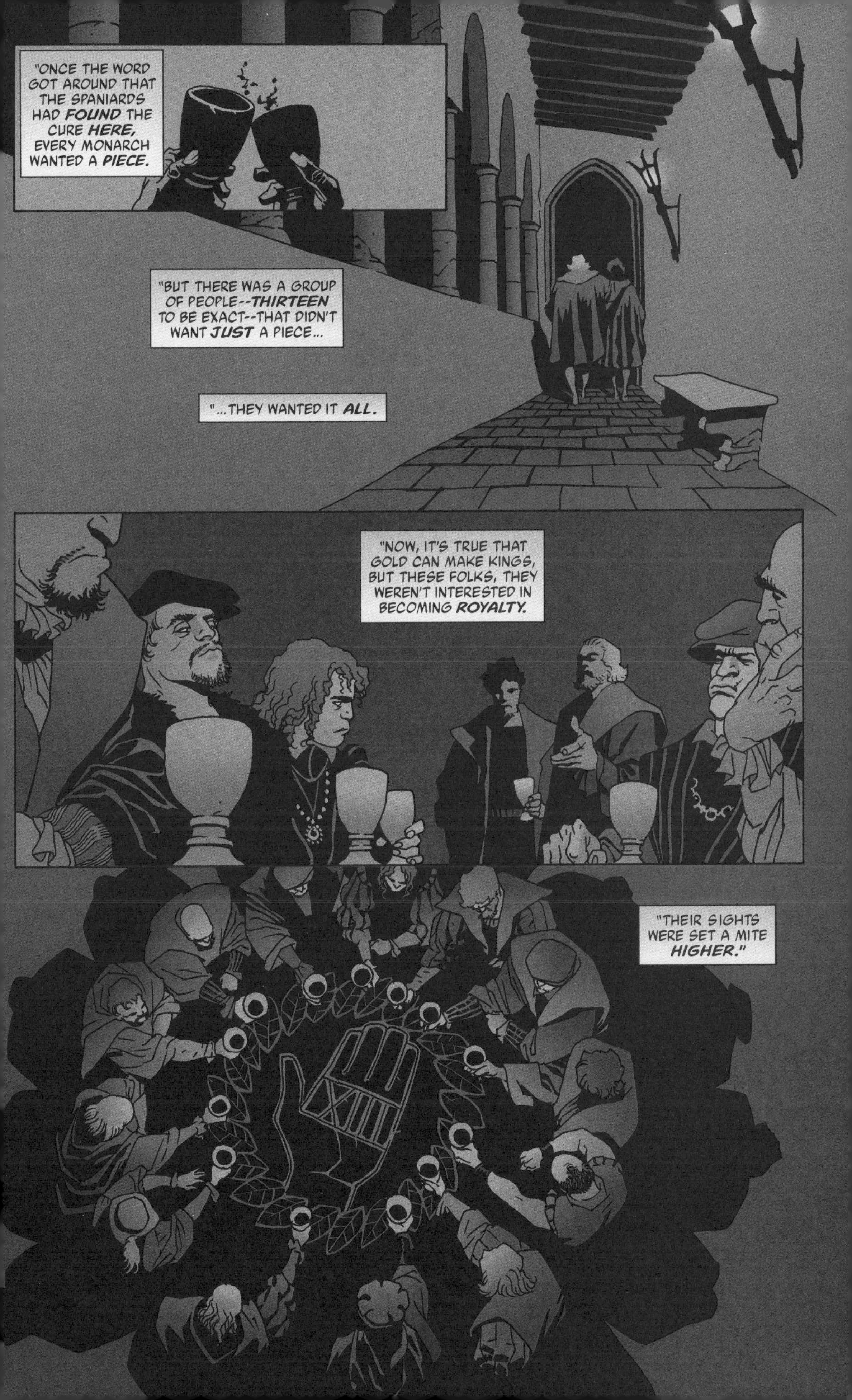
"ONCE THE WORD GOT AROUND THAT THE SPANIARDS HAD FOUND THE CURE HERE, EVERY MONARCH WANTED A PIECE.
"BUT THERE WAS A GROUP OF PEOPLE--THIRTEEN TO BE EXACT--THAT DIDN'T WANT JUST A PIECE...
"...THEY WANTED IT ALL.
"NOW, IT'S TRUE THAT GOLD CAN MAKE KINGS, BUT THESE FOLKS, THEY WEREN'T INTERESTED IN BECOMING ROYALTY.
"THEIR SIGHTS WERE SET A MITE HIGHER."

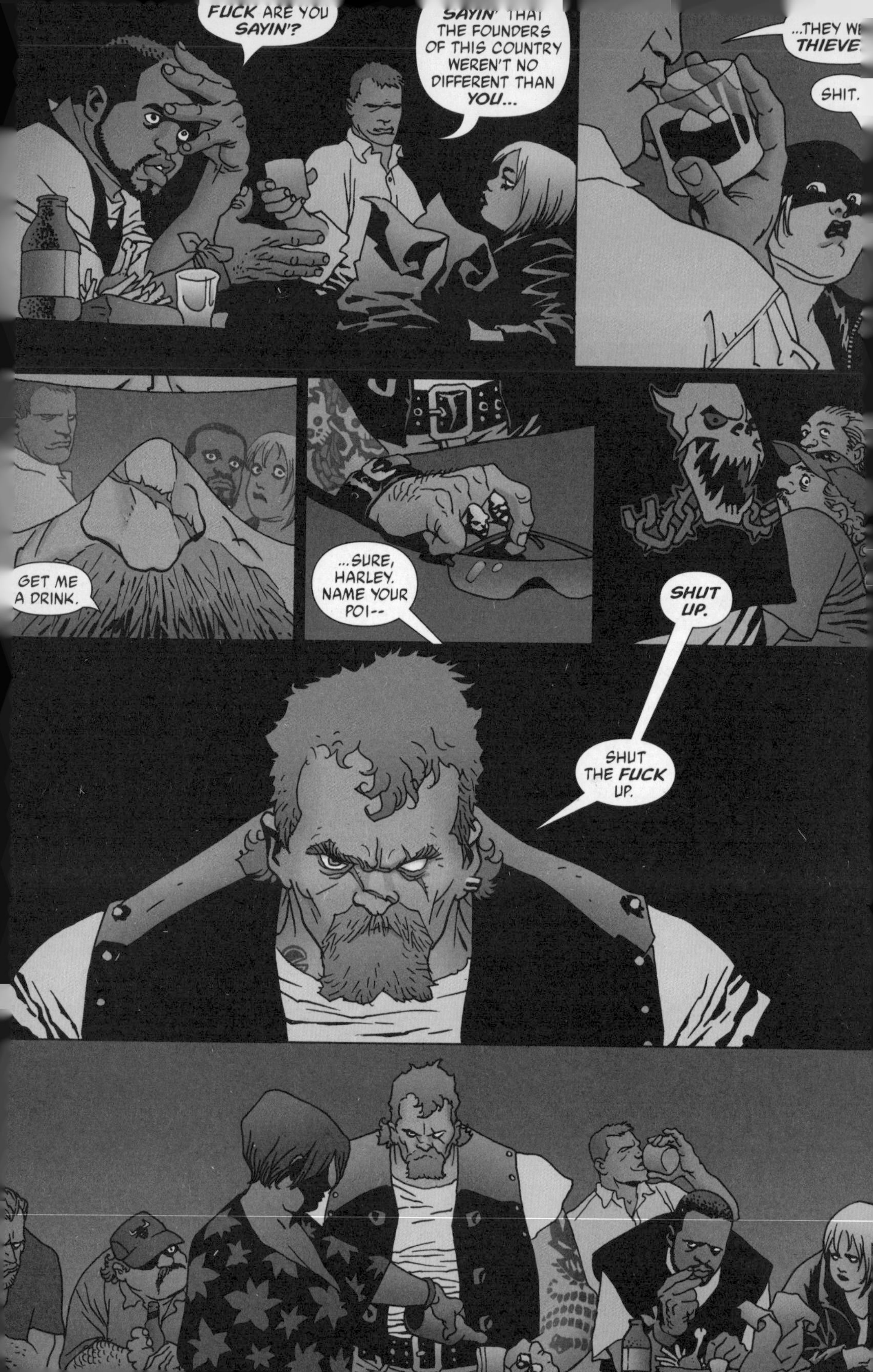
FUCK ARE YOU SAYIN'?
SAYIN' THAT THE FOUNDERS OF THIS COUNTRY WEREN'T NO DIFFERENT THAN YOU...
...THEY WE THIEVE
SHIT.
GET ME A DRINK.
...SURE, HARLEY. NAME YOUR POI--
SHUT UP.
SHUT THE FUCK UP.

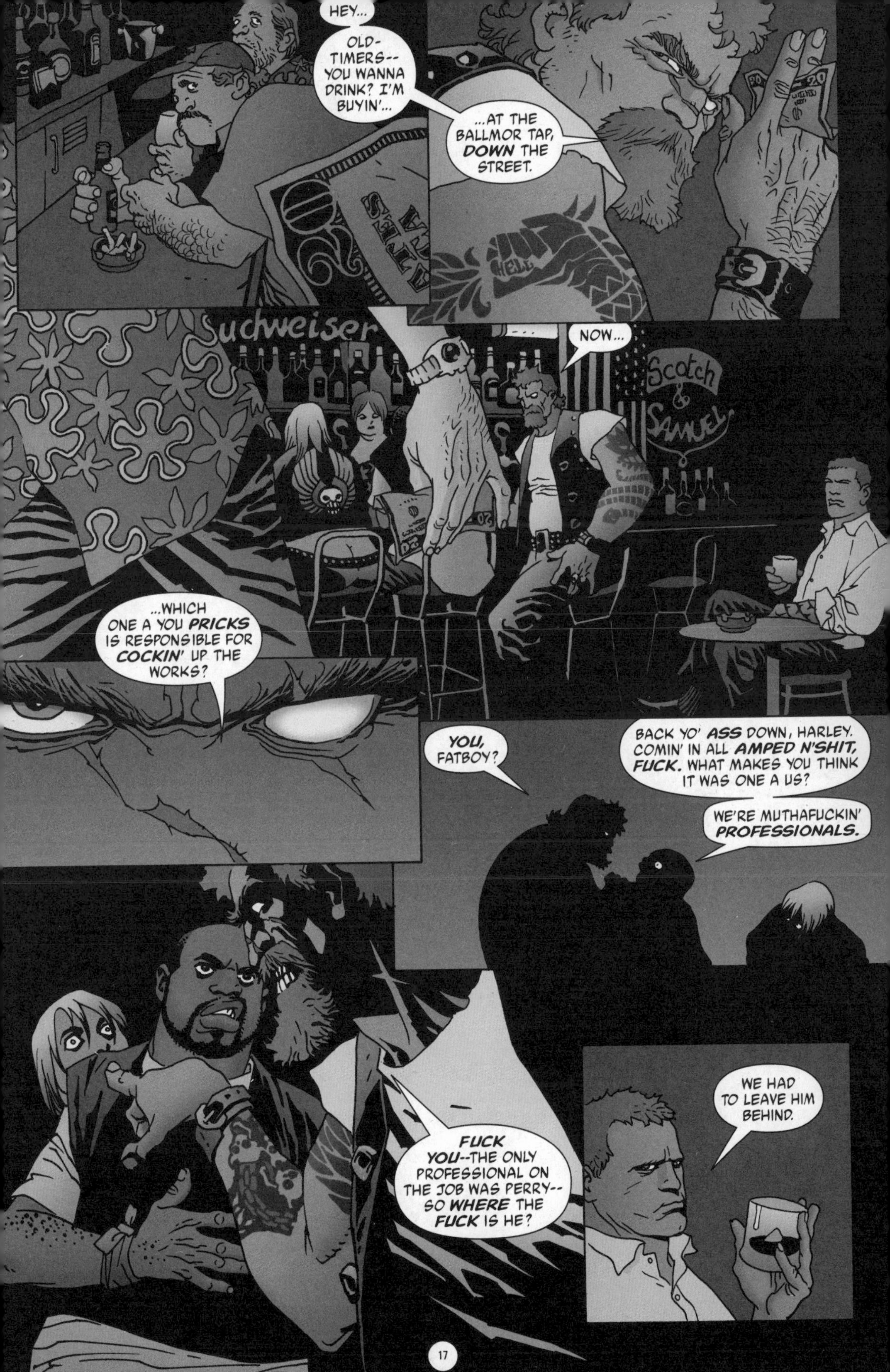

HEY... OLD-TIMERS--YOU WANNA DRINK? I'M BUYIN'...
...AT THE BALLMOR TAP, DOWN THE STREET.
Scotch & Samuel
NOW...
...WHICH ONE A YOU PRICKS IS RESPONSIBLE FOR COCKIN' UP THE WORKS?
YOU, FATBOY?
BACK YO' ASS DOWN, HARLEY. COMIN' IN ALL AMPED N'SHIT, FUCK. WHAT MAKES YOU THINK IT WAS ONE A US?
WE'RE MUTHAFUCKIN' PROFESSIONALS.
FUCK YOU--THE ONLY PROFESSIONAL ON THE JOB WAS PERRY--SO WHERE THE FUCK IS HE?
WE HAD TO LEAVE HIM BEHIND.

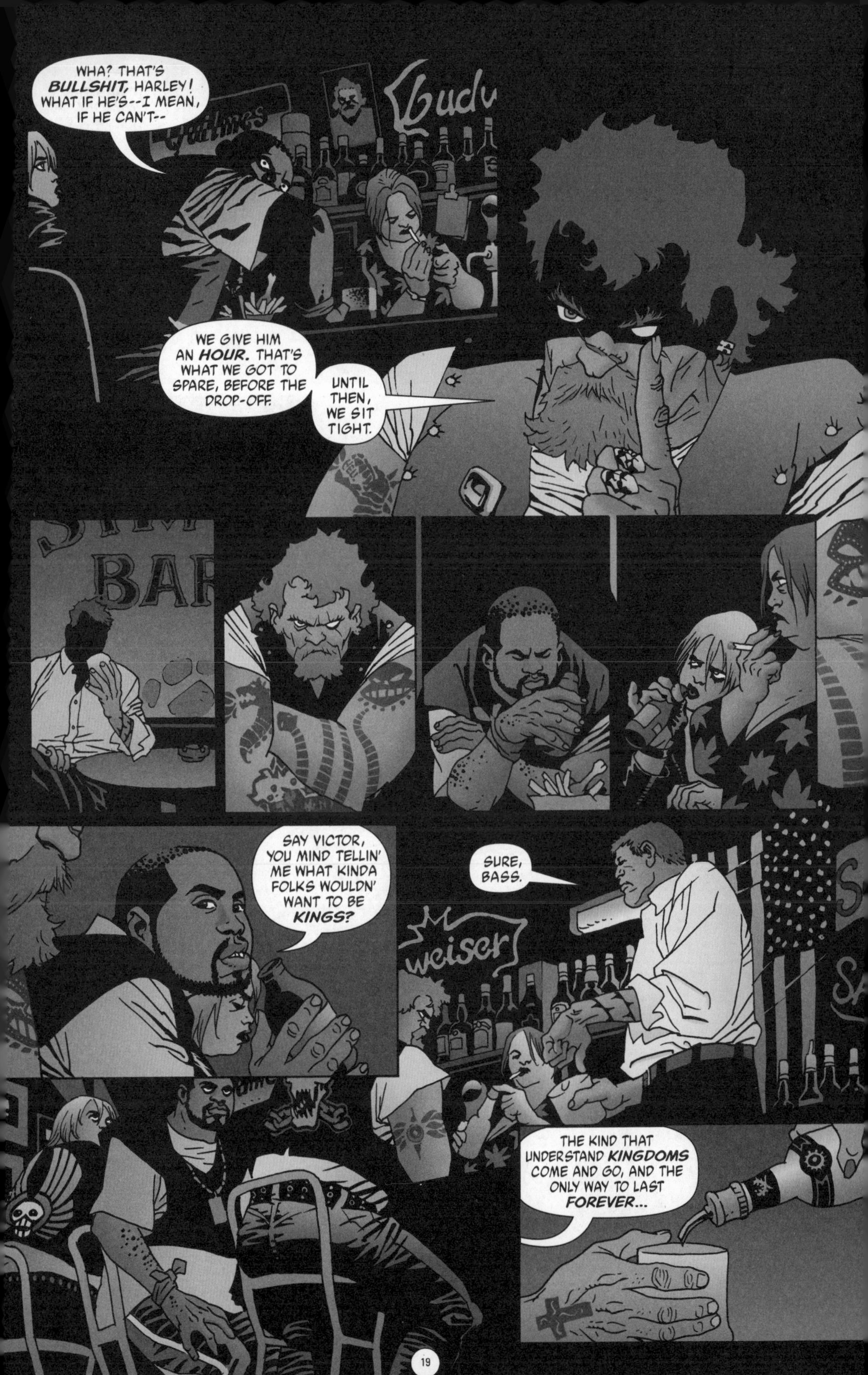
WHA? THAT'S BULLSHIT, HARLEY! WHAT IF HE'S--I MEAN, IF HE CAN'T--
WE GIVE HIM AN HOUR. THAT'S WHAT WE GOT TO SPARE, BEFORE THE DROP-OFF.
UNTIL THEN, WE SIT TIGHT.
SAY VICTOR, YOU MIND TELLIN' ME WHAT KINDA FOLKS WOULDN' WANT TO BE KINGS?
SURE, BASS.
THE KIND THAT UNDERSTAND KINGDOMS COME AND GO, AND THE ONLY WAY TO LAST FOREVER...

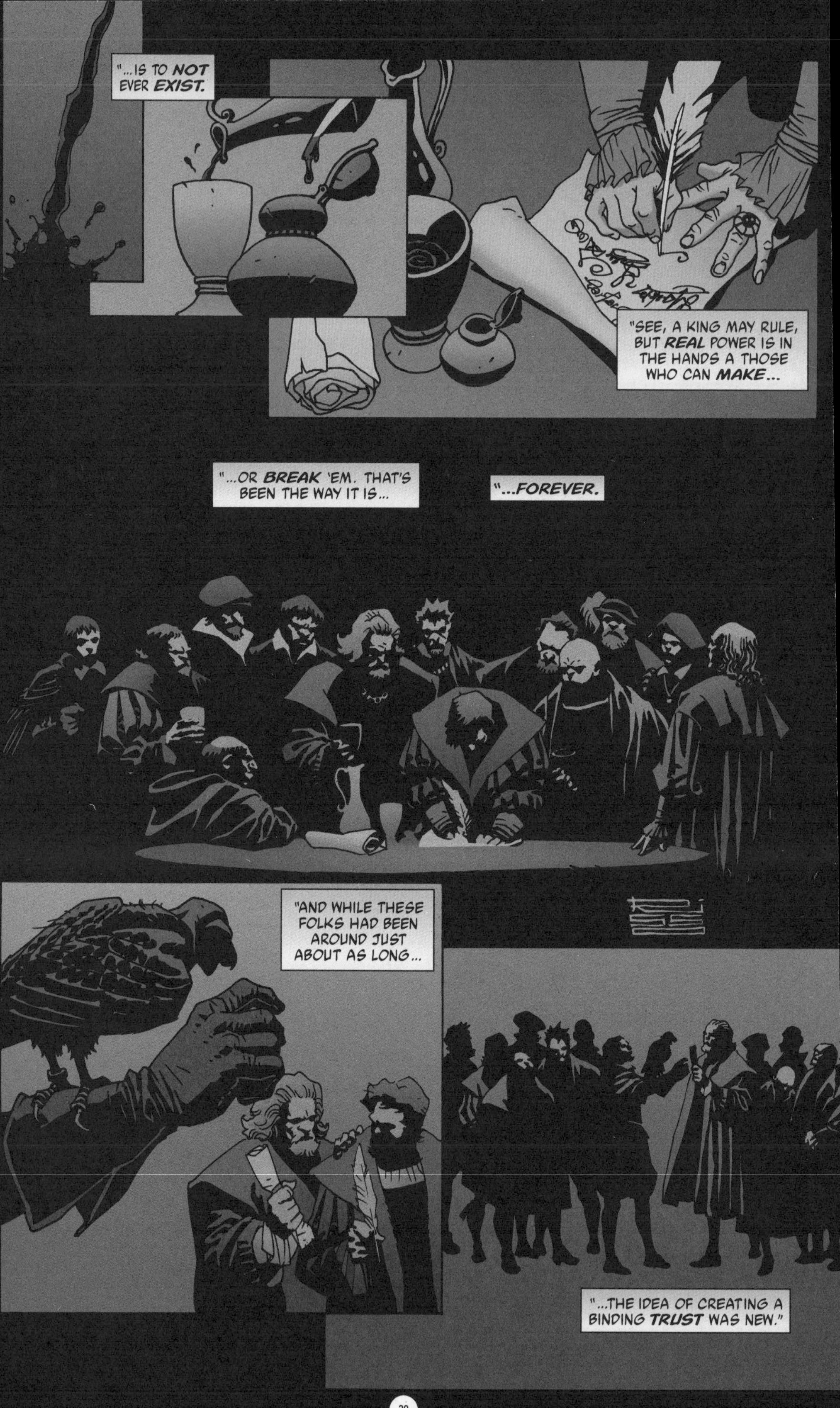
"...IS TO NOT EVER EXIST.
"SEE, A KING MAY RULE, BUT REAL POWER IS IN THE HANDS A THOSE WHO CAN MAKE...
"...OR BREAK 'EM. THAT'S BEEN THE WAY IT IS...
"...FOREVER.
"AND WHILE THESE FOLKS HAD BEEN AROUND JUST ABOUT AS LONG...
"...THE IDEA OF CREATING A BINDING TRUST WAS NEW."

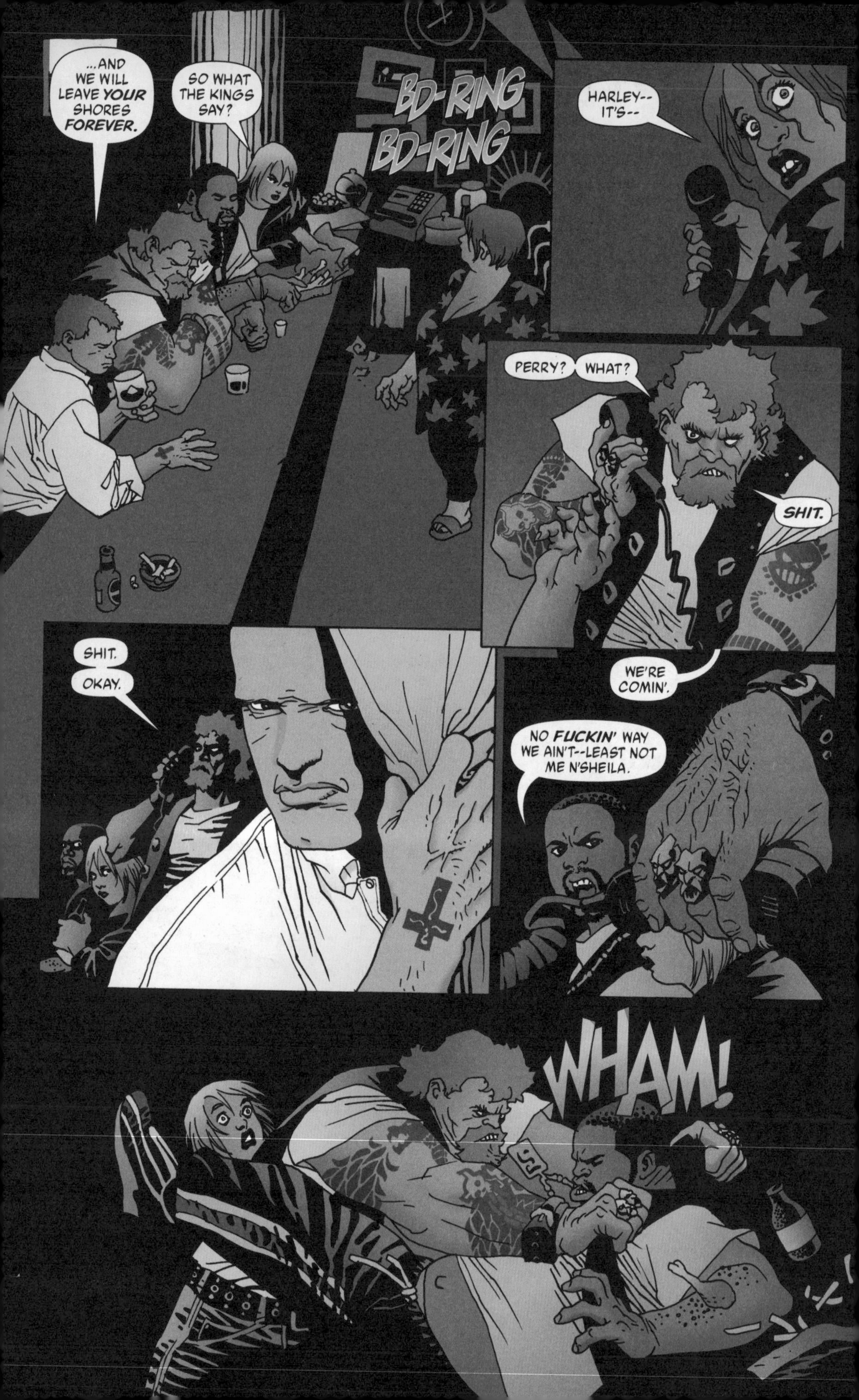
...AND WE WILL LEAVE YOUR SHORES FOREVER.
SO WHAT THE KINGS SAY?
BD-RING BD-RING
HARLEY-- IT'S--
PERRY? WHAT?
SHIT.
SHIT. OKAY.
WE'RE COMIN'.
NO FUCKIN' WAY WE AIN'T--LEAST NOT ME N'SHEILA.
WHAM!

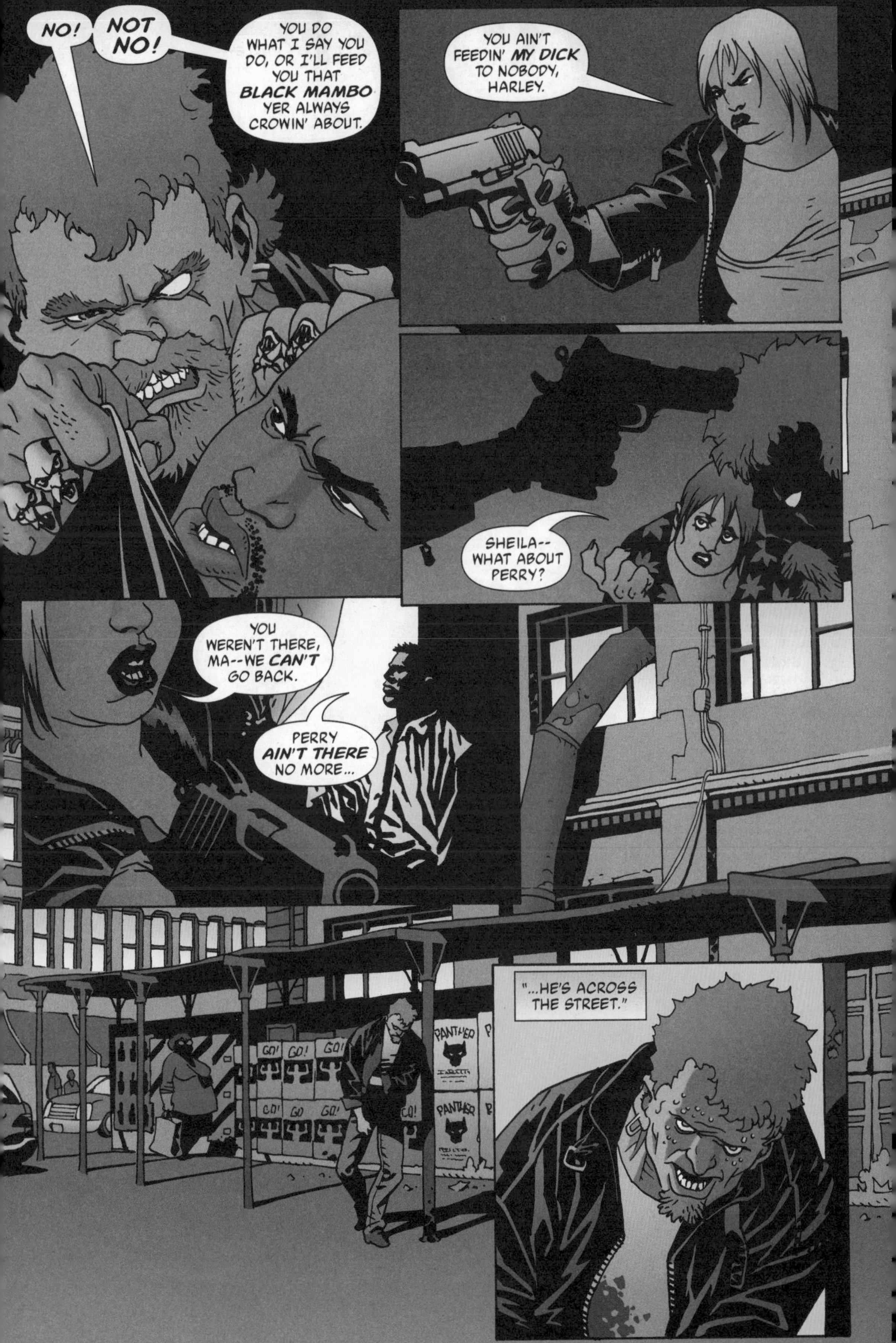
NO!
NOT NO!
YOU DO WHAT I SAY YOU DO, OR I'LL FEED YOU THAT BLACK MAMBO YER ALWAYS CROWIN' ABOUT.
YOU AIN'T FEEDIN' MY DICK TO NOBODY, HARLEY.
SHEILA-- WHAT ABOUT PERRY?
YOU WEREN'T THERE, MA--WE CAN'T GO BACK.
PERRY AIN'T THERE NO MORE...
"...HE'S ACROSS THE STREET."
GO!
PANTHER

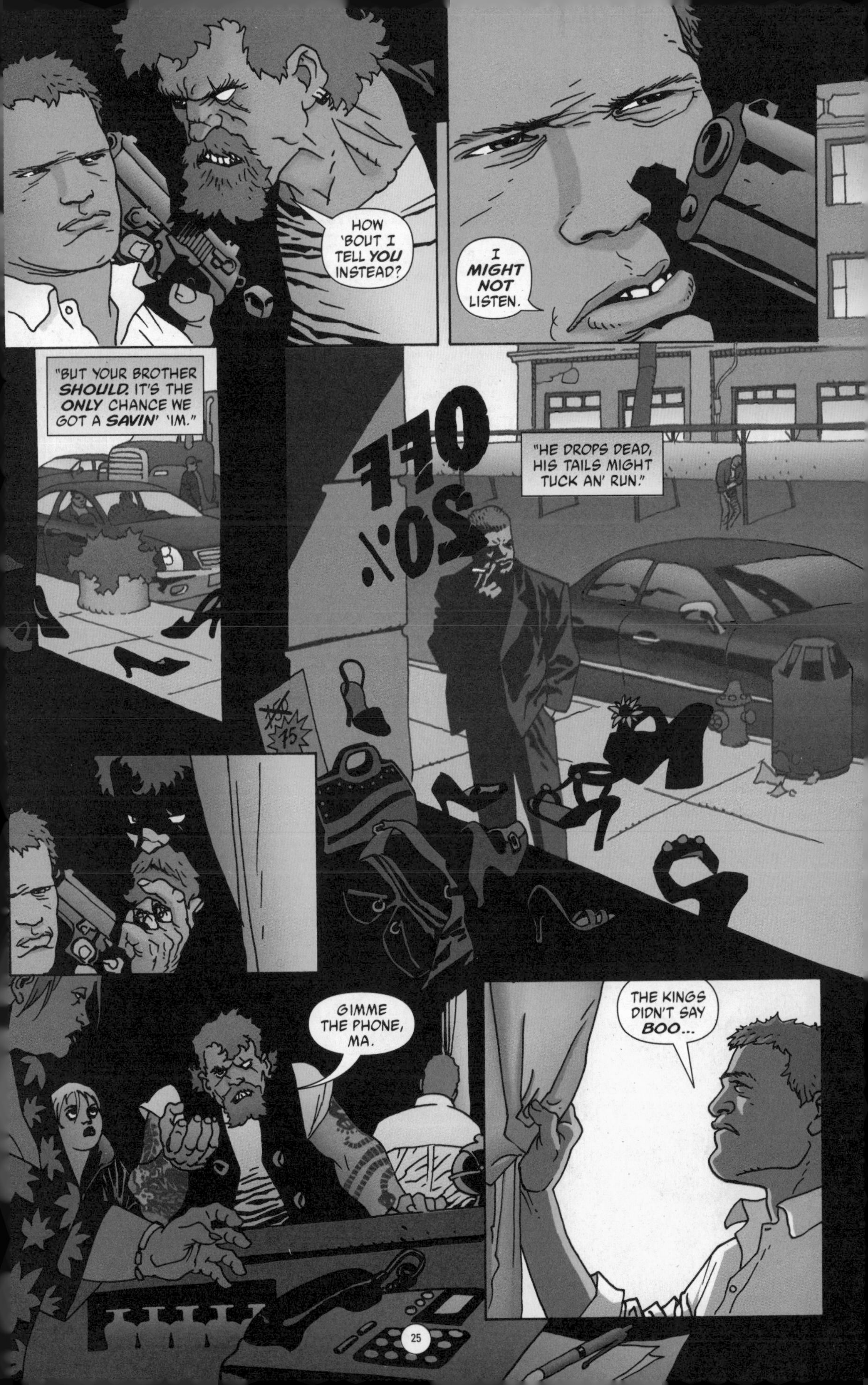
HOW 'BOUT I TELL YOU INSTEAD?
I MIGHT NOT LISTEN.
"BUT YOUR BROTHER SHOULD. IT'S THE ONLY CHANCE WE GOT A SAVIN' 'IM."
"HE DROPS DEAD, HIS TAILS MIGHT TUCK AN' RUN."
GIMME THE PHONE, MA.
THE KINGS DIDN'T SAY BOO...

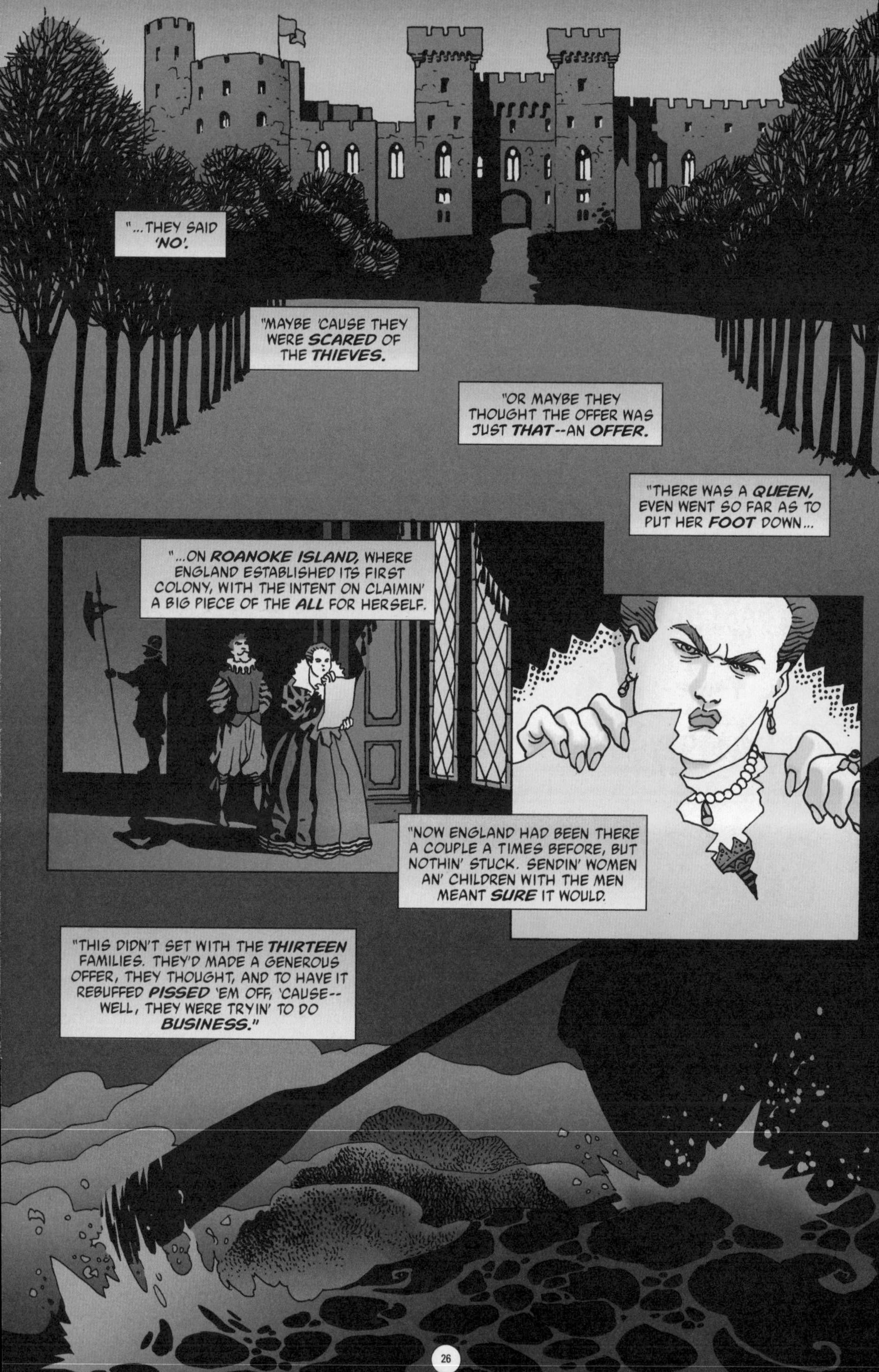
"...THEY SAID 'NO'.
"MAYBE 'CAUSE THEY WERE SCARED OF THE THIEVES.
"OR MAYBE THEY THOUGHT THE OFFER WAS JUST THAT--AN OFFER.
"THERE WAS A QUEEN, EVEN WENT SO FAR AS TO PUT HER FOOT DOWN...
"...ON ROANOKE ISLAND, WHERE ENGLAND ESTABLISHED ITS FIRST COLONY, WITH THE INTENT ON CLAIMIN' A BIG PIECE OF THE ALL FOR HERSELF.
"NOW ENGLAND HAD BEEN THERE A COUPLE A TIMES BEFORE, BUT NOTHIN' STUCK. SENDIN' WOMEN AN' CHILDREN WITH THE MEN MEANT SURE IT WOULD.
"THIS DIDN'T SET WITH THE THIRTEEN FAMILIES. THEY'D MADE A GENEROUS OFFER, THEY THOUGHT, AND TO HAVE IT REBUFFED PISSED 'EM OFF, 'CAUSE--WELL, THEY WERE TRYIN' TO DO BUSINESS."

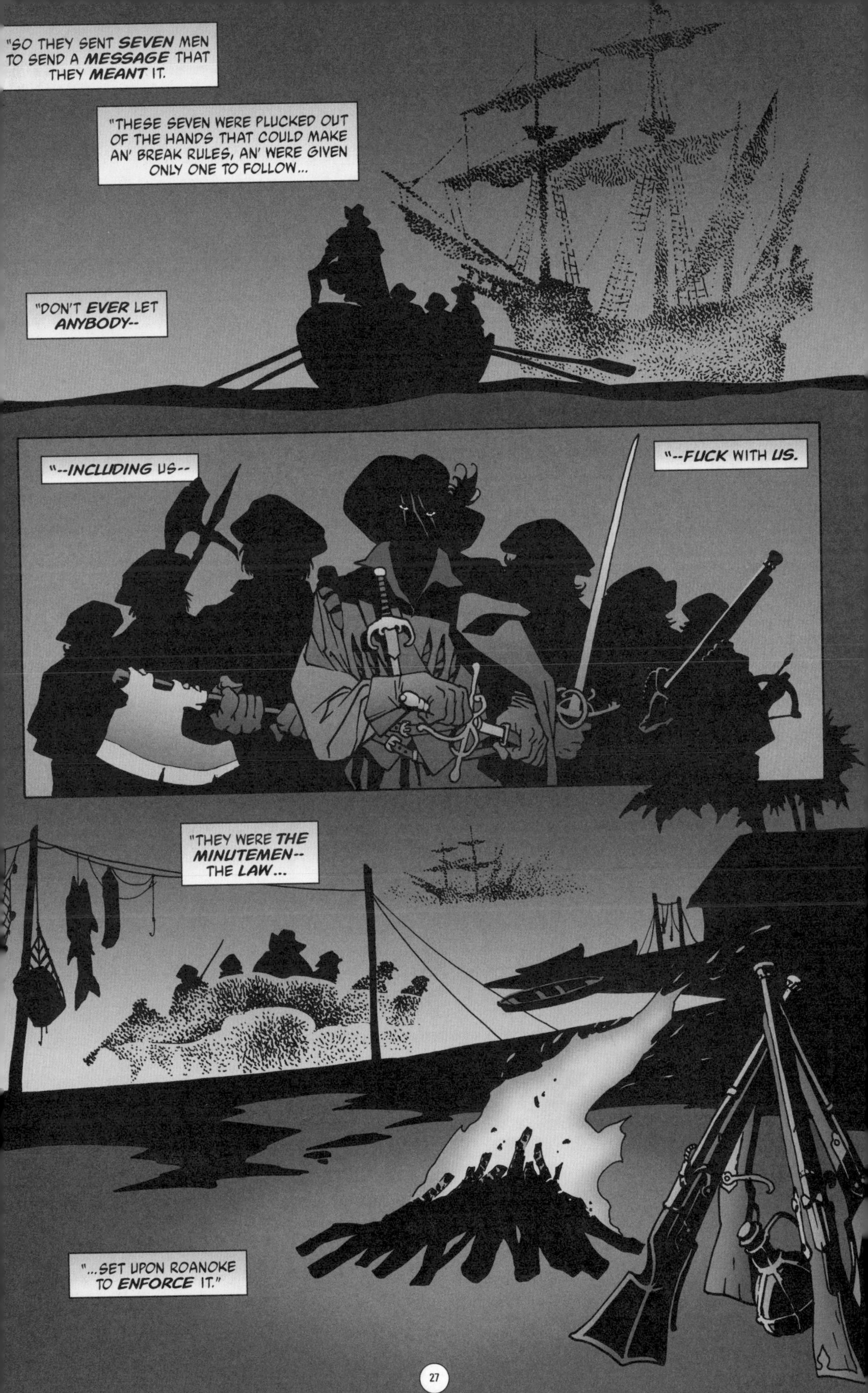
"SO THEY SENT SEVEN MEN TO SEND A MESSAGE THAT THEY MEANT IT.
"THESE SEVEN WERE PLUCKED OUT OF THE HANDS THAT COULD MAKE AN' BREAK RULES, AN' WERE GIVEN ONLY ONE TO FOLLOW...
"DON'T EVER LET ANYBODY--
"--INCLUDING US--
"--FUCK WITH US.
"THEY WERE THE MINUTEMEN-- THE LAW...
"...SET UPON ROANOKE TO ENFORCE IT."

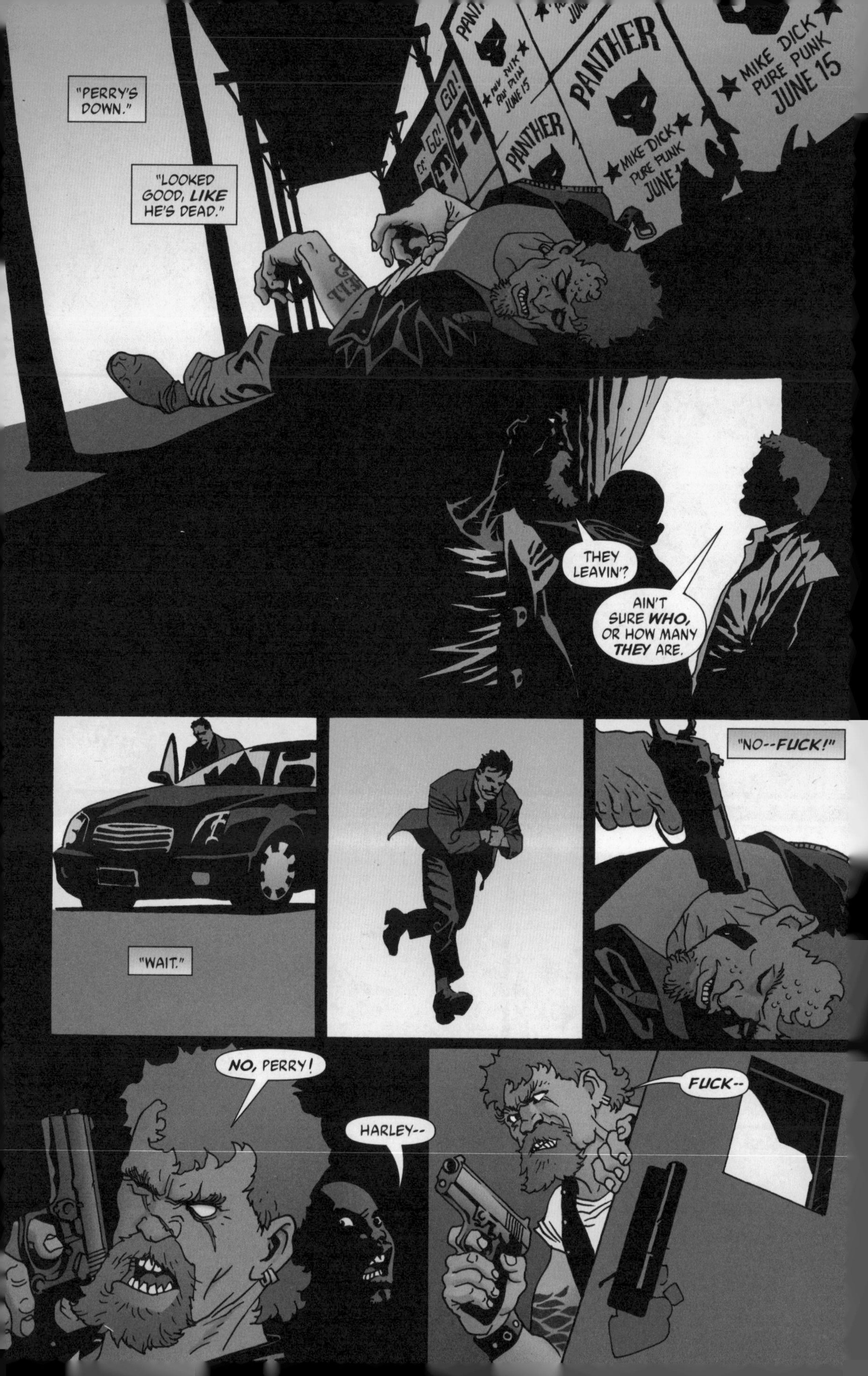
"PERRY'S DOWN."
"LOOKED GOOD, LIKE HE'S DEAD."
PANTHER
MIKE DICK PURE PUNK JUNE 15
THEY LEAVIN'?
AIN'T SURE WHO, OR HOW MANY THEY ARE.
"WAIT."
"NO--FUCK!"
NO, PERRY!
HARLEY--
FUCK--

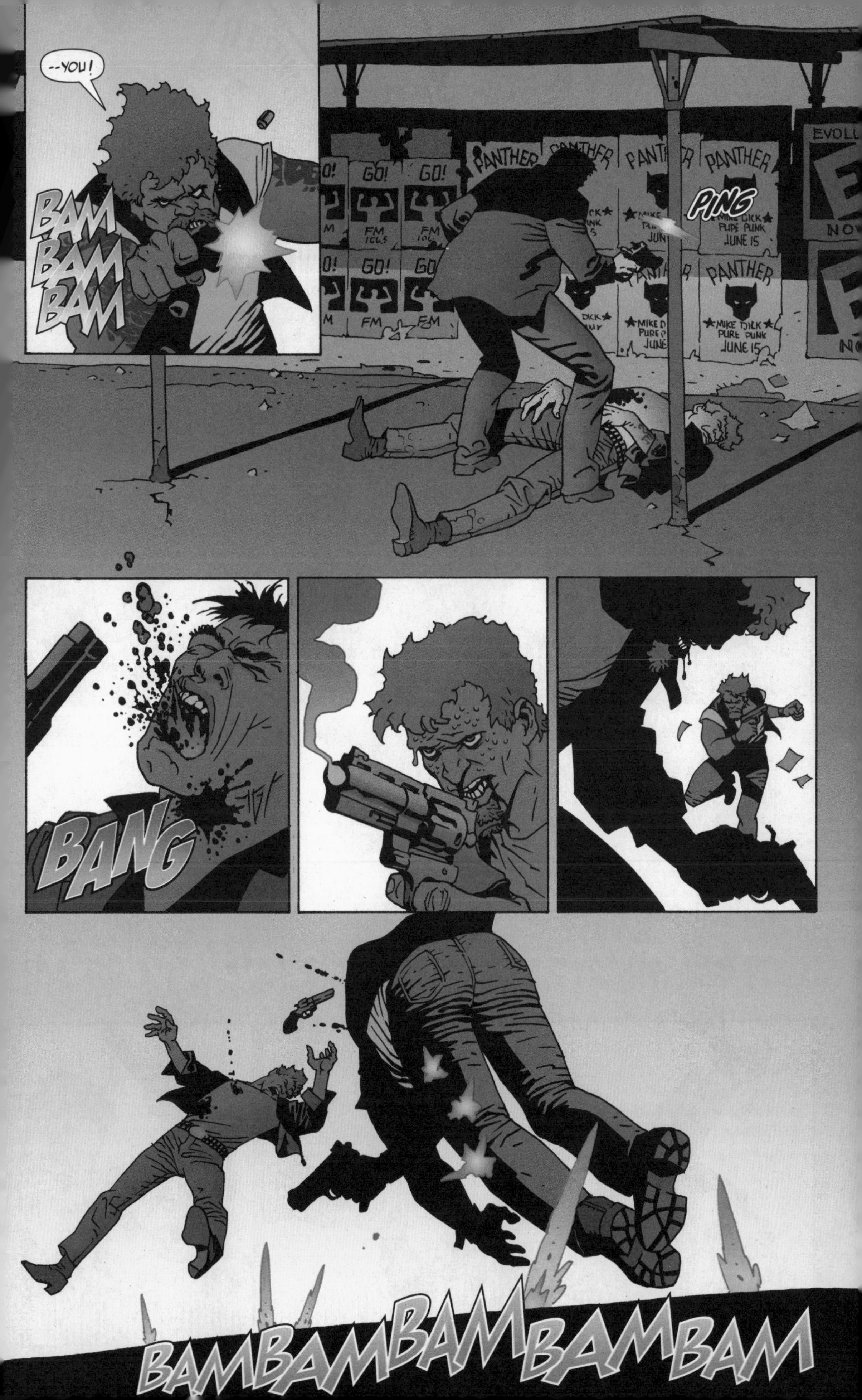
--YOU!
BAM BAM BAM
GO!
FM
PANTHER
MIKE DICK PURE PUNK JUNE 15
EVOLU
PING
BANG
BAMBAMBAMBAMBAM

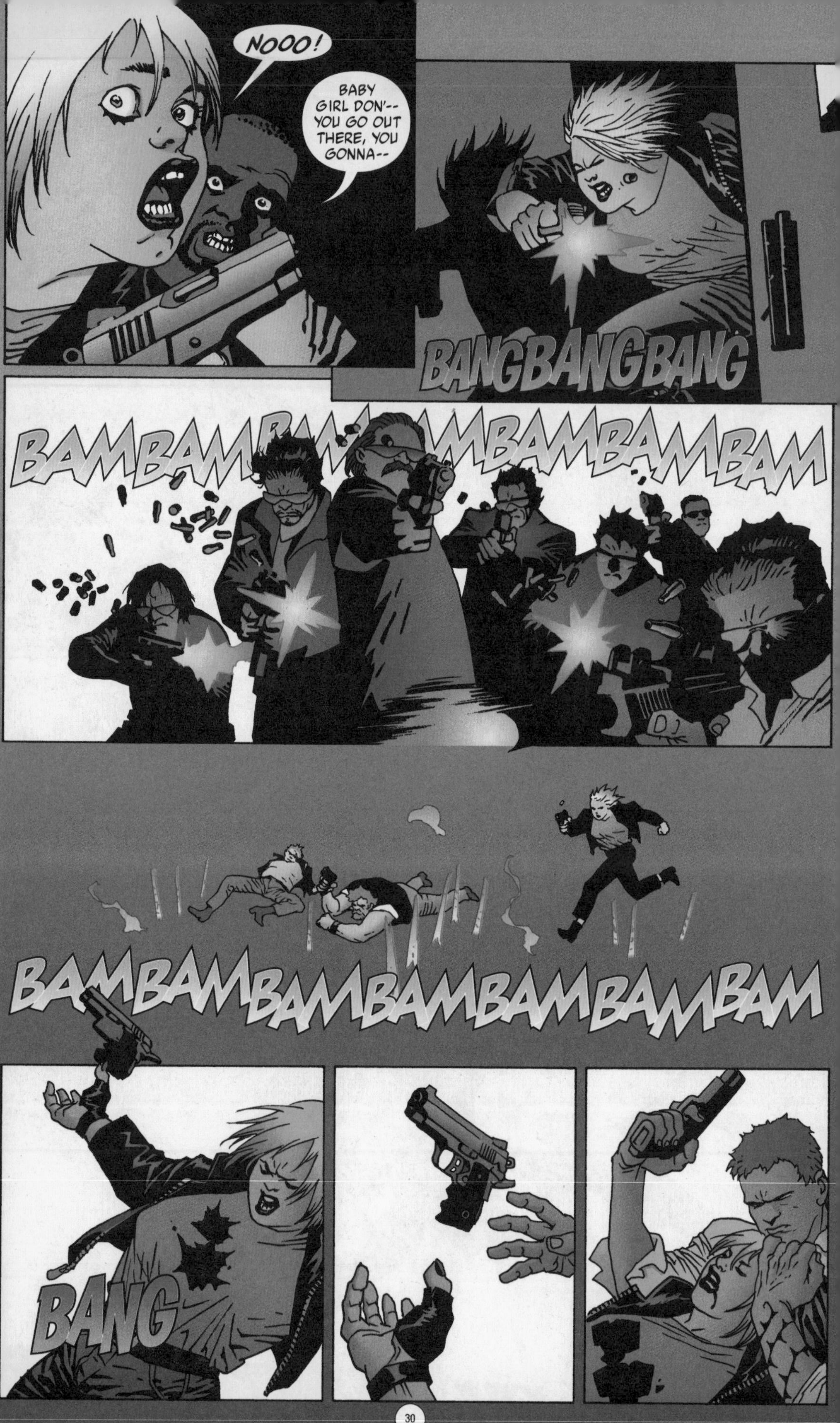
NOOO!
BABY GIRL DON'-- YOU GO OUT THERE, YOU GONNA--
BANGBANGBANG
BAMBAMBAMBAMBAMBAMBAMBAM
BAMBAMBAMBAMBAMBAMBAMBAM
BANG

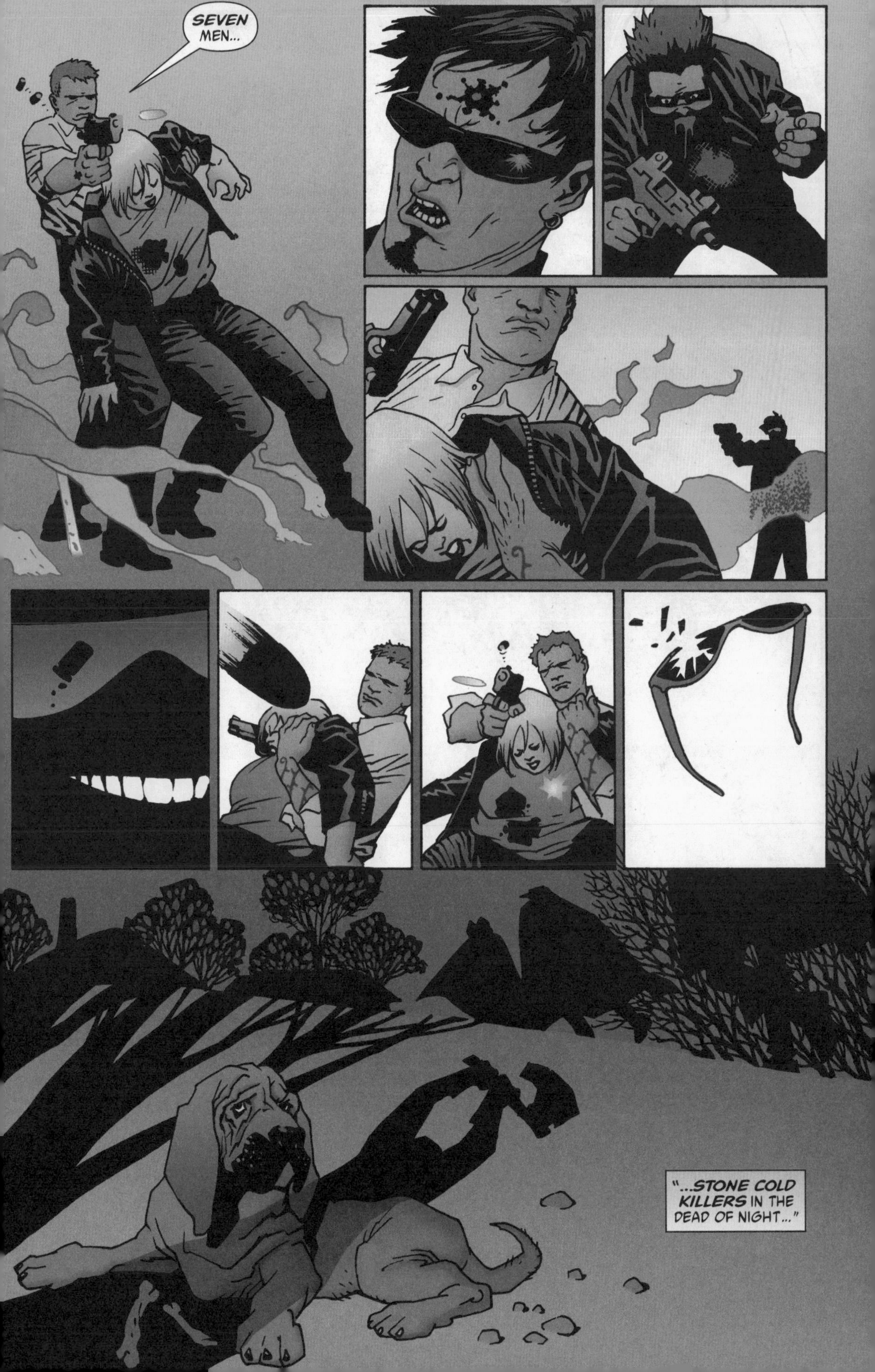
SEVEN MEN...
"...STONE COLD KILLERS IN THE DEAD OF NIGHT..."

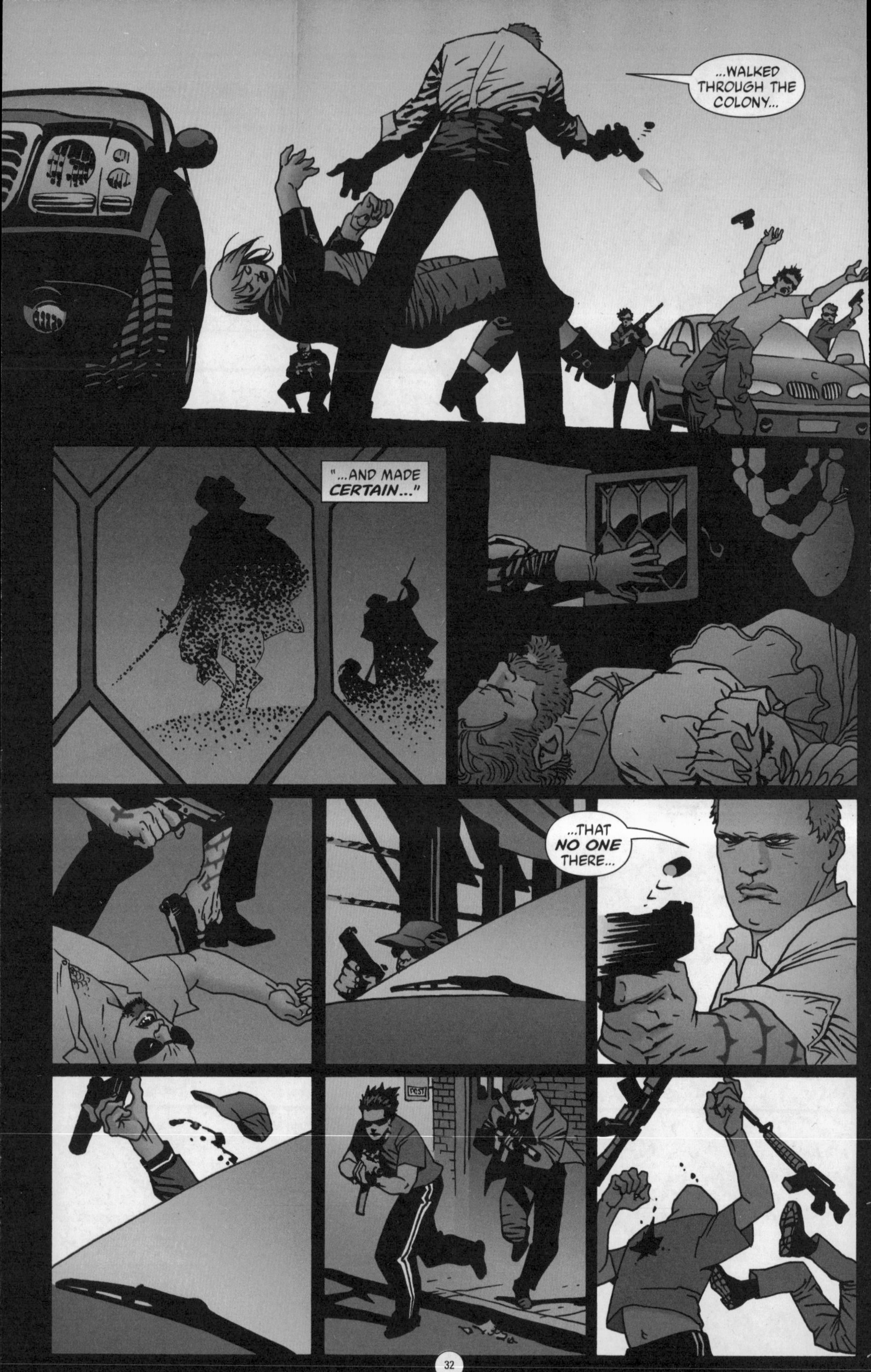
...WALKED THROUGH THE COLONY...
"...AND MADE CERTAIN..."
...THAT NO ONE THERE...
POST

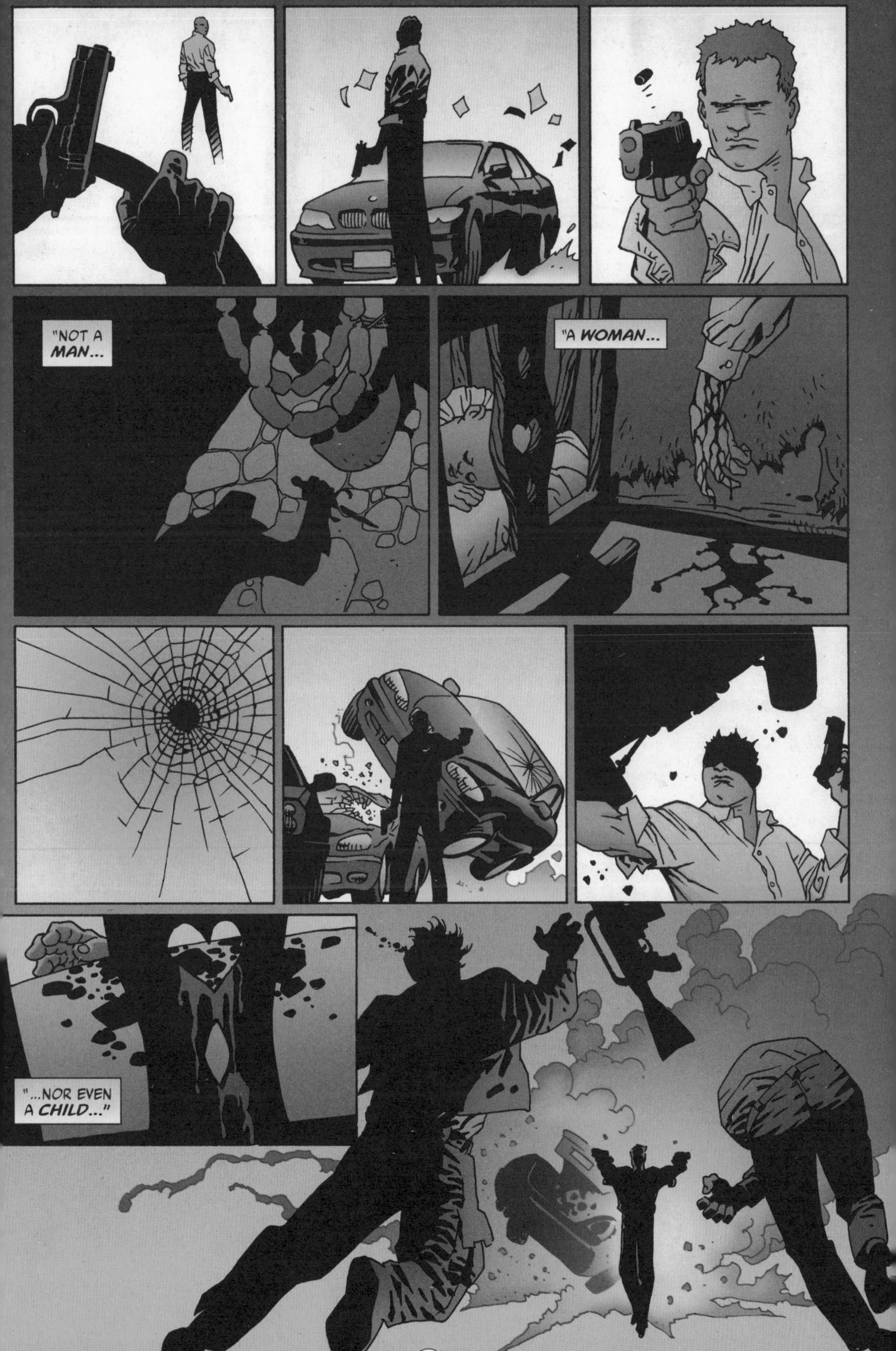
"NOT A MAN...
"A WOMAN...
"...NOR EVEN A CHILD..."

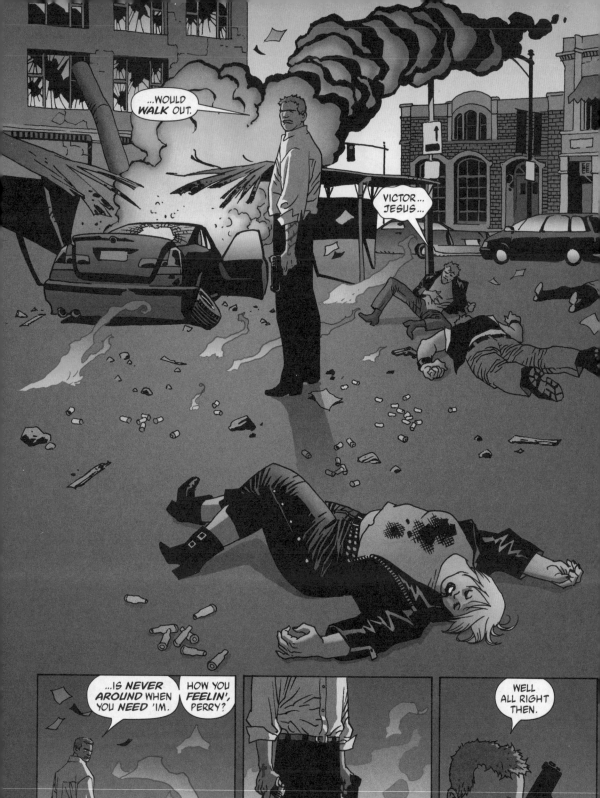

...WOULD **WALK** OUT.

VICTOR... **JESUS**...

...IS **NEVER** AROUND WHEN YOU **NEED** 'IM.

HOW YOU **FEELIN'**, PERRY?

WELL ALL RIGHT THEN.

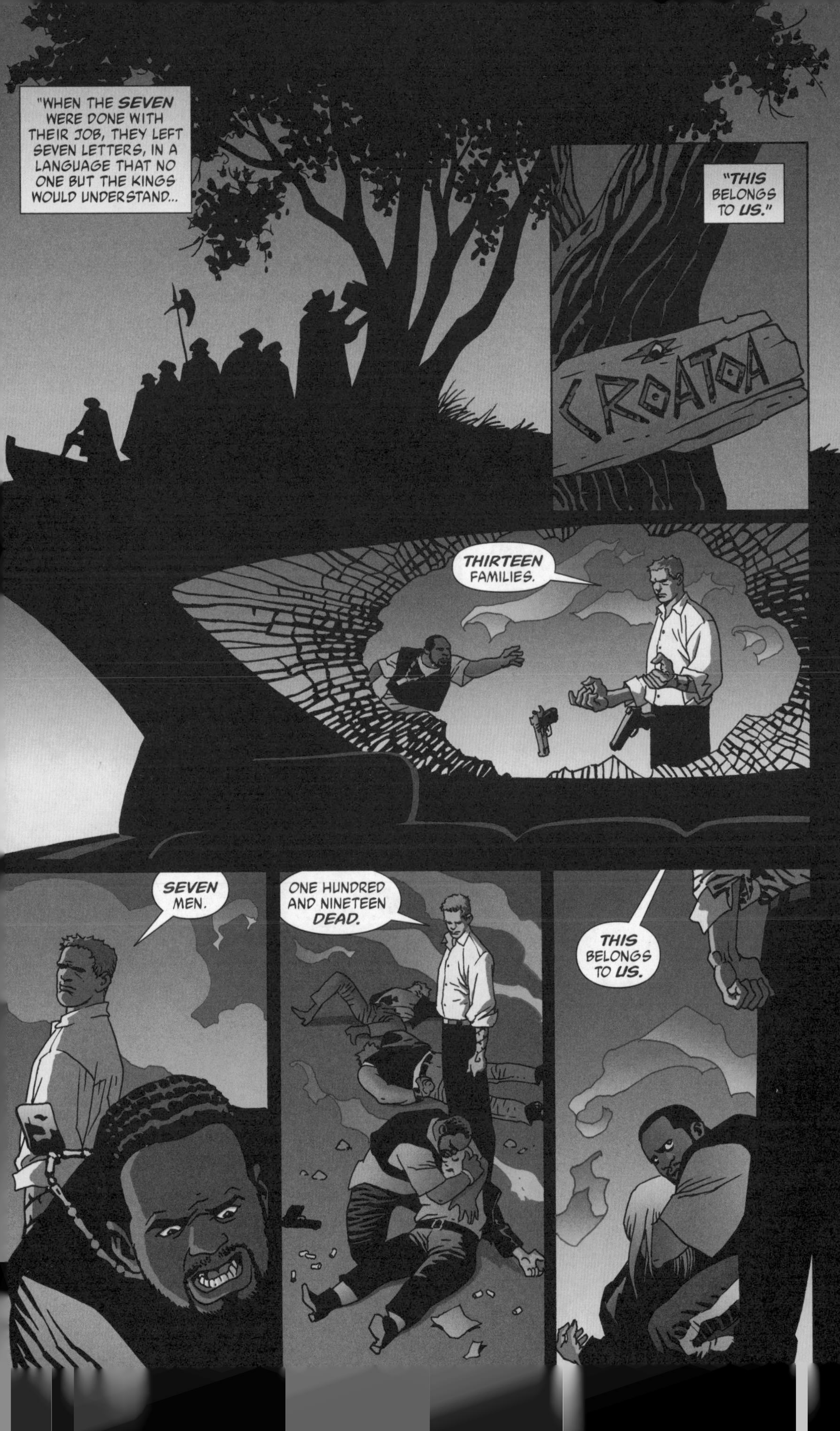
"WHEN THE SEVEN WERE DONE WITH THEIR JOB, THEY LEFT SEVEN LETTERS, IN A LANGUAGE THAT NO ONE BUT THE KINGS WOULD UNDERSTAND...
"THIS BELONGS TO US."
CROATOA
THIRTEEN FAMILIES.
SEVEN MEN.
ONE HUNDRED AND NINETEEN DEAD.
THIS BELONGS TO US.

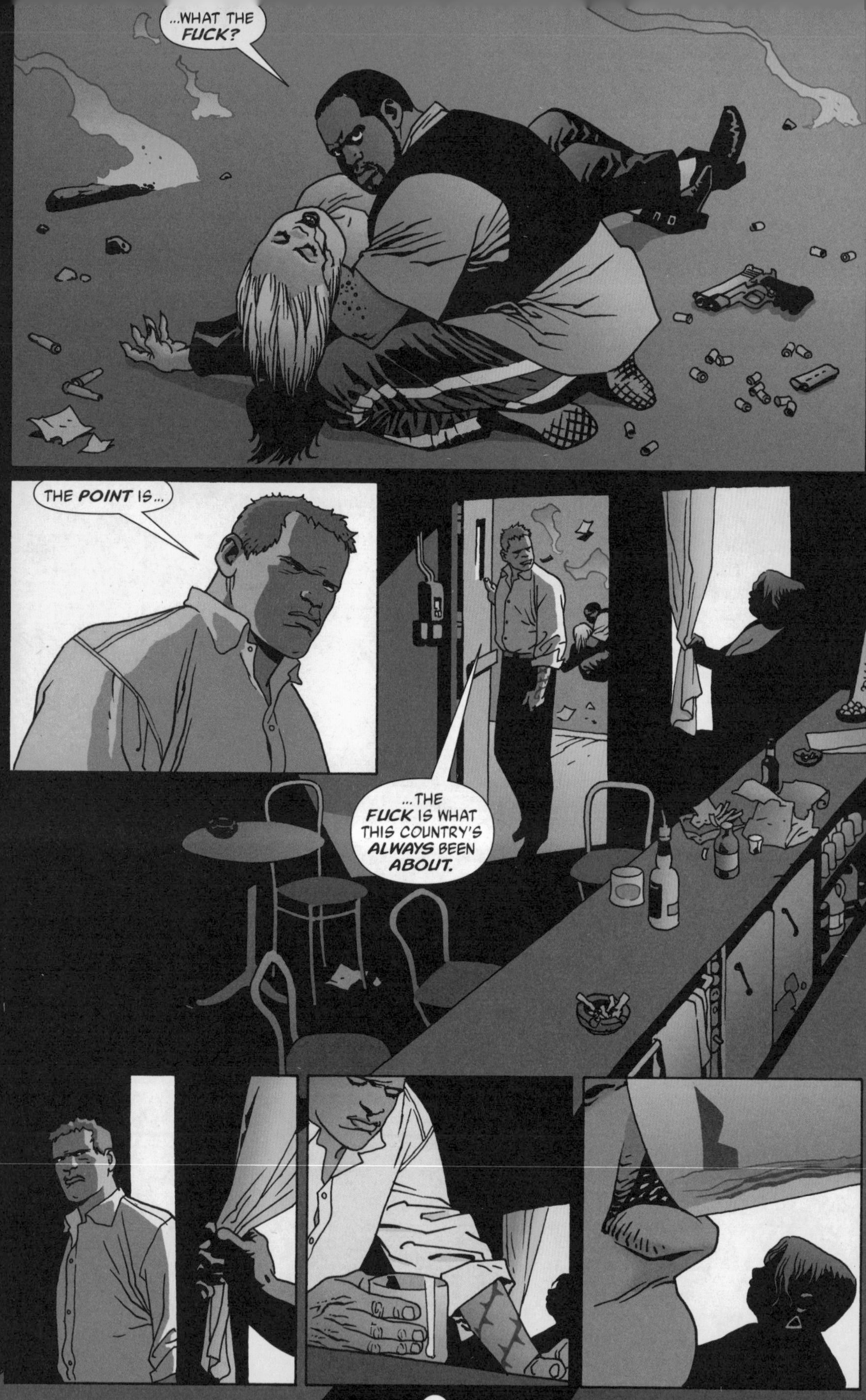
...WHAT THE FUCK?
THE POINT IS...
...THE FUCK IS WHAT THIS COUNTRY'S ALWAYS BEEN ABOUT.

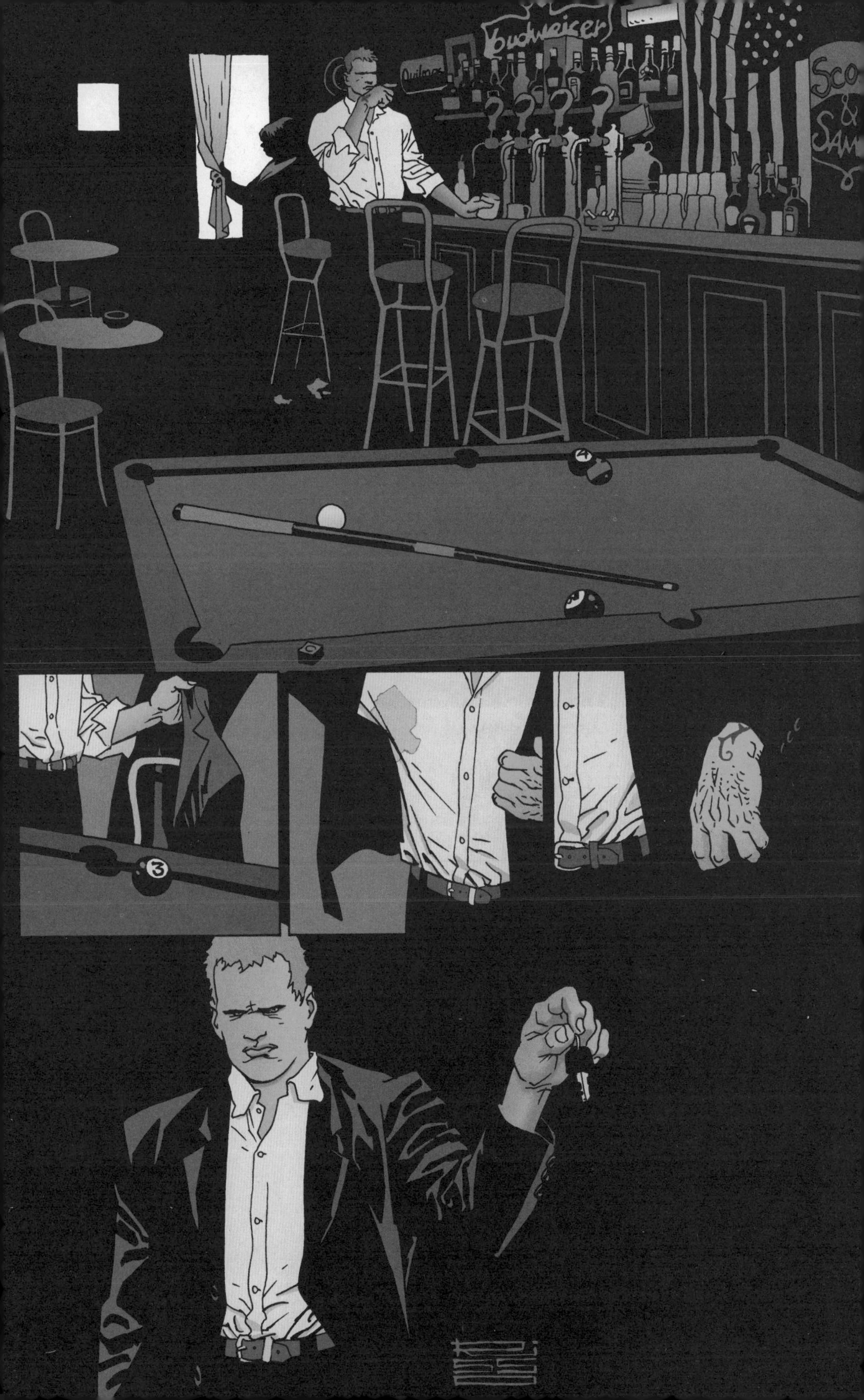
Budweiser

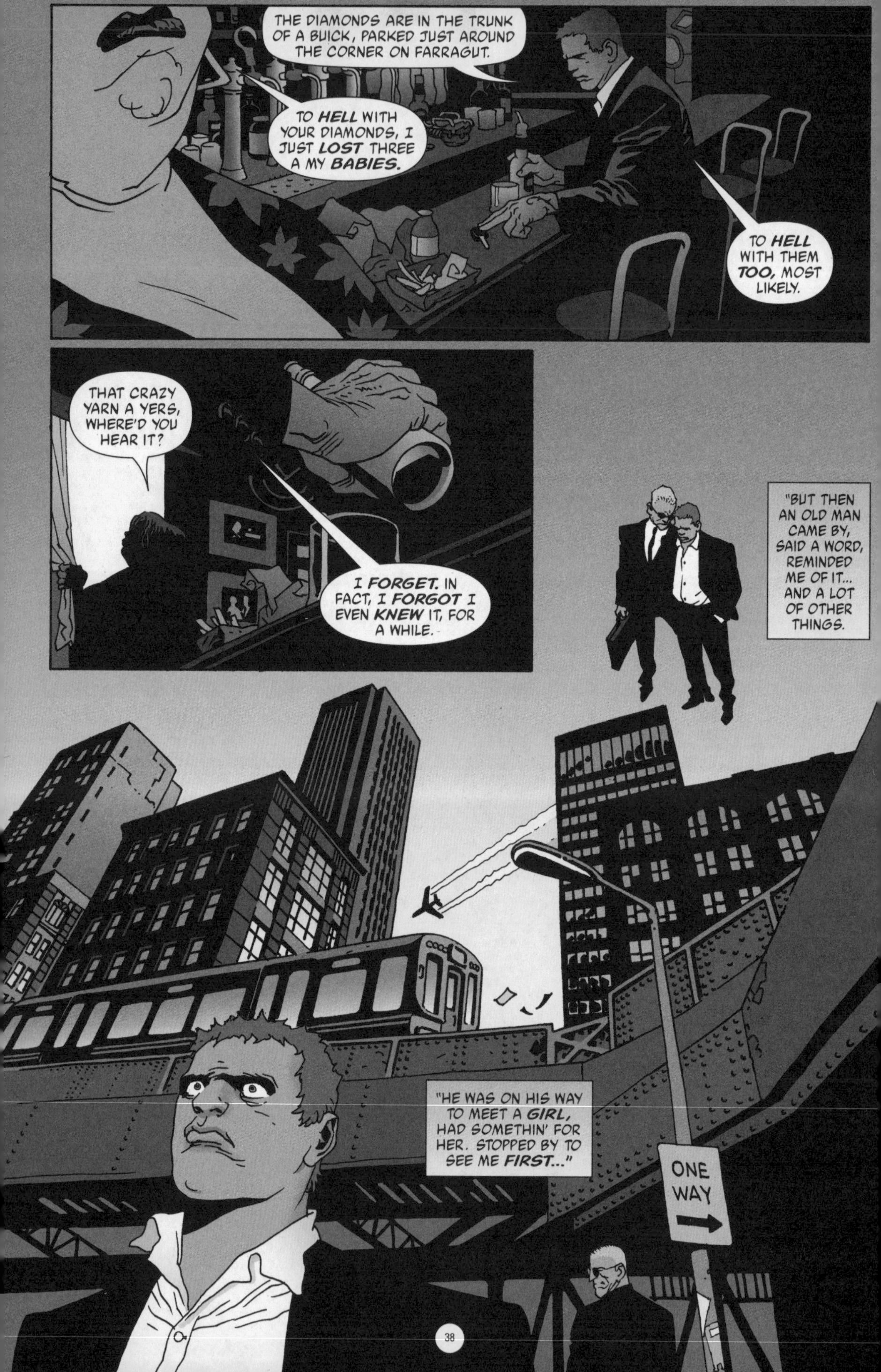
THE DIAMONDS ARE IN THE TRUNK OF A BUICK, PARKED JUST AROUND THE CORNER ON FARRAGUT.
TO HELL WITH YOUR DIAMONDS, I JUST LOST THREE A MY BABIES.
TO HELL WITH THEM TOO, MOST LIKELY.
THAT CRAZY YARN A YERS, WHERE'D YOU HEAR IT?
I FORGET. IN FACT, I FORGOT I EVEN KNEW IT, FOR A WHILE.
"BUT THEN AN OLD MAN CAME BY, SAID A WORD, REMINDED ME OF IT... AND A LOT OF OTHER THINGS.
"HE WAS ON HIS WAY TO MEET A GIRL, HAD SOMETHIN' FOR HER. STOPPED BY TO SEE ME FIRST..."
ONE WAY

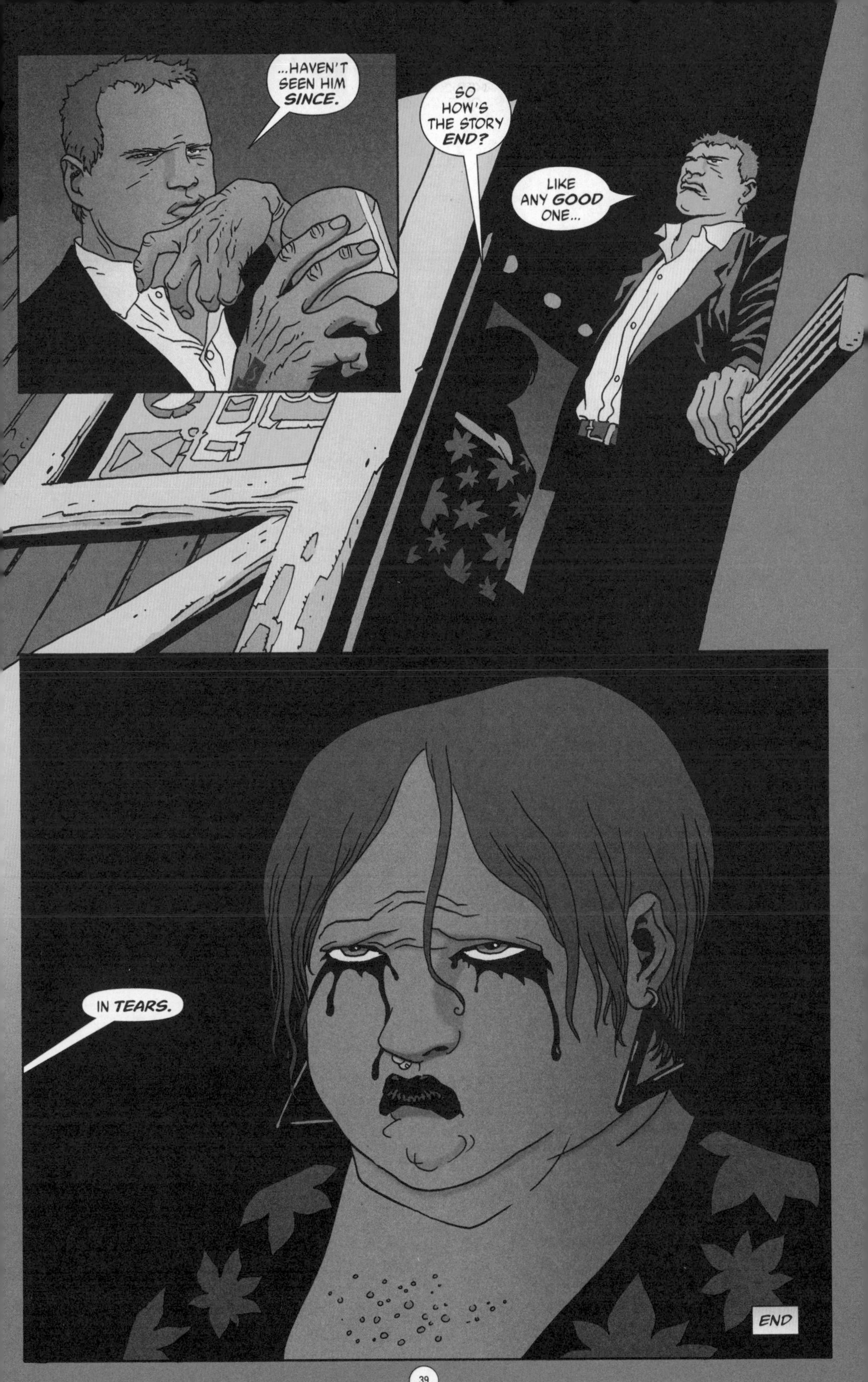
...HAVEN'T SEEN HIM *SINCE.*
SO HOW'S THE STORY *END?*
LIKE ANY *GOOD* ONE...
IN *TEARS.*
END

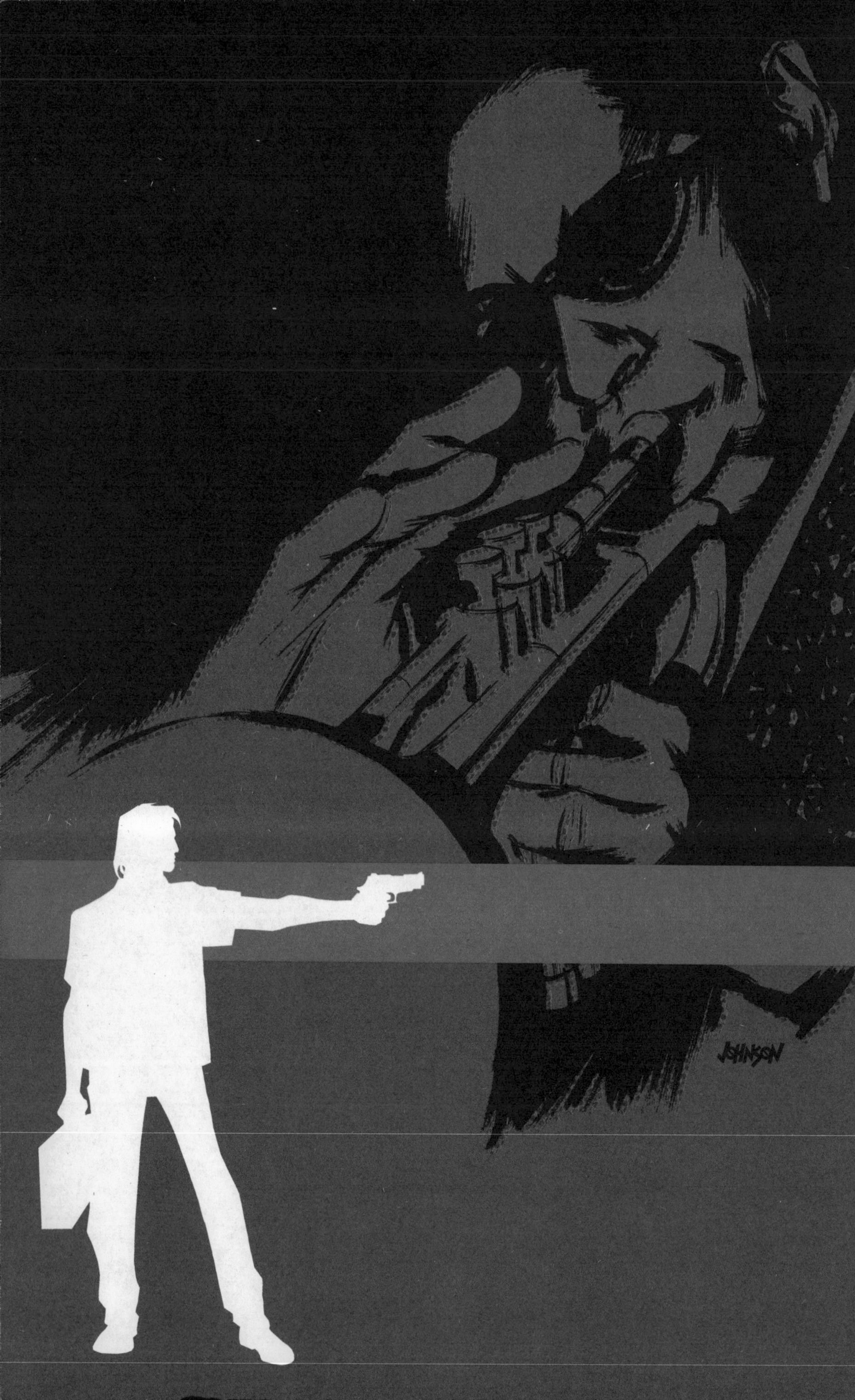
JOHNSON

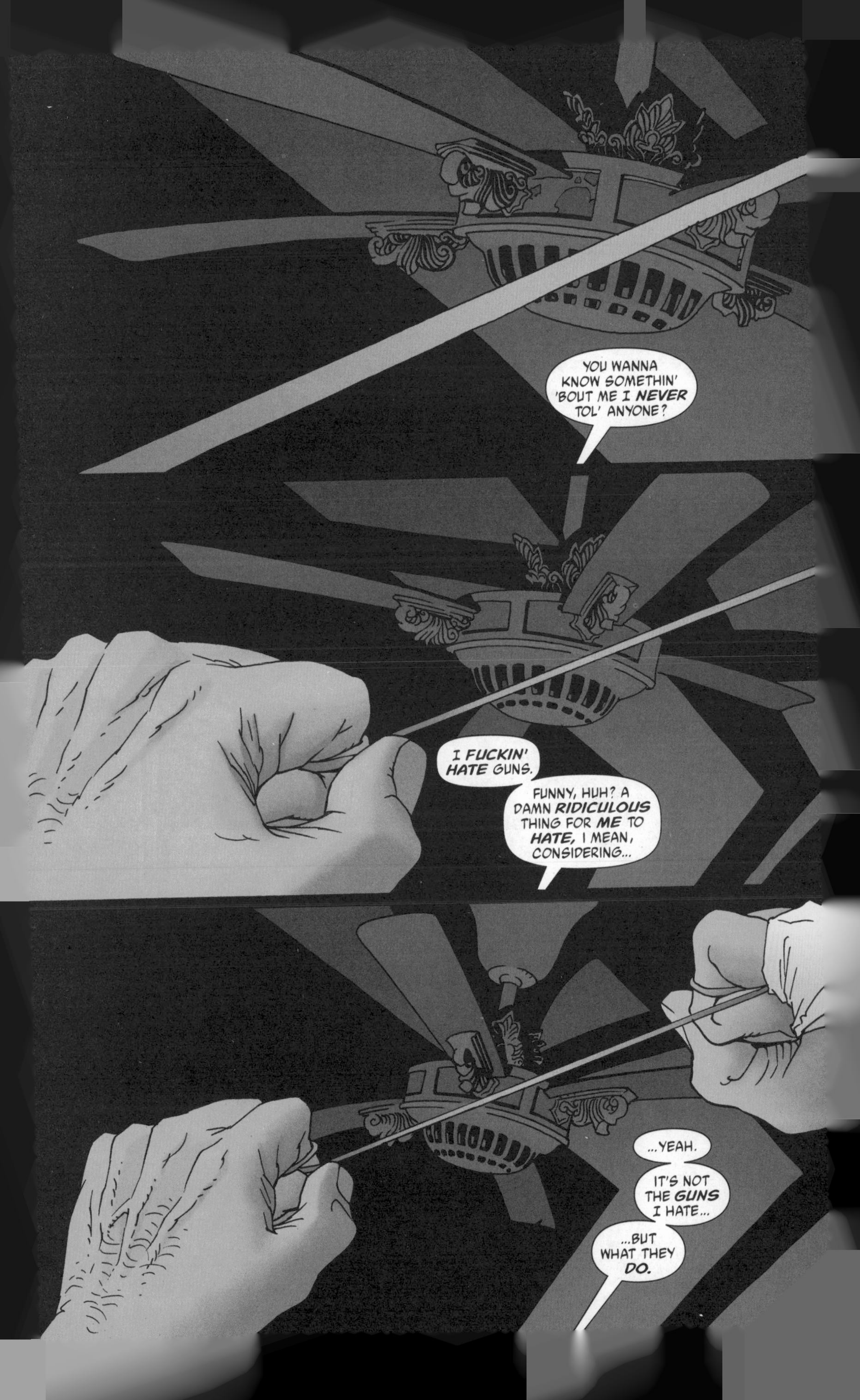
YOU WANNA KNOW SOMETHIN' 'BOUT ME I NEVER TOL' ANYONE?
I FUCKIN' HATE GUNS.
FUNNY, HUH? A DAMN RIDICULOUS THING FOR ME TO HATE, I MEAN, CONSIDERING...
...YEAH.
IT'S NOT THE GUNS I HATE...
...BUT WHAT THEY DO.

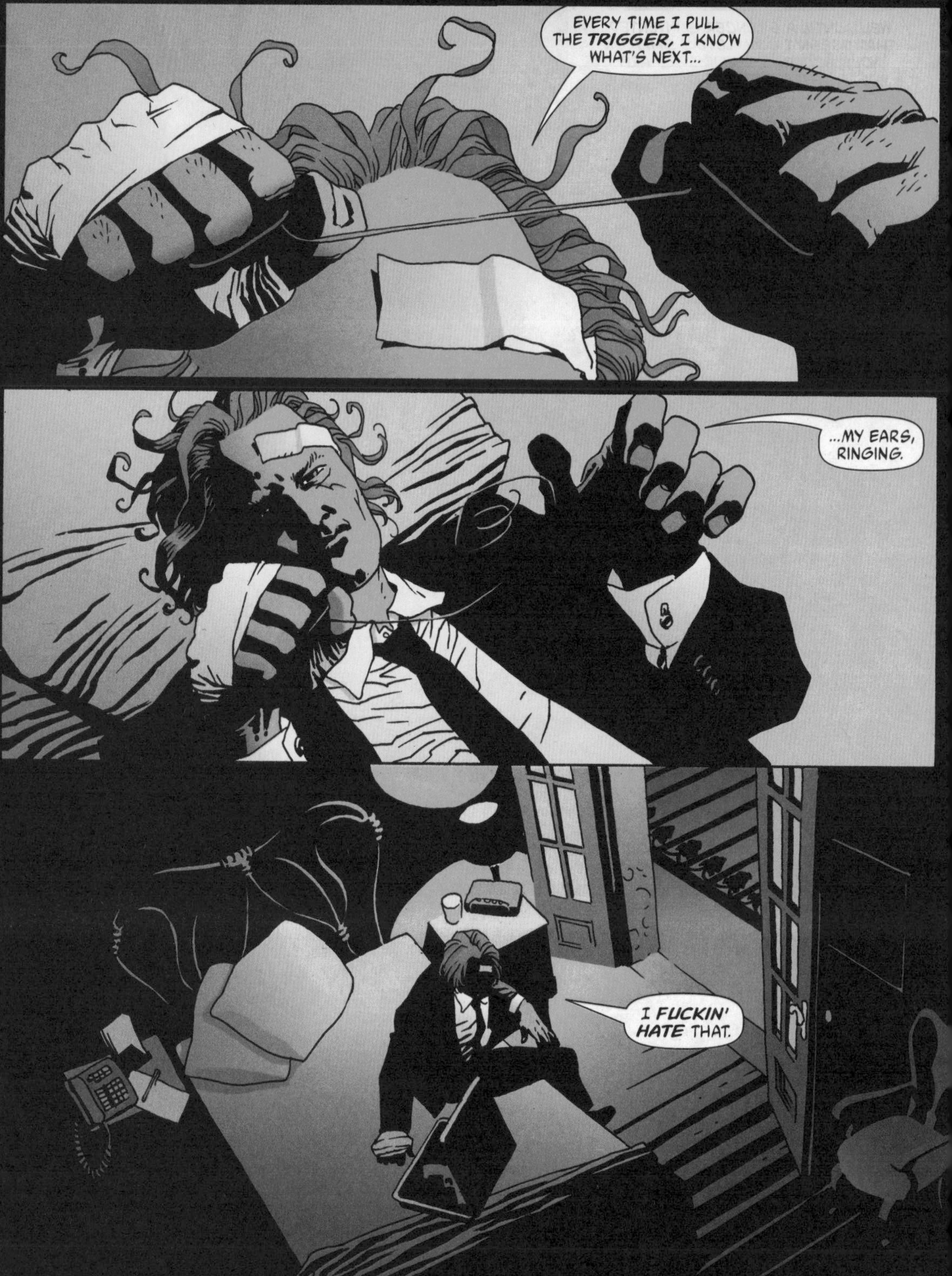
EVERY TIME I PULL THE TRIGGER, I KNOW WHAT'S NEXT...
...MY EARS, RINGING.
I FUCKIN' HATE THAT.

Wylie Runs the Voodoo Down

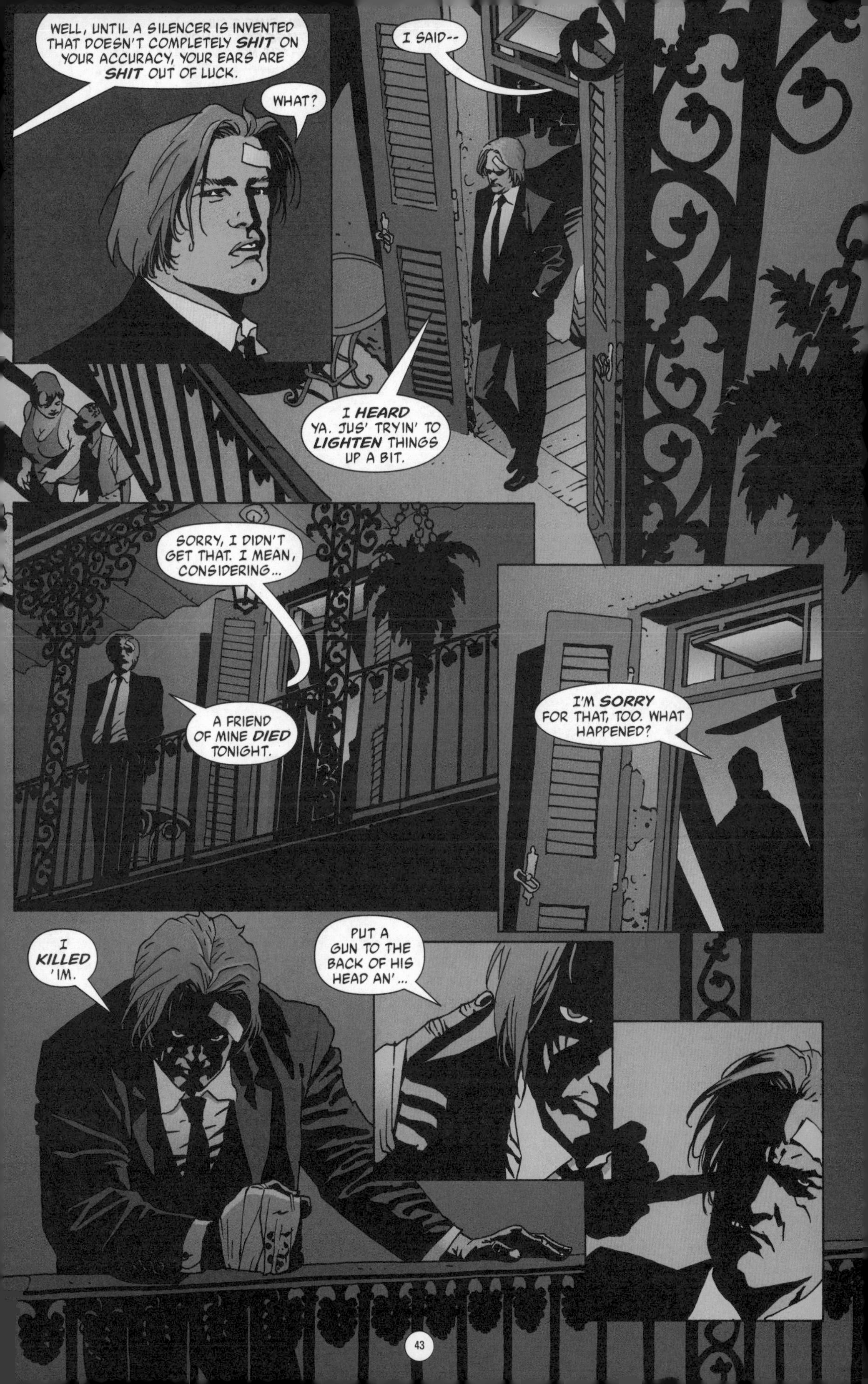

WELL, UNTIL A SILENCER IS INVENTED THAT DOESN'T COMPLETELY SHIT ON YOUR ACCURACY, YOUR EARS ARE SHIT OUT OF LUCK.
WHAT?
I SAID--
I HEARD YA. JUS' TRYIN' TO LIGHTEN THINGS UP A BIT.
SORRY, I DIDN'T GET THAT. I MEAN, CONSIDERING...
A FRIEND OF MINE DIED TONIGHT.
I'M SORRY FOR THAT, TOO. WHAT HAPPENED?
I KILLED 'IM.
PUT A GUN TO THE BACK OF HIS HEAD AN'...

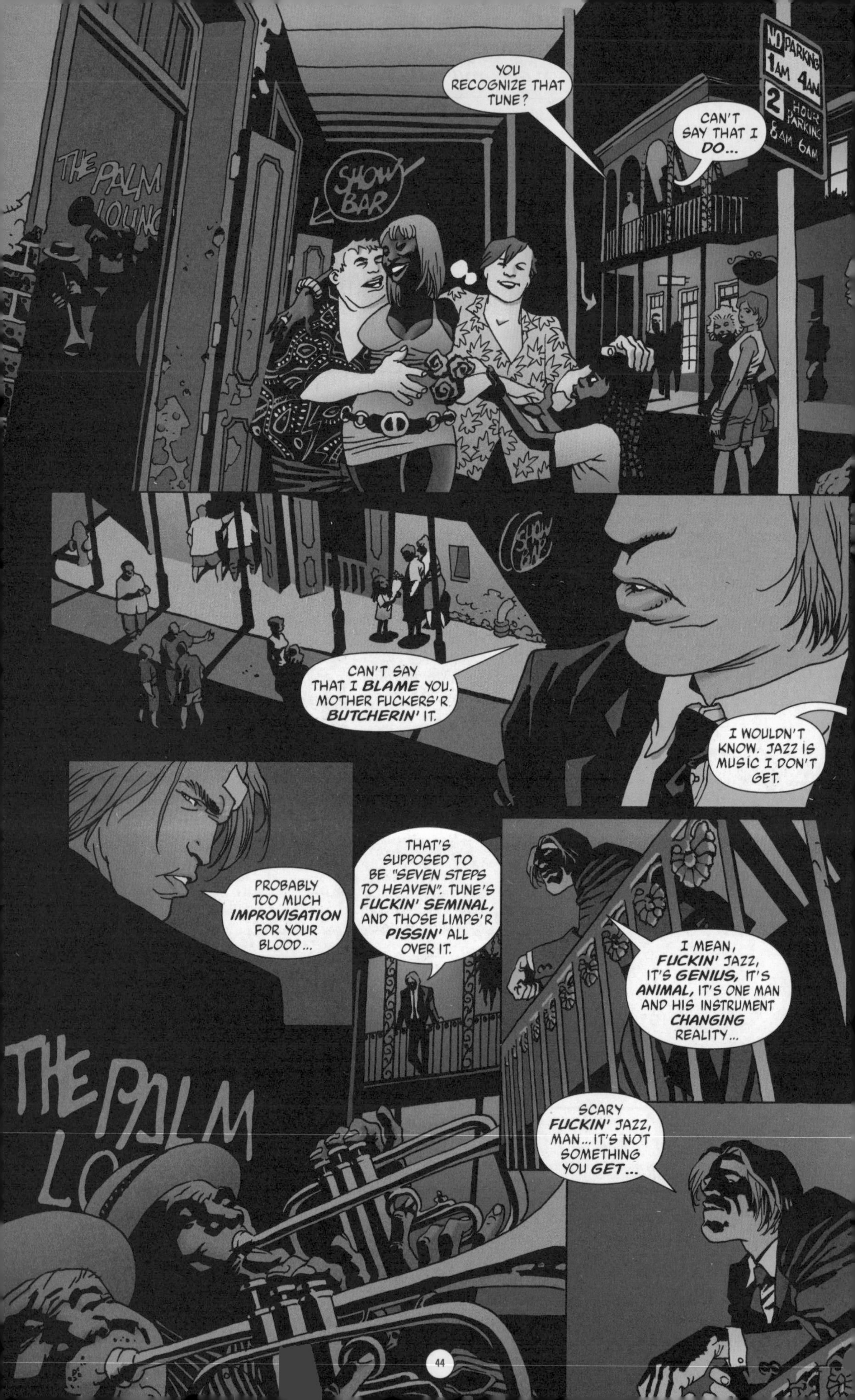
YOU RECOGNIZE THAT TUNE?
CAN'T SAY THAT I DO...
NO PARKING 1AM 4AM
2 HOUR PARKING 8AM 6AM
SHOW BAR
THE PALM LOUNGE
CAN'T SAY THAT I BLAME YOU. MOTHER FUCKERS'R BUTCHERIN' IT.
I WOULDN'T KNOW. JAZZ IS MUSIC I DON'T GET.
PROBABLY TOO MUCH IMPROVISATION FOR YOUR BLOOD...
THAT'S SUPPOSED TO BE "SEVEN STEPS TO HEAVEN". TUNE'S FUCKIN' SEMINAL, AND THOSE LIMPS'R PISSIN' ALL OVER IT.
I MEAN, FUCKIN' JAZZ, IT'S GENIUS, IT'S ANIMAL, IT'S ONE MAN AND HIS INSTRUMENT CHANGING REALITY...
SCARY FUCKIN' JAZZ, MAN... IT'S NOT SOMETHING YOU GET...

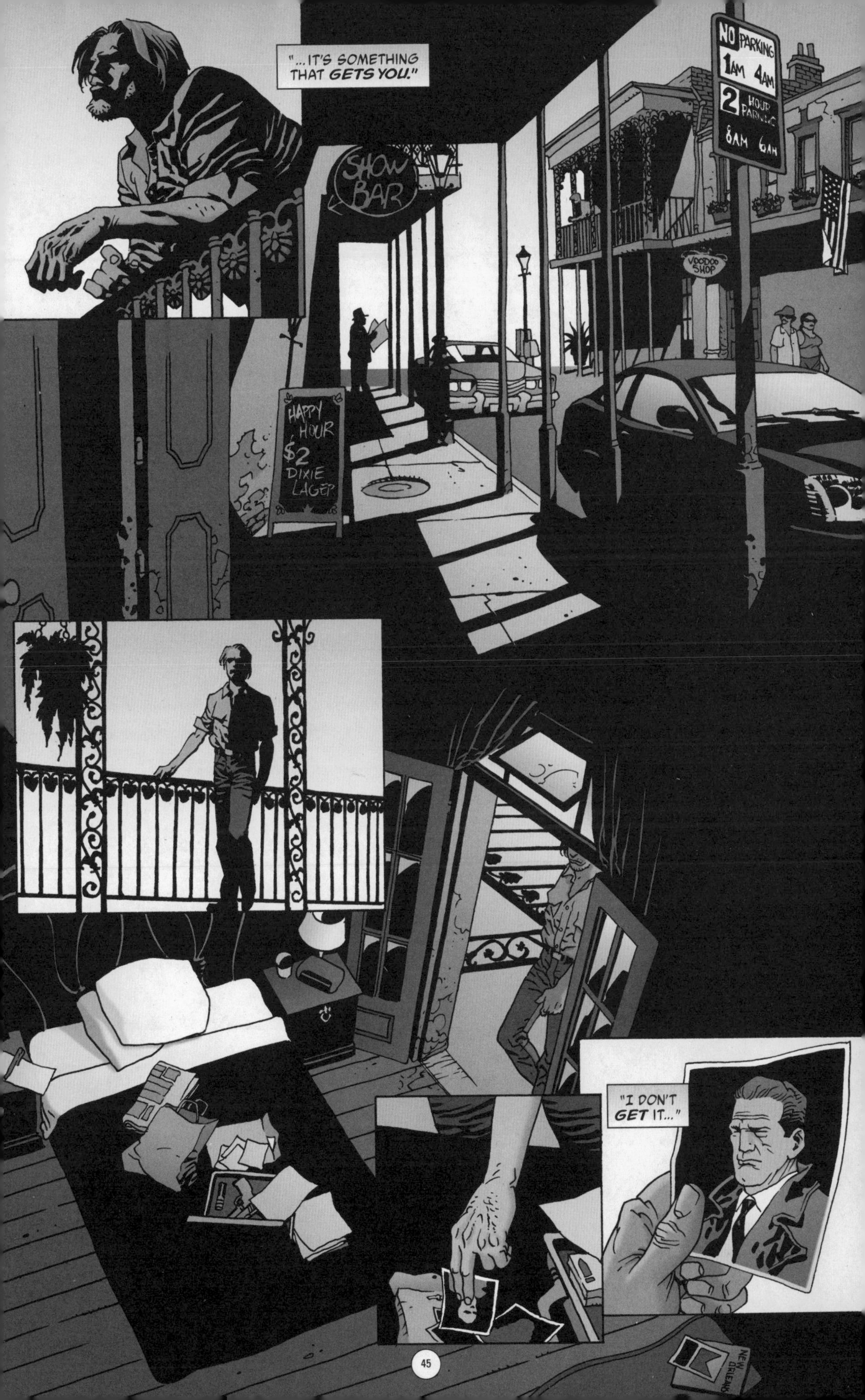
"...IT'S SOMETHING THAT GETS YOU."
NO PARKING
1AM 4AM
2 HOUR PARKING
8AM 6AM
SHOW BAR
VOODOO SHOP
HAPPY HOUR
$2
DIXIE LAGER
"I DON'T GET IT..."
NEW ORLEANS

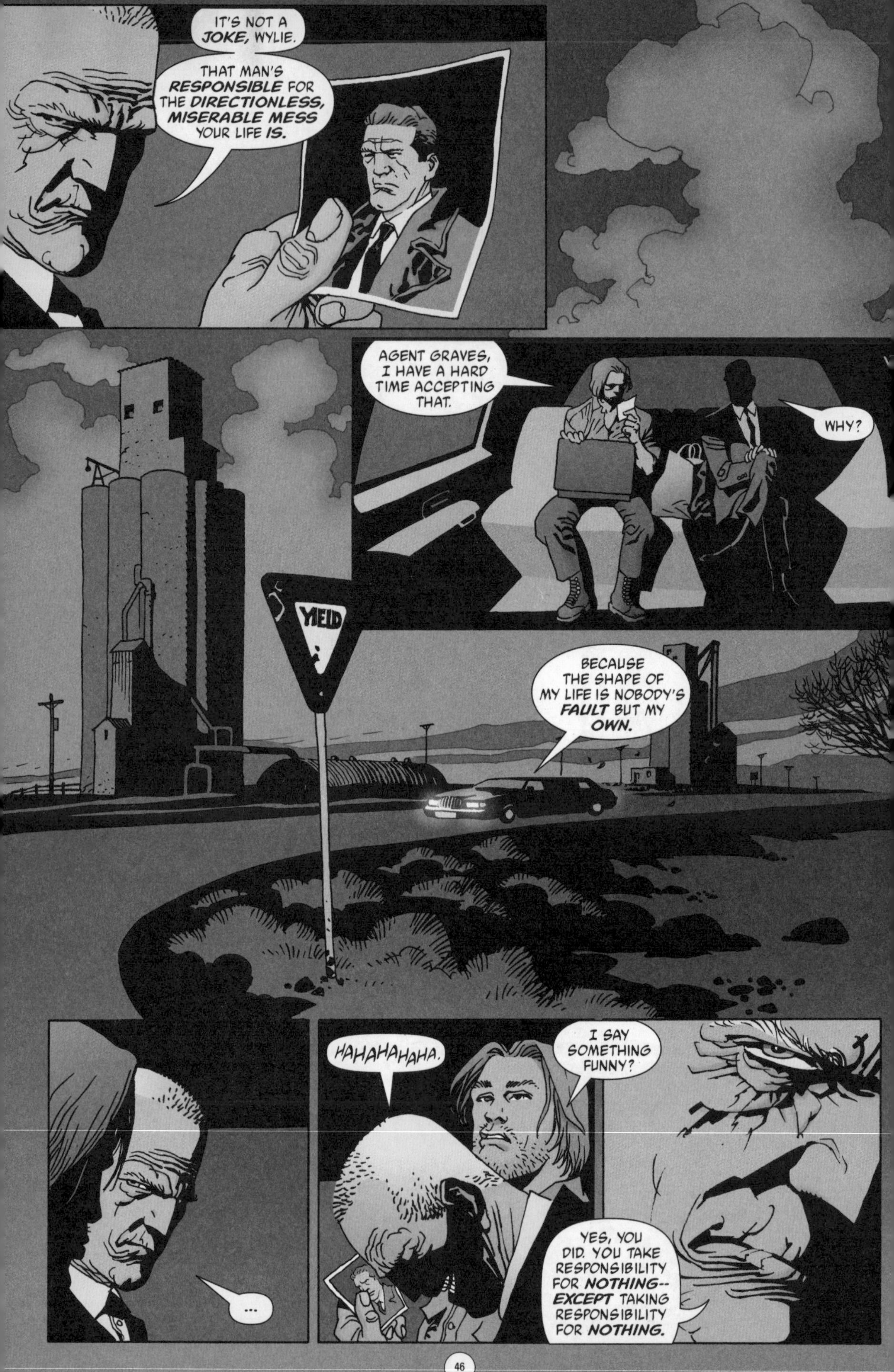
IT'S NOT A JOKE, WYLIE.
THAT MAN'S RESPONSIBLE FOR THE DIRECTIONLESS, MISERABLE MESS YOUR LIFE IS.
AGENT GRAVES, I HAVE A HARD TIME ACCEPTING THAT.
WHY?
YIELD
BECAUSE THE SHAPE OF MY LIFE IS NOBODY'S FAULT BUT MY OWN.
...
HAHAHAHAHA.
I SAY SOMETHING FUNNY?
YES, YOU DID. YOU TAKE RESPONSIBILITY FOR NOTHING-- EXCEPT TAKING RESPONSIBILITY FOR NOTHING.

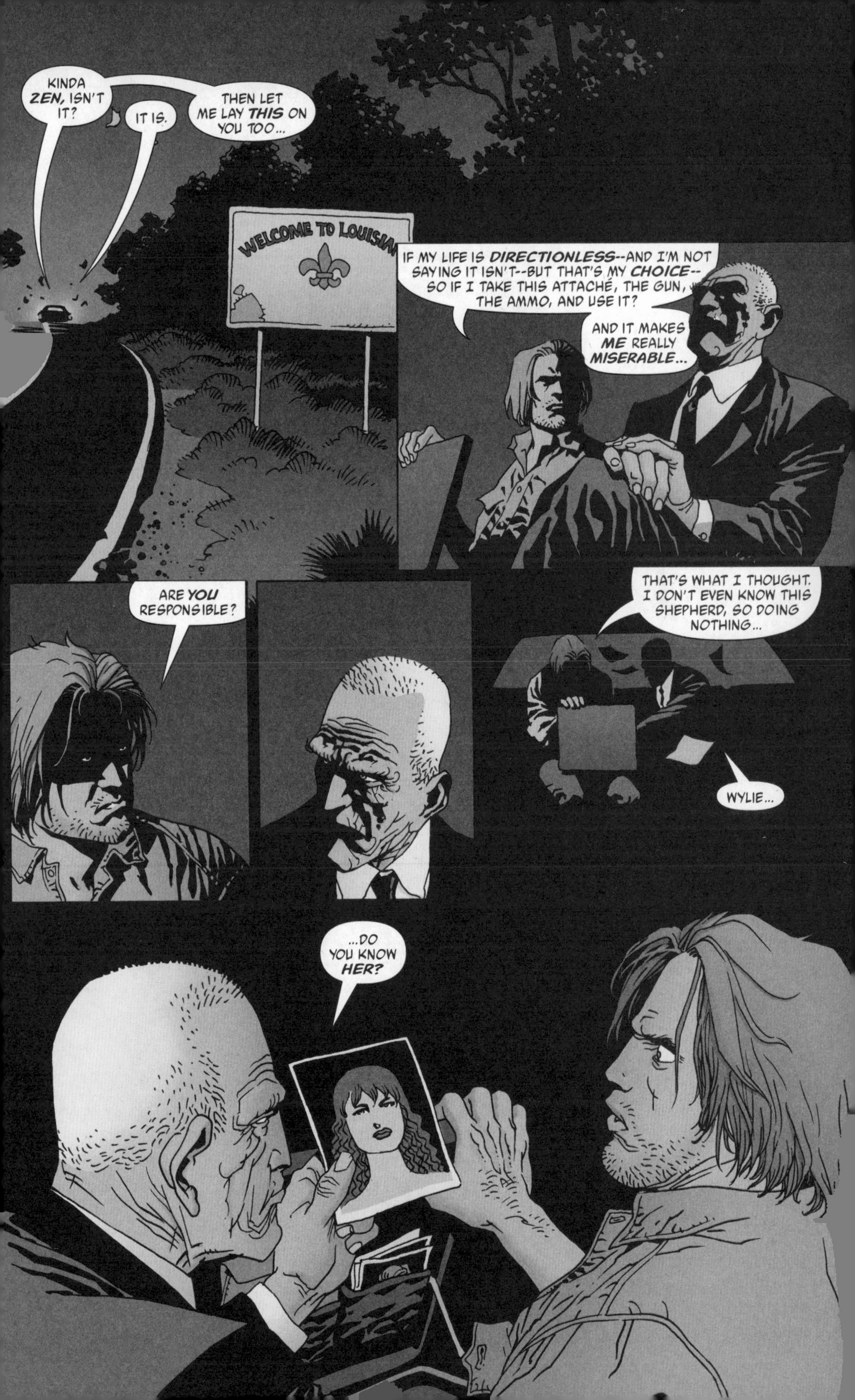
KINDA ZEN, ISN'T IT?
IT IS.
THEN LET ME LAY THIS ON YOU TOO...
WELCOME TO LOUISIAN
IF MY LIFE IS DIRECTIONLESS--AND I'M NOT SAYING IT ISN'T--BUT THAT'S MY CHOICE--SO IF I TAKE THIS ATTACHÉ, THE GUN, THE AMMO, AND USE IT?
AND IT MAKES ME REALLY MISERABLE...
ARE YOU RESPONSIBLE?
THAT'S WHAT I THOUGHT. I DON'T EVEN KNOW THIS SHEPHERD, SO DOING NOTHING...
WYLIE...
...DO YOU KNOW HER?

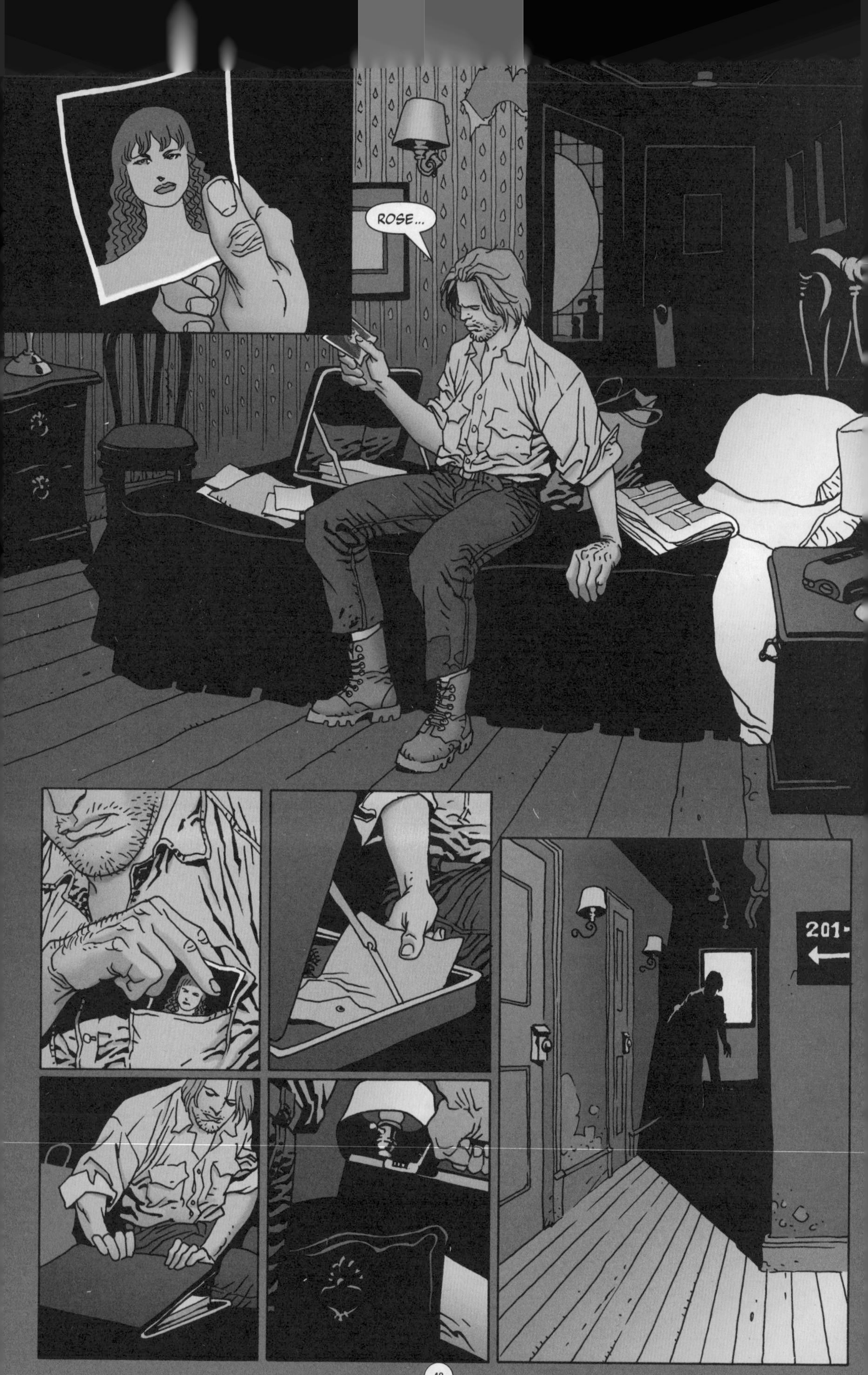
ROSE...
201-

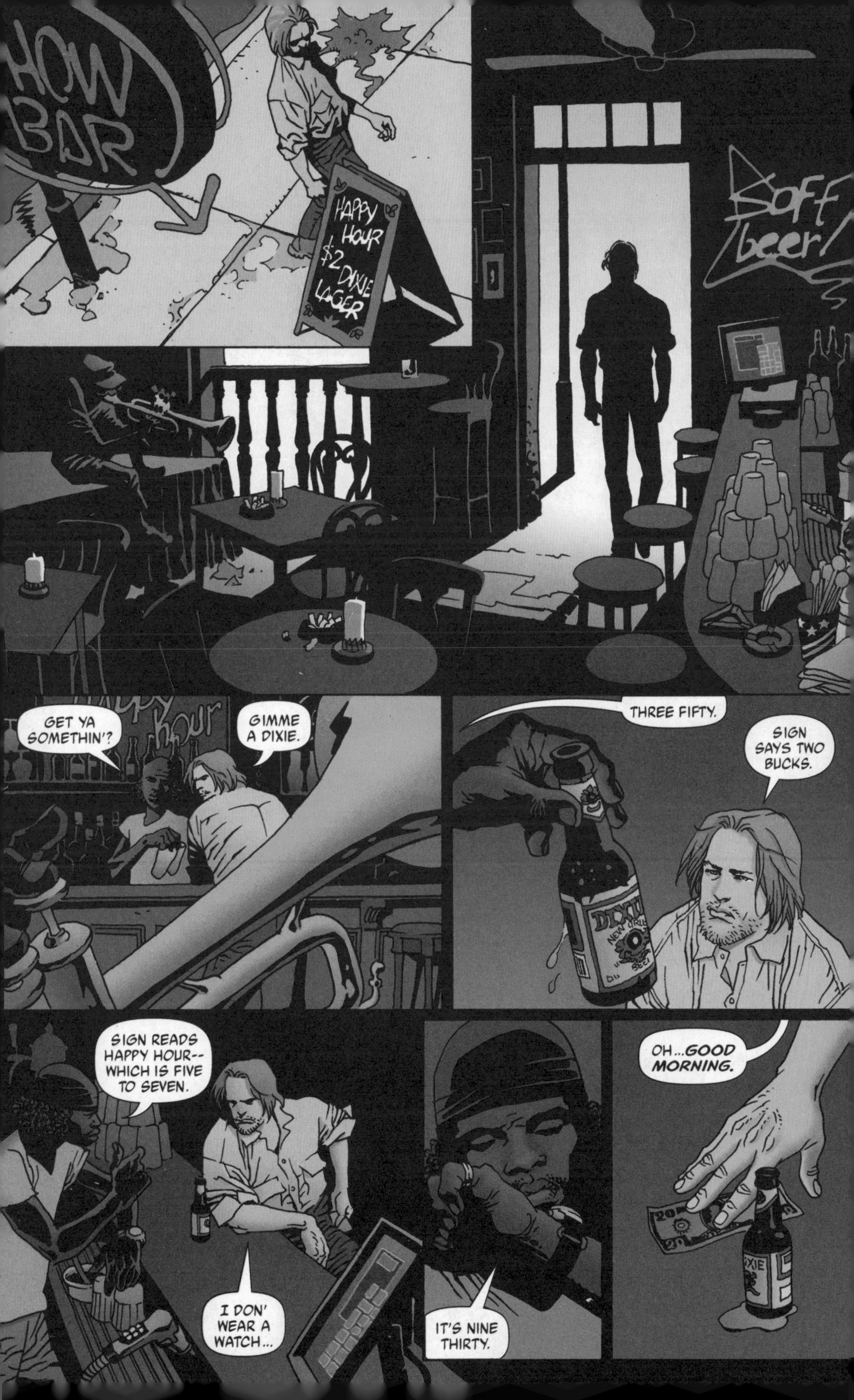

HOW BAR
HAPPY HOUR $2 DIXIE LAGER
beer!
GET YA SOMETHIN'?
GIMME A DIXIE.
THREE FIFTY.
SIGN SAYS TWO BUCKS.
SIGN READS HAPPY HOUR-- WHICH IS FIVE TO SEVEN.
I DON' WEAR A WATCH...
IT'S NINE THIRTY.
OH...GOOD MORNING.

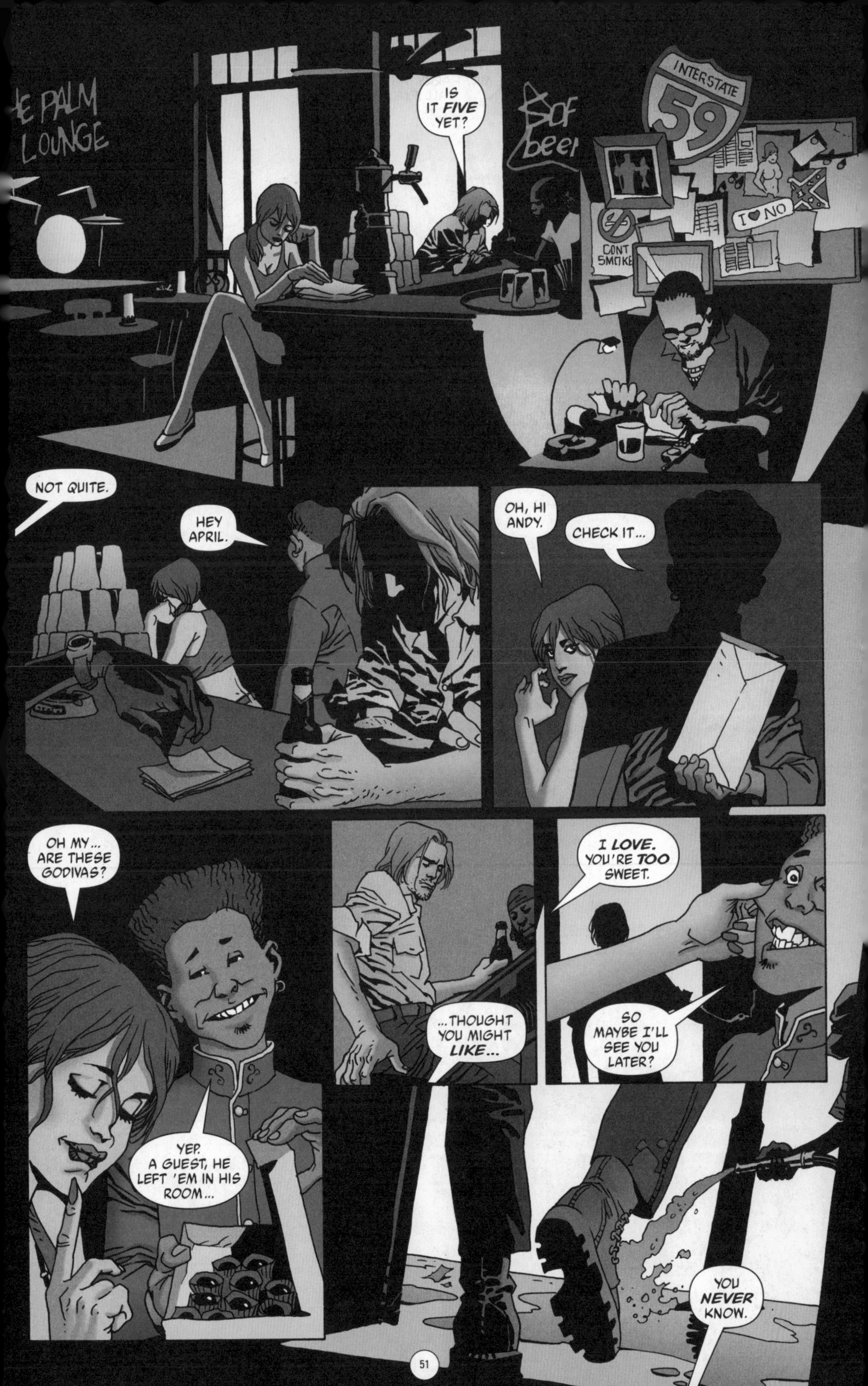
HE PALM
LOUNGE
IS IT FIVE YET?
Soft beer
INTERSTATE 59
I ♥ NO
CONT SMOKE
NOT QUITE.
HEY APRIL.
OH, HI ANDY.
CHECK IT...
OH MY... ARE THESE GODIVAS?
YEP. A GUEST, HE LEFT 'EM IN HIS ROOM...
...THOUGHT YOU MIGHT LIKE...
I LOVE. YOU'RE TOO SWEET.
SO MAYBE I'LL SEE YOU LATER?
YOU NEVER KNOW.

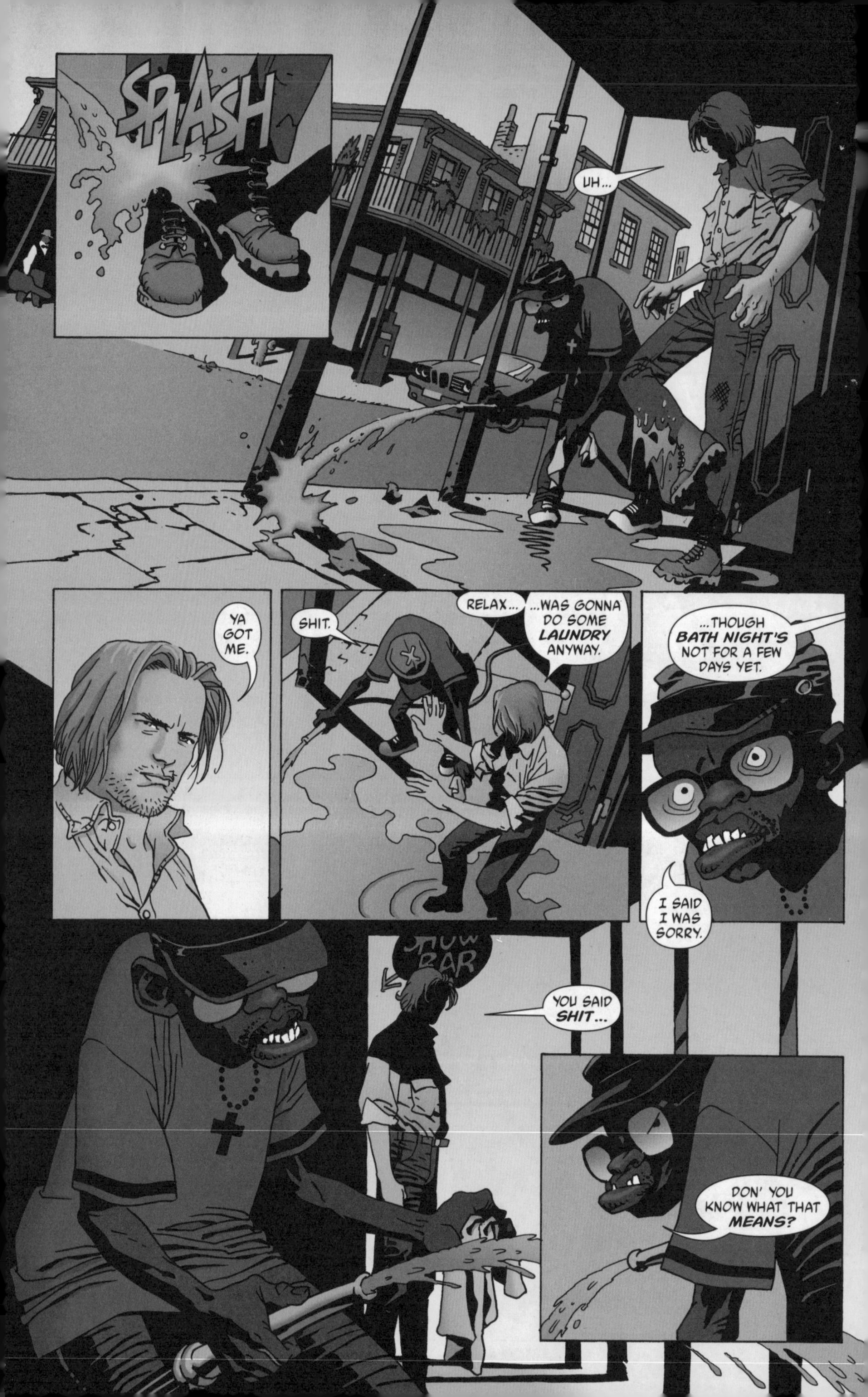
SPLASH
UH...
YA GOT ME.
SHIT.
RELAX...
...WAS GONNA DO SOME **LAUNDRY** ANYWAY.
...THOUGH **BATH NIGHT'S** NOT FOR A FEW DAYS YET.
I SAID I WAS SORRY.
YOU SAID **SHIT...**
DON' YOU KNOW WHAT THAT **MEANS?**

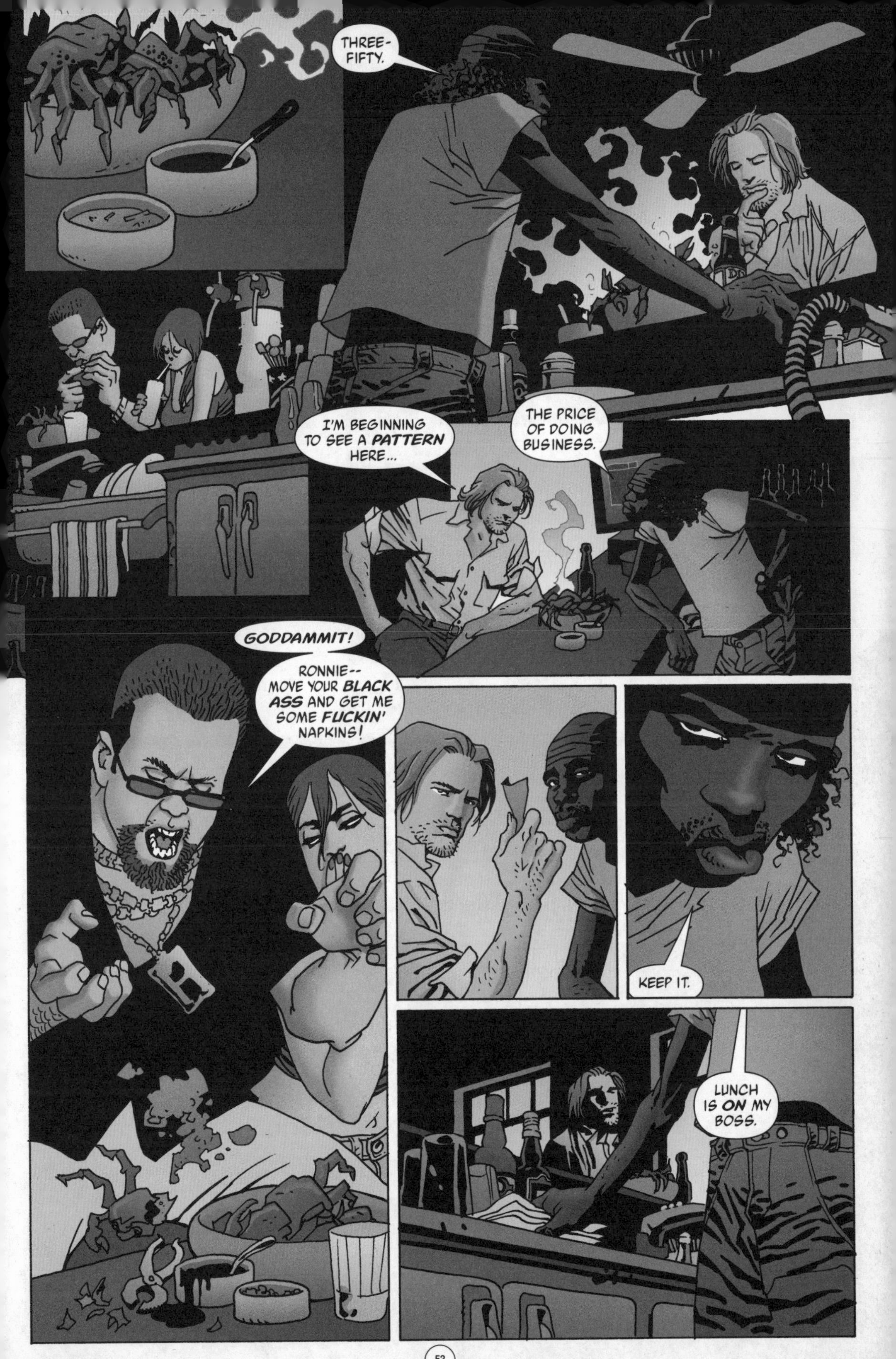
THREE-FIFTY.
I'M BEGINNING TO SEE A PATTERN HERE...
THE PRICE OF DOING BUSINESS.
GODDAMMIT!
RONNIE-- MOVE YOUR BLACK ASS AND GET ME SOME FUCKIN' NAPKINS!
KEEP IT.
LUNCH IS ON MY BOSS.

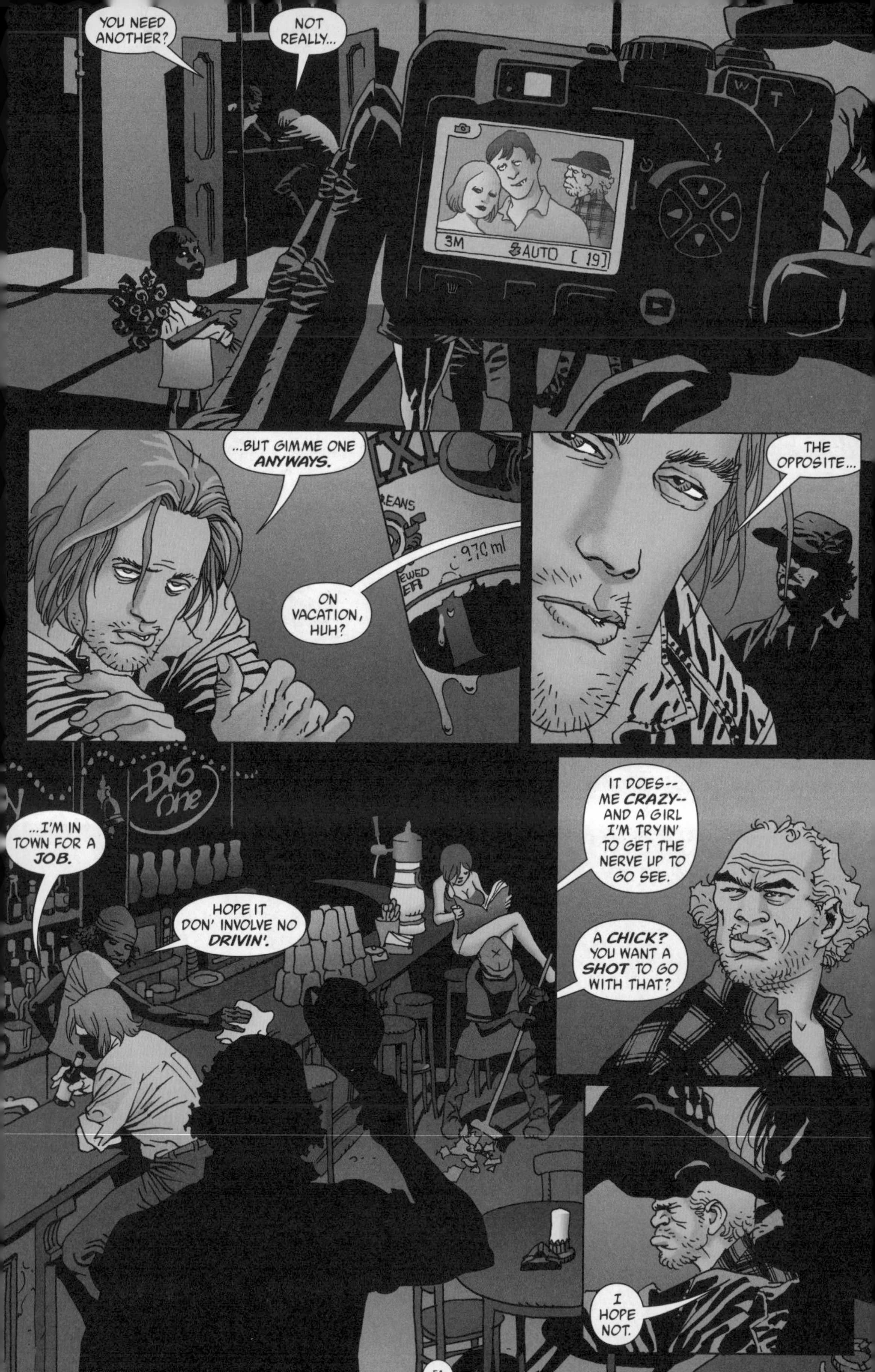
YOU NEED ANOTHER?
NOT REALLY...
3M AUTO [19]
...BUT GIMME ONE ANYWAYS.
ON VACATION, HUH?
THE OPPOSITE...
...I'M IN TOWN FOR A JOB.
HOPE IT DON' INVOLVE NO DRIVIN'.
IT DOES-- ME CRAZY-- AND A GIRL I'M TRYIN' TO GET THE NERVE UP TO GO SEE.
A CHICK? YOU WANT A SHOT TO GO WITH THAT?
I HOPE NOT.

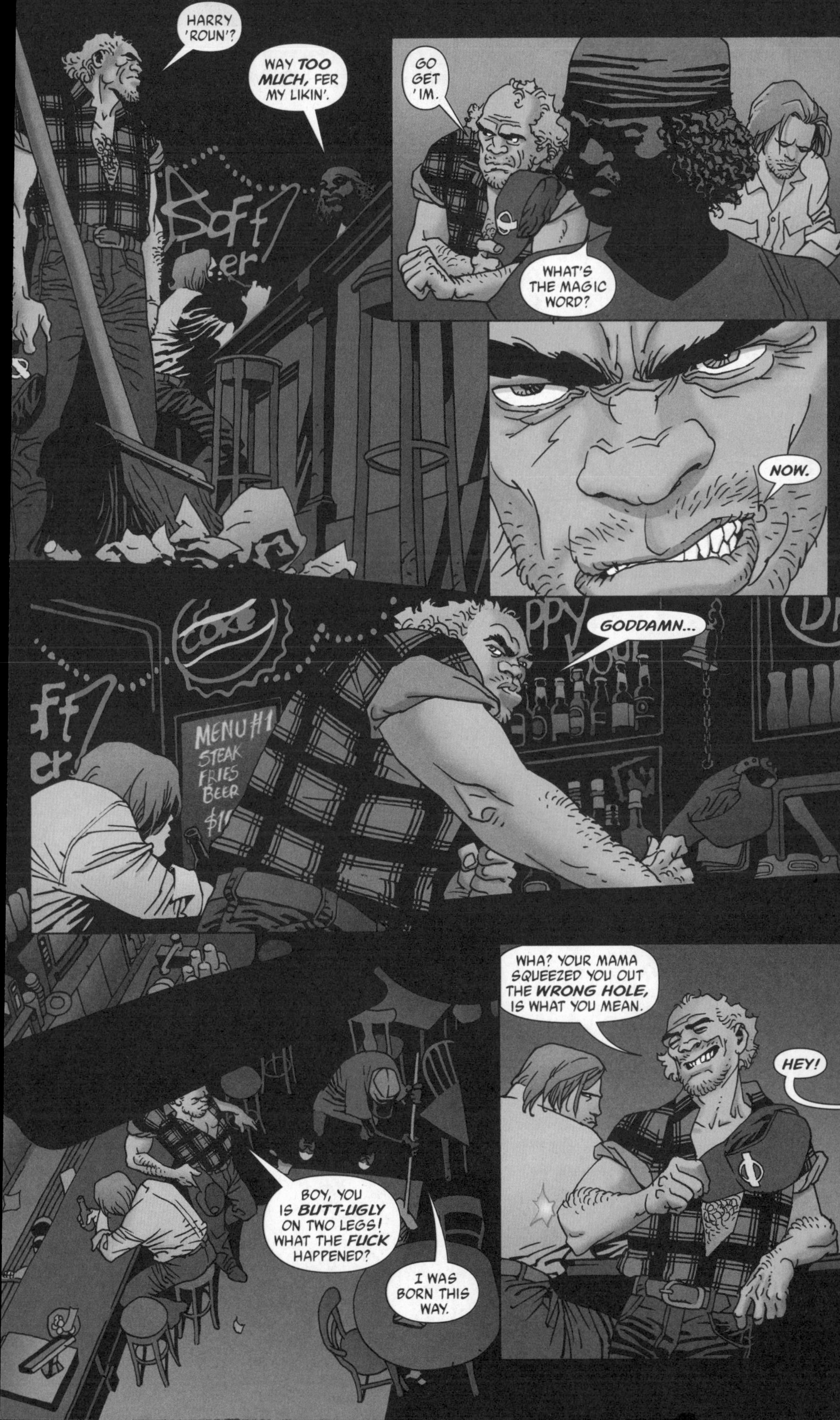
HARRY 'ROUN'?
WAY TOO MUCH, FER MY LIKIN'.
Soft
GO GET 'IM.
WHAT'S THE MAGIC WORD?
NOW.
COKE
GODDAMN...
MENU #1 STEAK FRIES BEER
BOY, YOU IS BUTT-UGLY ON TWO LEGS! WHAT THE FUCK HAPPENED?
I WAS BORN THIS WAY.
WHA? YOUR MAMA SQUEEZED YOU OUT THE WRONG HOLE, IS WHAT YOU MEAN.
HEY!

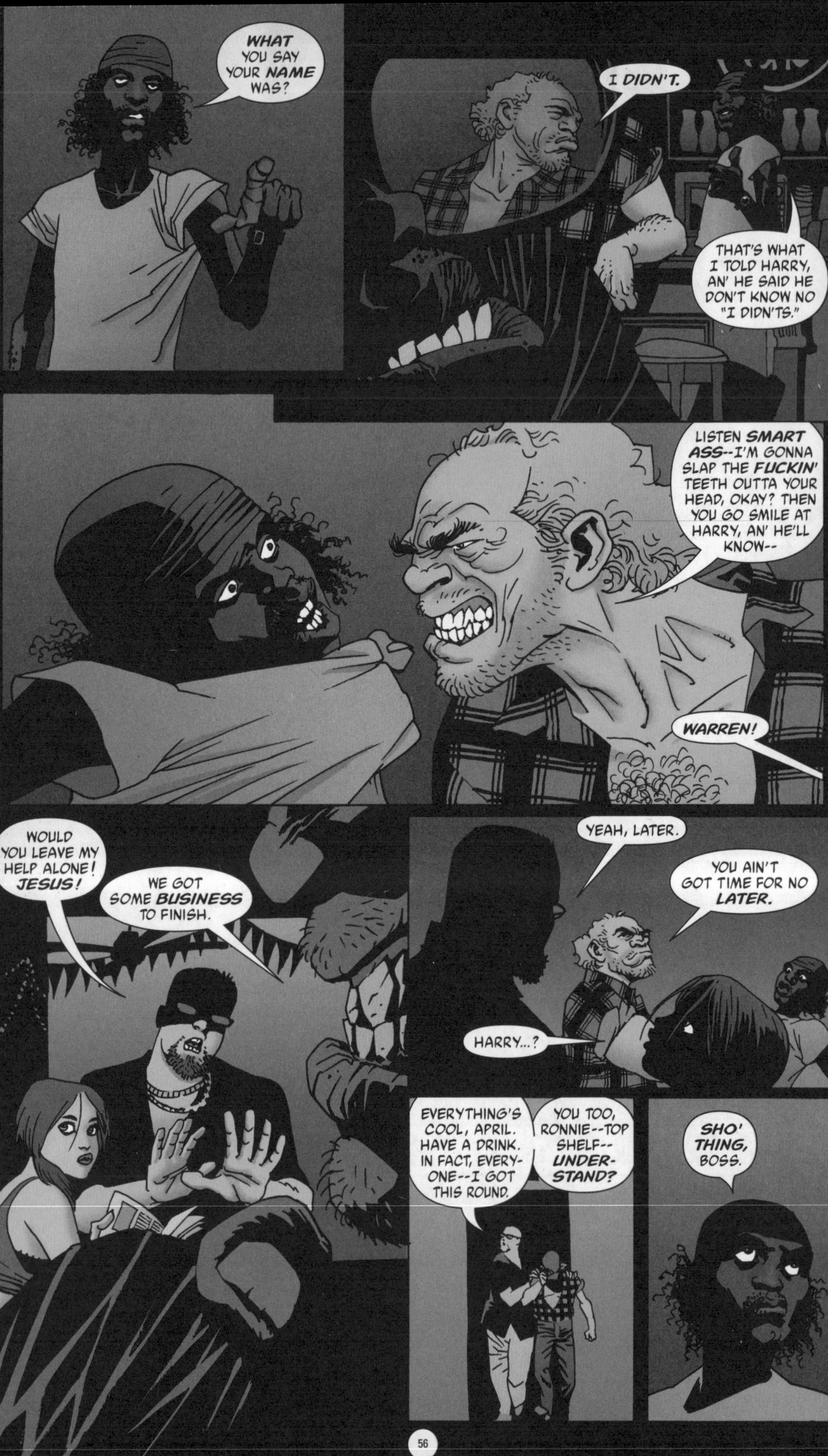

WHAT YOU SAY YOUR NAME WAS?
I DIDN'T.
THAT'S WHAT I TOLD HARRY, AN' HE SAID HE DON'T KNOW NO "I DIDN'TS."
LISTEN SMART ASS--I'M GONNA SLAP THE FUCKIN' TEETH OUTTA YOUR HEAD, OKAY? THEN YOU GO SMILE AT HARRY, AN' HE'LL KNOW--
WARREN!
WOULD YOU LEAVE MY HELP ALONE! JESUS!
WE GOT SOME BUSINESS TO FINISH.
YEAH, LATER.
YOU AIN'T GOT TIME FOR NO LATER.
HARRY...?
EVERYTHING'S COOL, APRIL. HAVE A DRINK. IN FACT, EVERY-ONE--I GOT THIS ROUND.
YOU TOO, RONNIE--TOP SHELF--UNDER-STAND?
SHO' THING, BOSS.

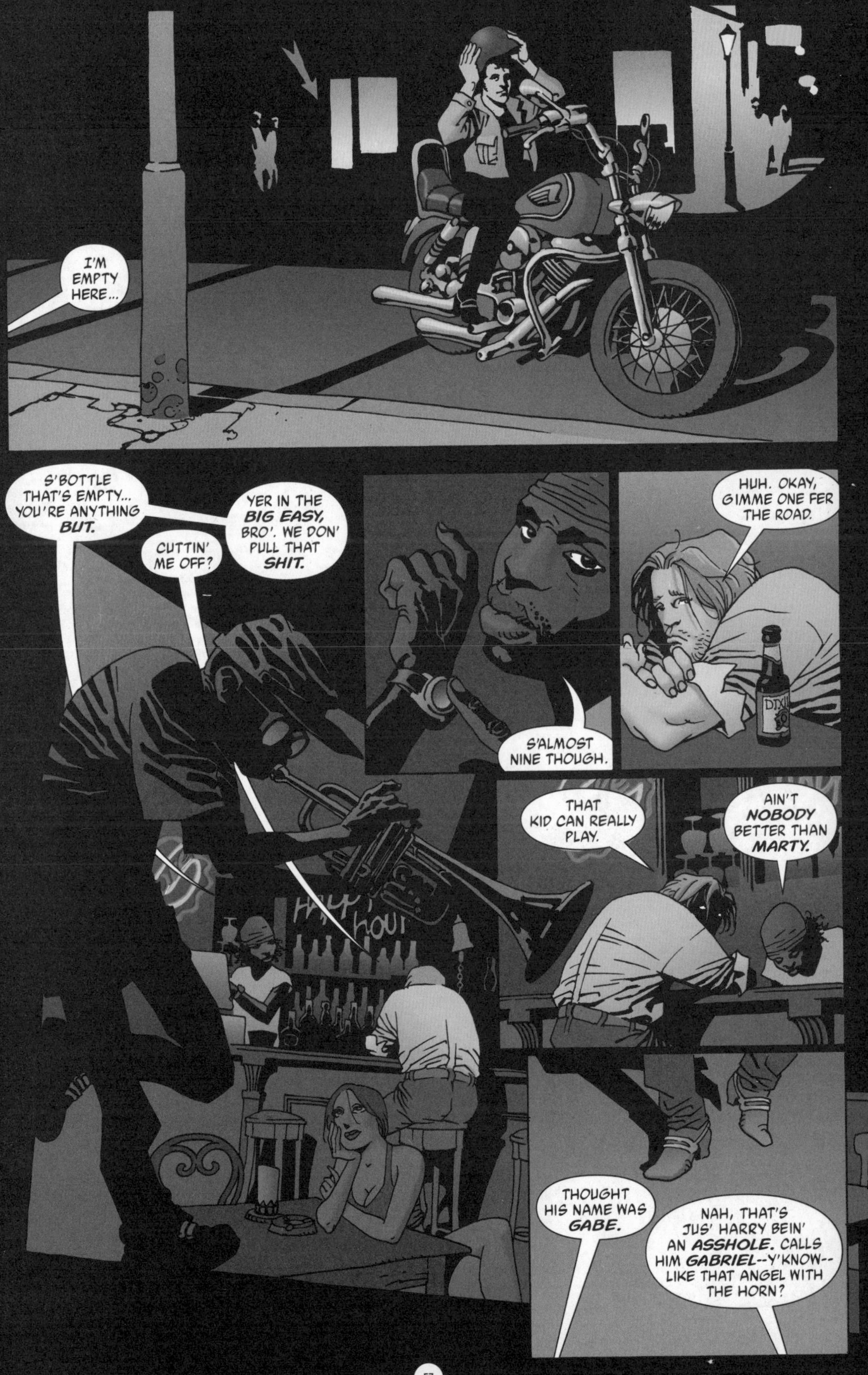

I'M EMPTY HERE...
S'BOTTLE THAT'S EMPTY... YOU'RE ANYTHING BUT.
CUTTIN' ME OFF?
YER IN THE BIG EASY, BRO'. WE DON' PULL THAT SHIT.
S'ALMOST NINE THOUGH.
HUH. OKAY, GIMME ONE FER THE ROAD.
THAT KID CAN REALLY PLAY.
AIN'T NOBODY BETTER THAN MARTY.
THOUGHT HIS NAME WAS GABE.
NAH, THAT'S JUS' HARRY BEIN' AN ASSHOLE. CALLS HIM GABRIEL--Y'KNOW--LIKE THAT ANGEL WITH THE HORN?

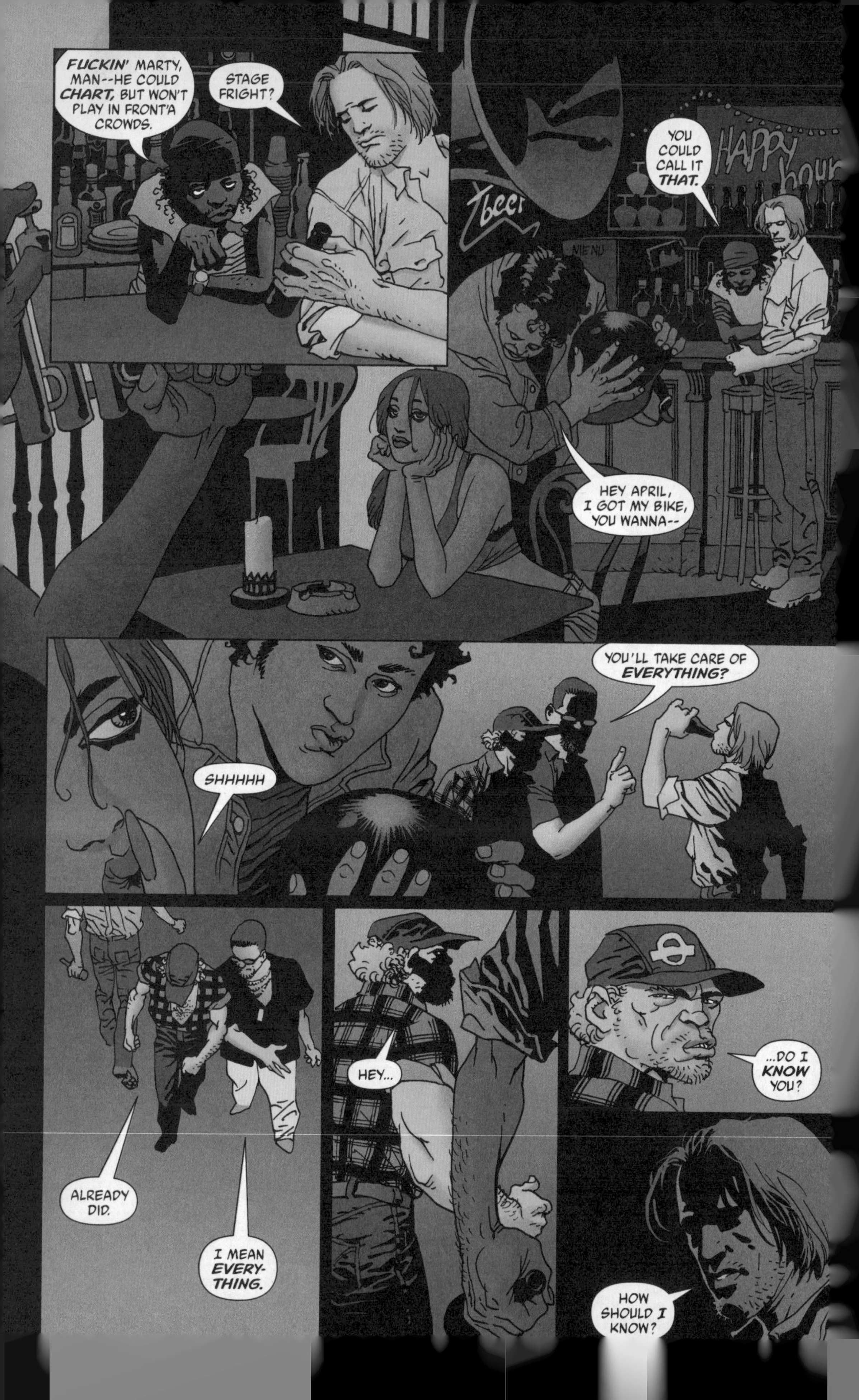
FUCKIN' MARTY, MAN--HE COULD CHART, BUT WON'T PLAY IN FRONT'A CROWDS.
STAGE FRIGHT?
YOU COULD CALL IT THAT.
HAPPY hour
beer
MENU
HEY APRIL, I GOT MY BIKE, YOU WANNA--
YOU'LL TAKE CARE OF EVERYTHING?
SHHHHH
ALREADY DID.
I MEAN EVERY-THING.
HEY...
...DO I KNOW YOU?
HOW SHOULD I KNOW?

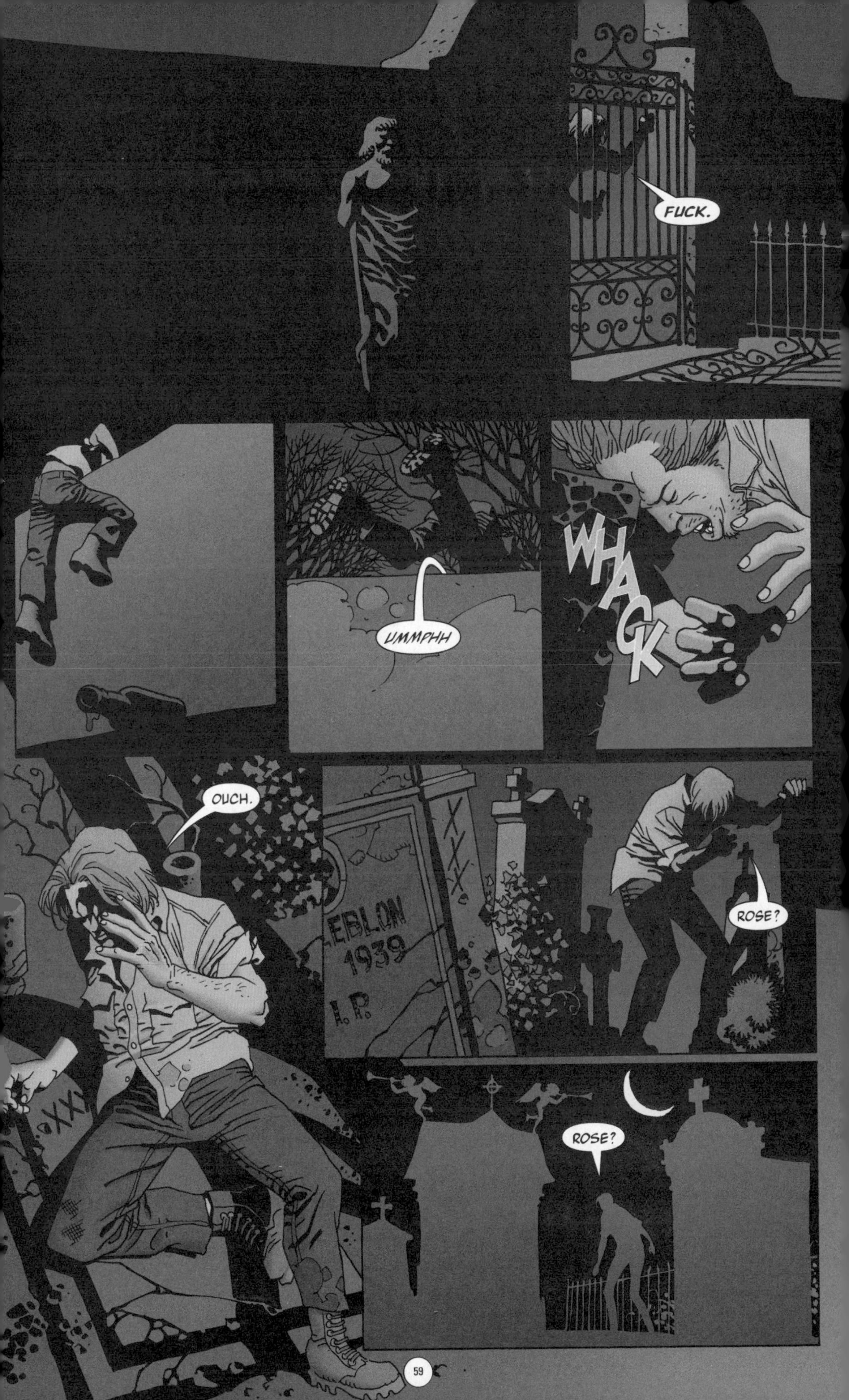
FUCK.
UMMPHH
WHACK
OUCH.
EBLON
1939
I.P.
ROSE?
ROSE?

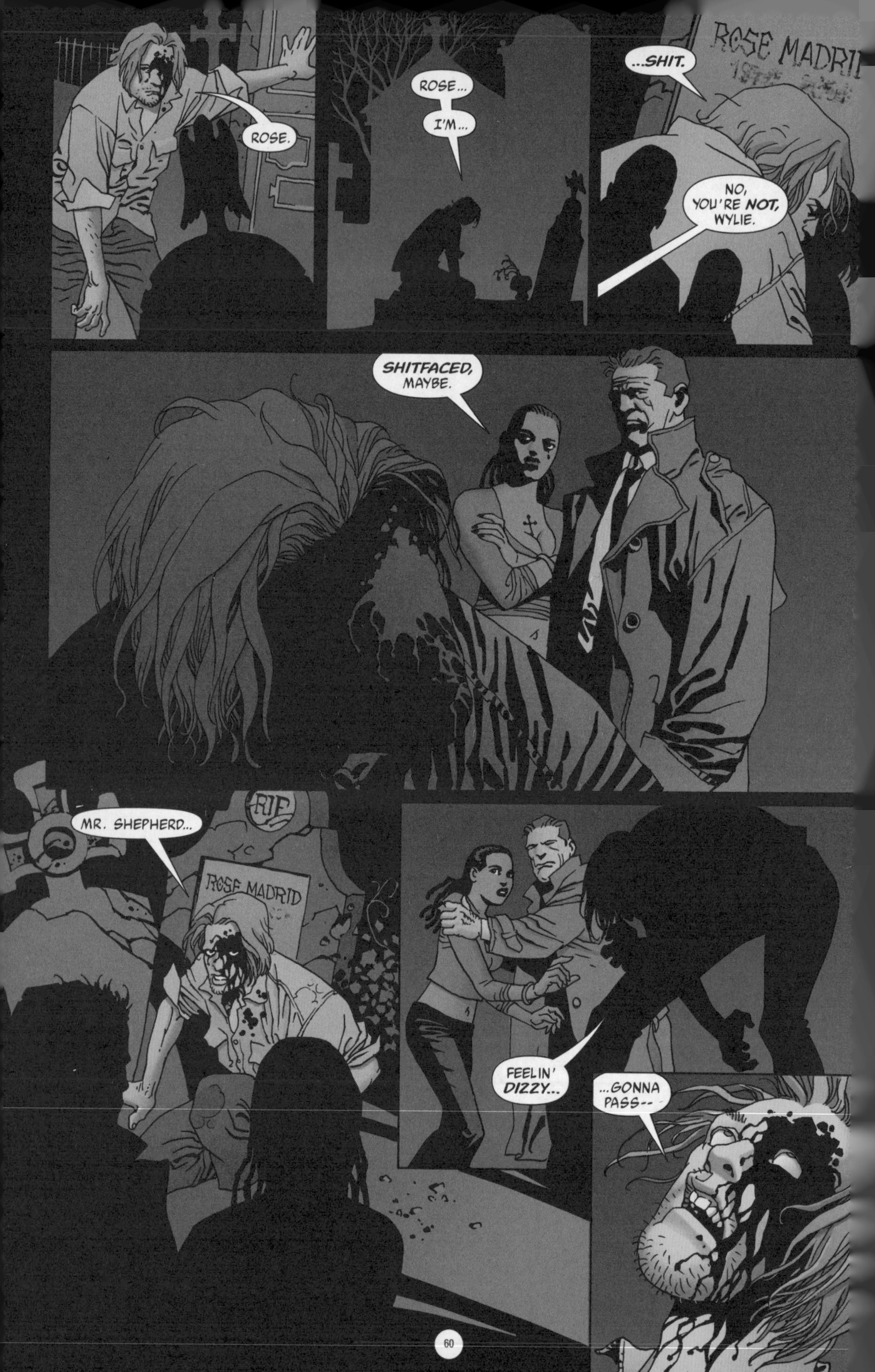
ROSE.
ROSE...
I'M...
ROSE MADRID
...SHIT.
NO, YOU'RE NOT, WYLIE.
SHITFACED, MAYBE.
RIP
MR. SHEPHERD...
ROSE MADRID
FEELIN' DIZZY...
...GONNA PASS--

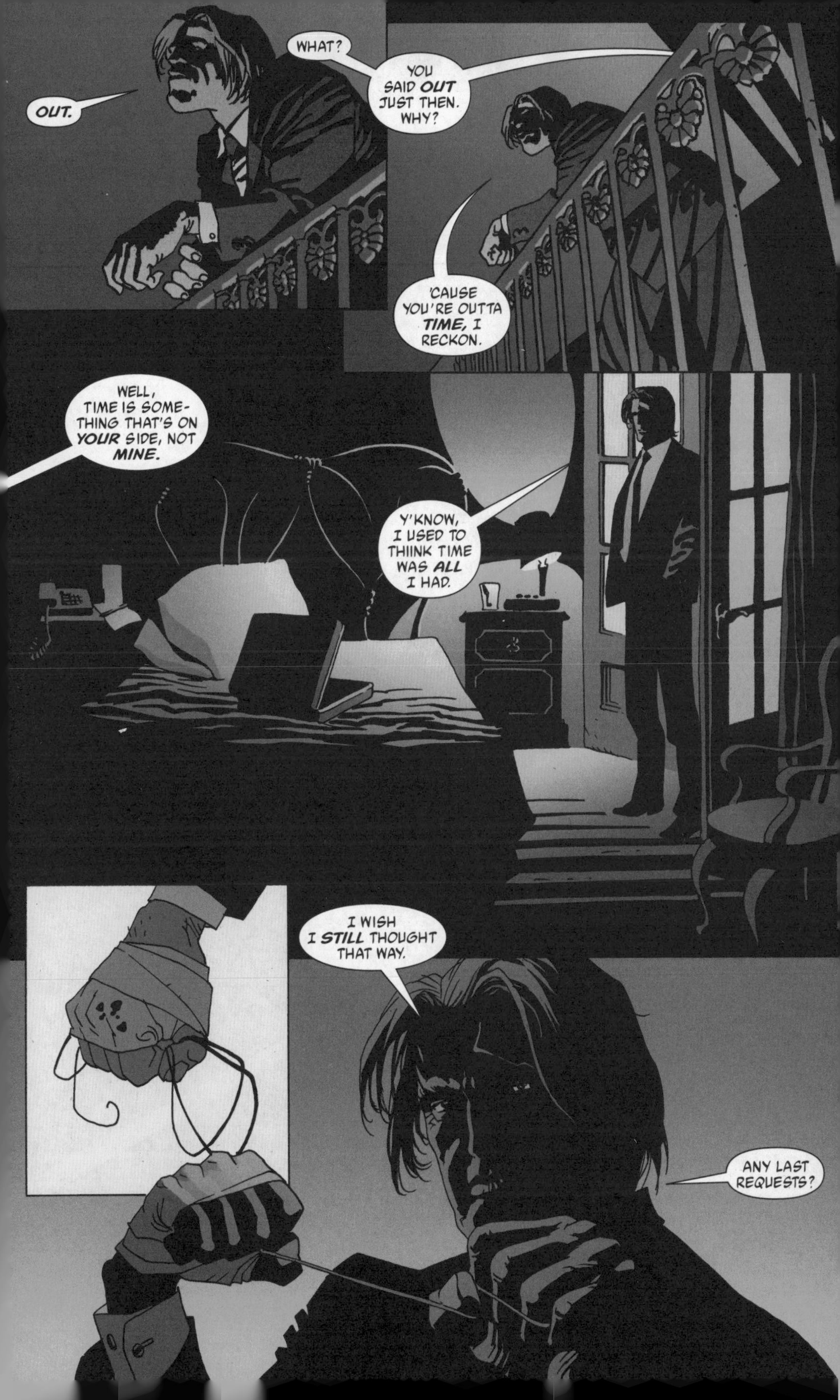
OUT.
WHAT?
YOU SAID OUT JUST THEN. WHY?
'CAUSE YOU'RE OUTTA TIME, I RECKON.
WELL, TIME IS SOME-THING THAT'S ON YOUR SIDE, NOT MINE.
Y'KNOW, I USED TO THIINK TIME WAS ALL I HAD.
I WISH I STILL THOUGHT THAT WAY.
ANY LAST REQUESTS?

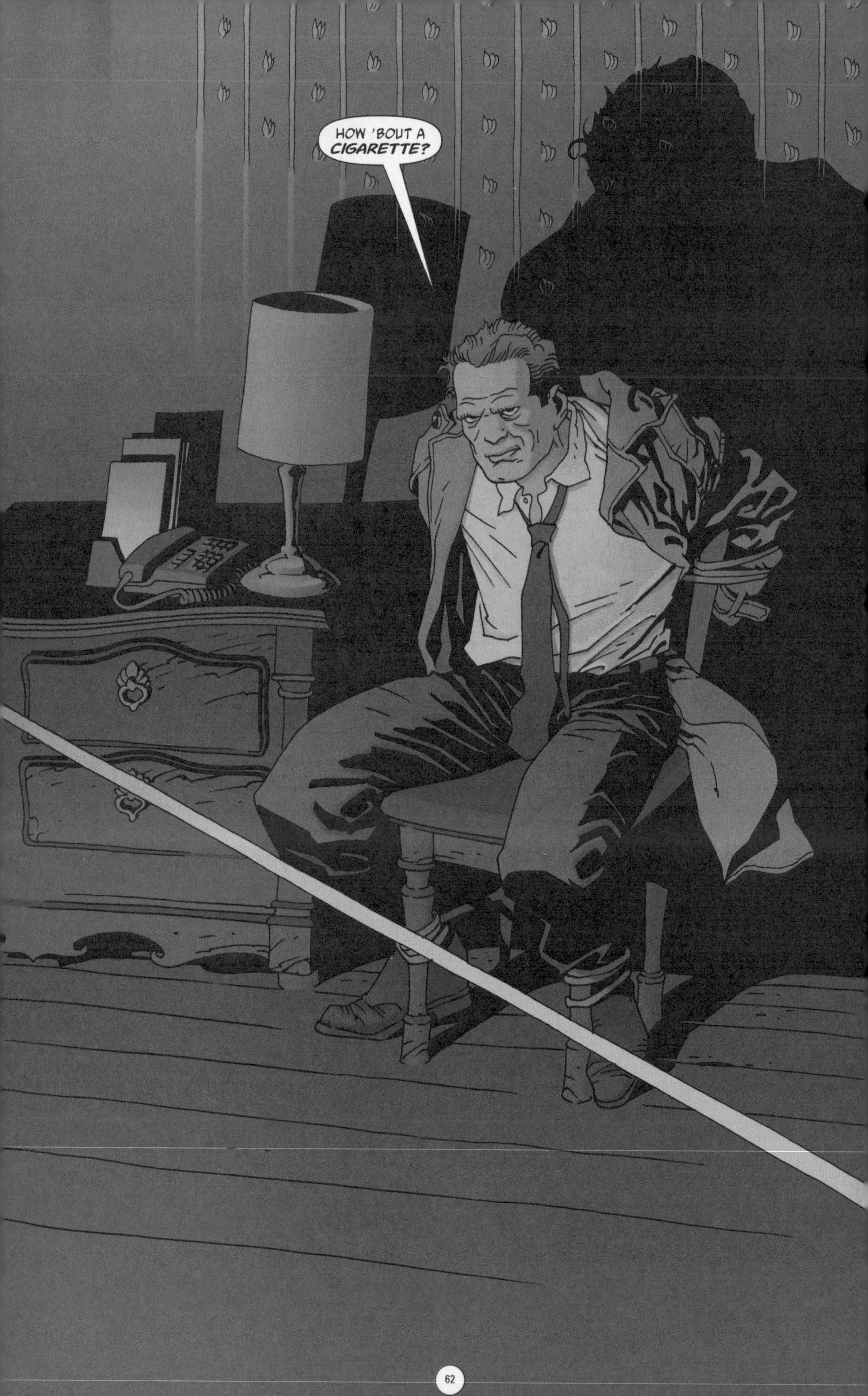
HOW 'BOUT A *CIGARETTE?*

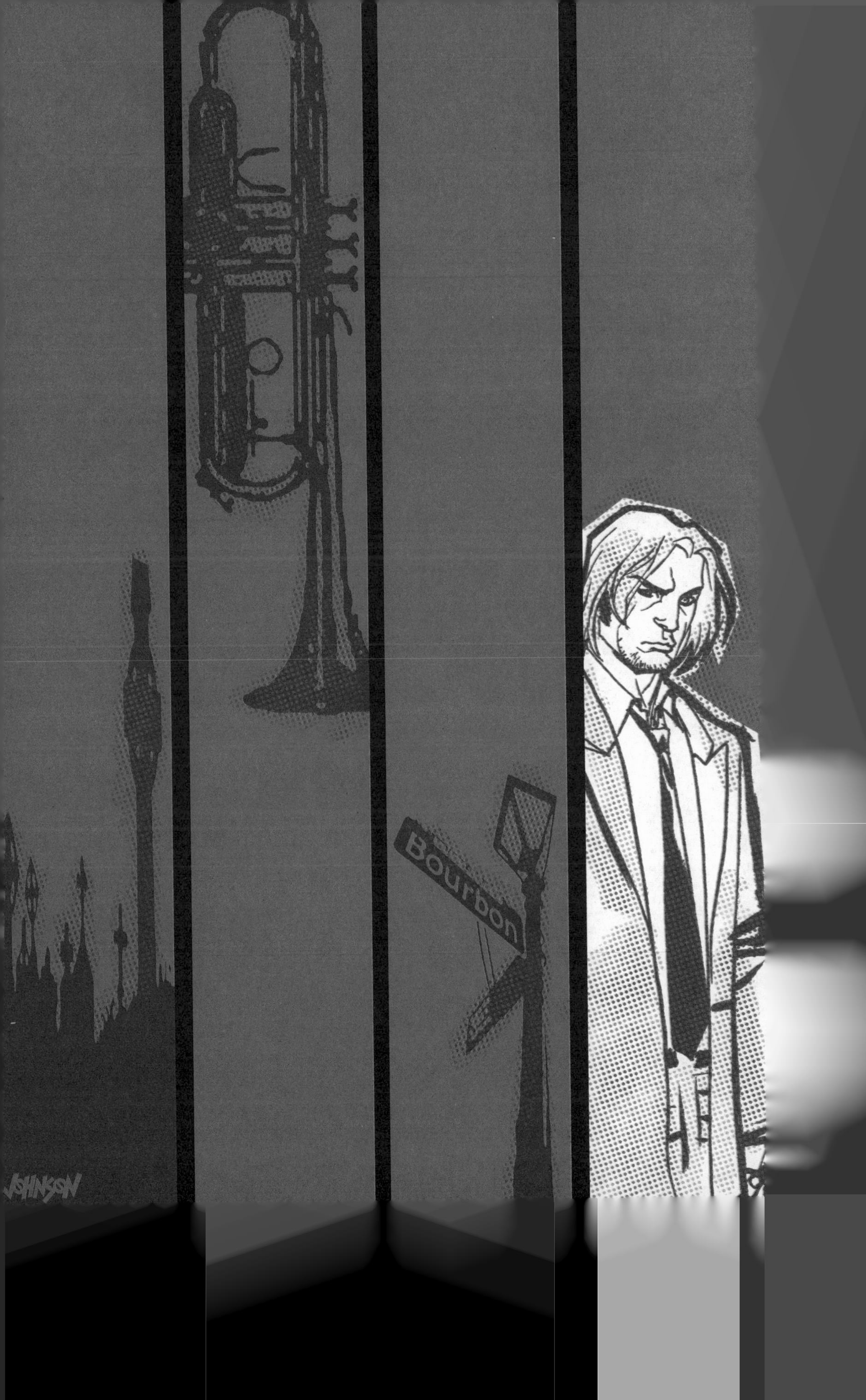

Bourbon
JOHNSON

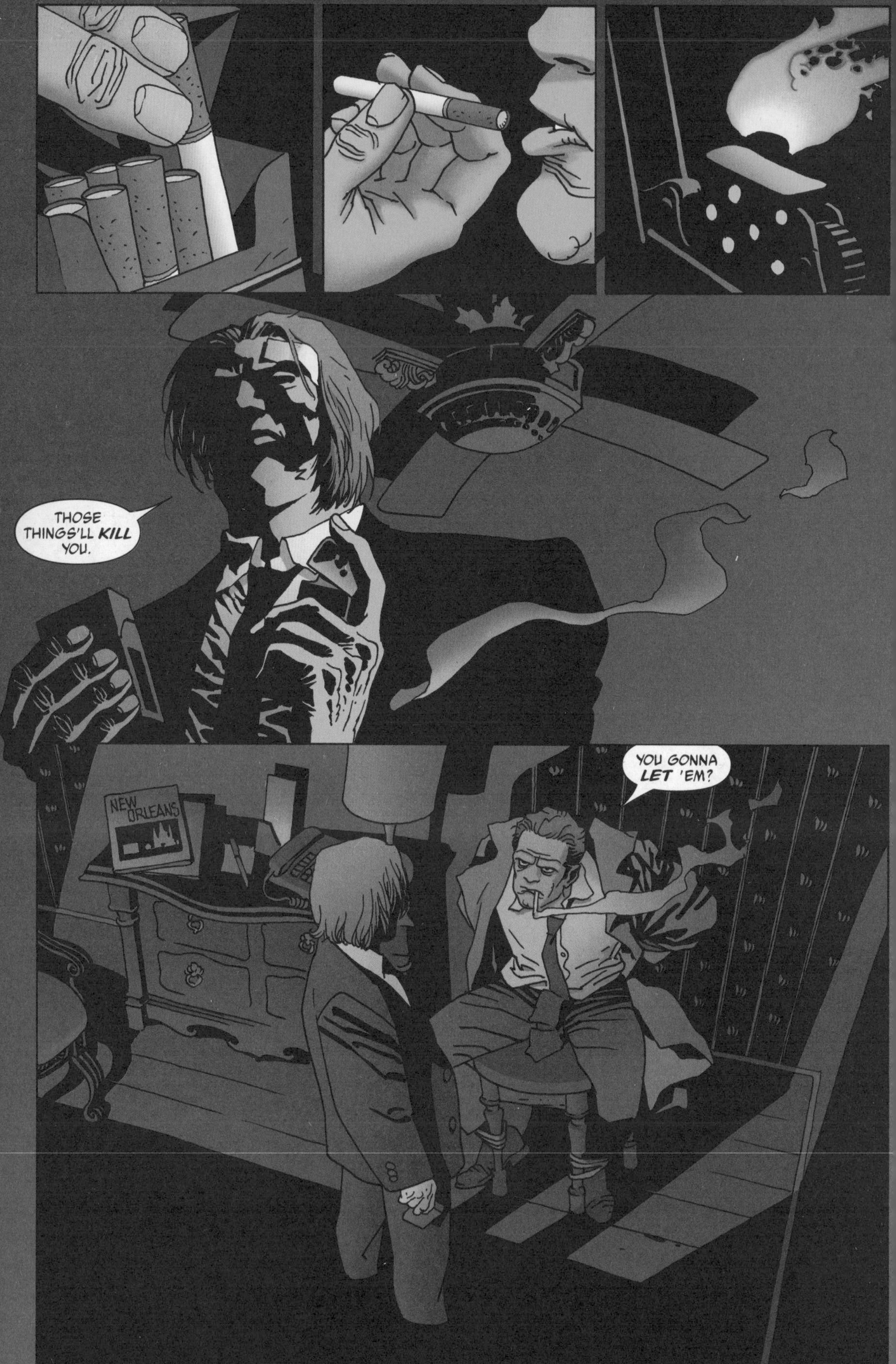
THOSE THINGS'LL **KILL** YOU.
YOU GONNA **LET** 'EM?
NEW ORLEANS

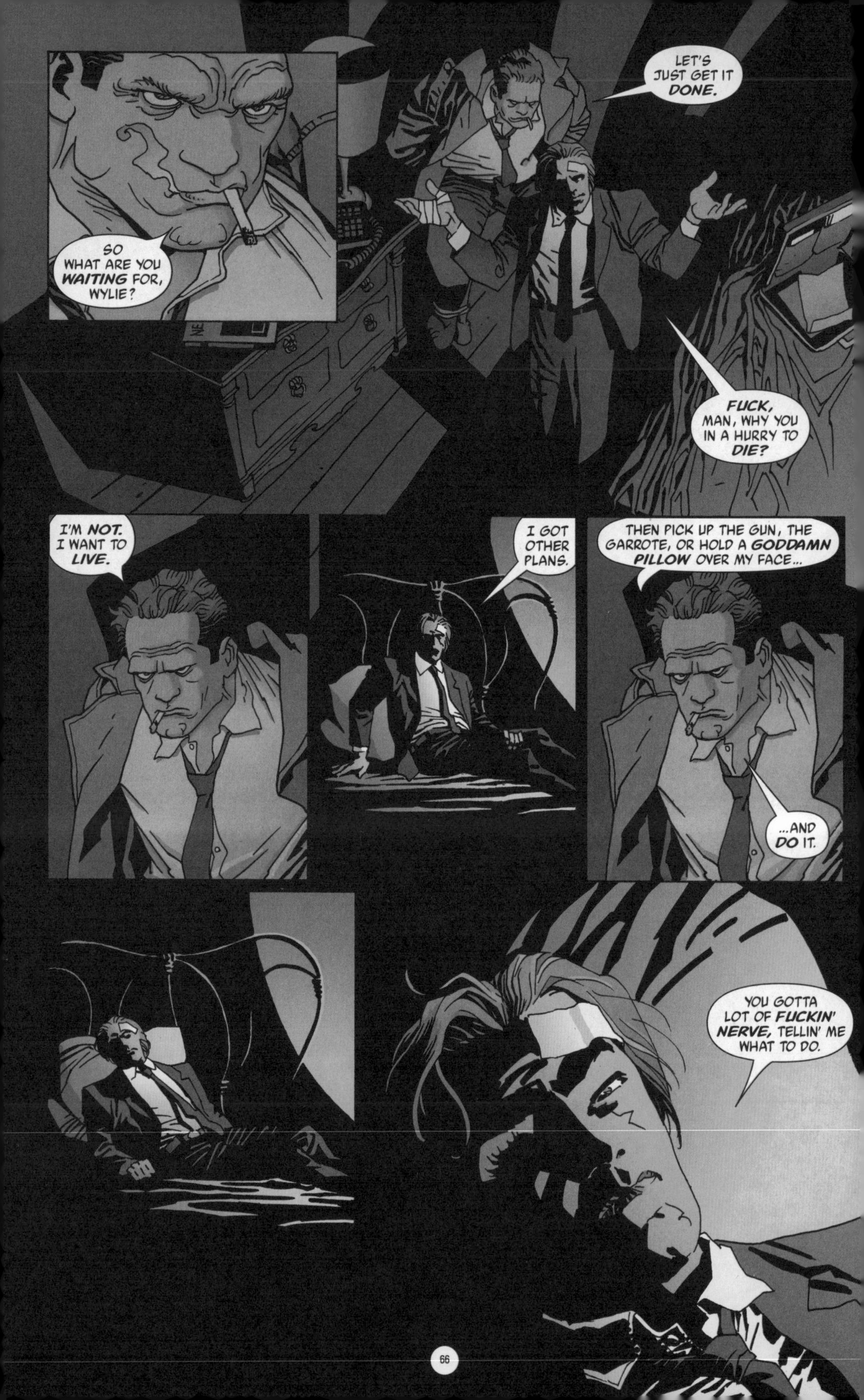
SO WHAT ARE YOU WAITING FOR, WYLIE?
LET'S JUST GET IT DONE.
FUCK, MAN, WHY YOU IN A HURRY TO DIE?
I'M NOT. I WANT TO LIVE.
I GOT OTHER PLANS.
THEN PICK UP THE GUN, THE GARROTE, OR HOLD A GODDAMN PILLOW OVER MY FACE...
...AND DO IT.
YOU GOTTA LOT OF FUCKIN' NERVE, TELLIN' ME WHAT TO DO.

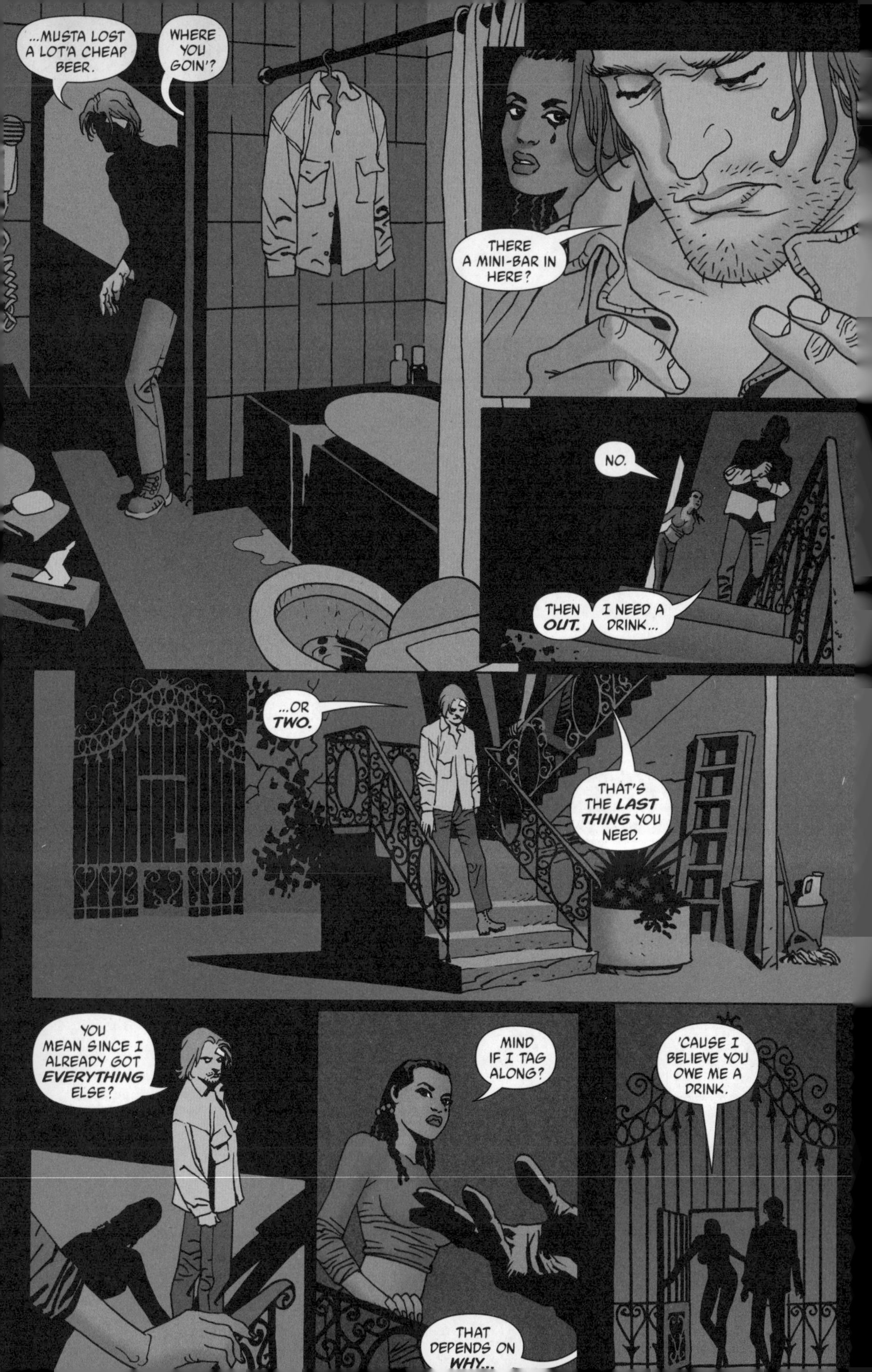
...MUSTA LOST A LOT'A CHEAP BEER.
WHERE YOU GOIN'?
THERE A MINI-BAR IN HERE?
NO.
I NEED A DRINK...
THEN OUT.
...OR TWO.
THAT'S THE LAST THING YOU NEED.
YOU MEAN SINCE I ALREADY GOT EVERYTHING ELSE?
MIND IF I TAG ALONG?
THAT DEPENDS ON WHY...
'CAUSE I BELIEVE YOU OWE ME A DRINK.

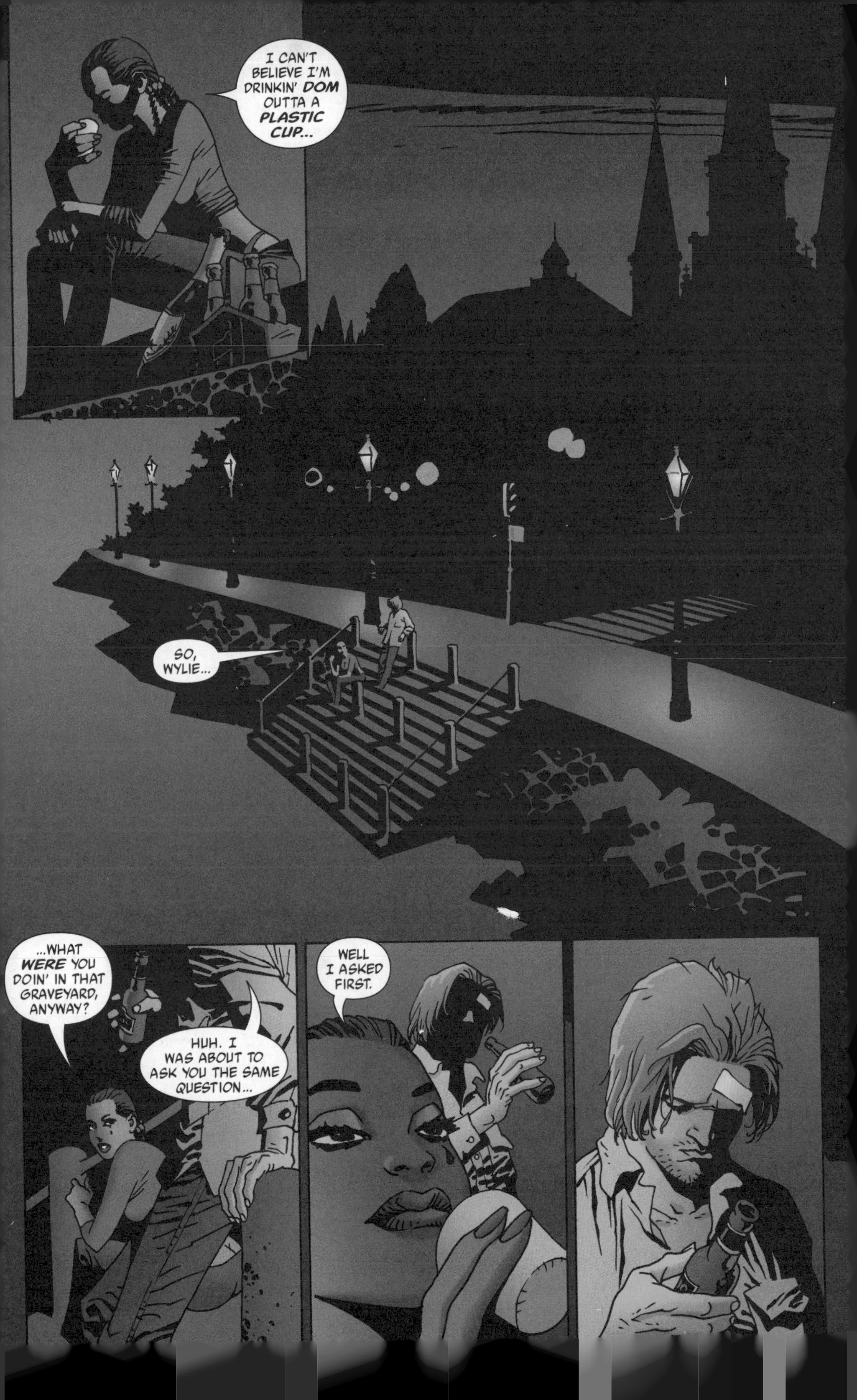
I CAN'T BELIEVE I'M DRINKIN' DOM OUTTA A PLASTIC CUP...
SO, WYLIE...
...WHAT WERE YOU DOIN' IN THAT GRAVEYARD, ANYWAY?
HUH. I WAS ABOUT TO ASK YOU THE SAME QUESTION...
WELL I ASKED FIRST.

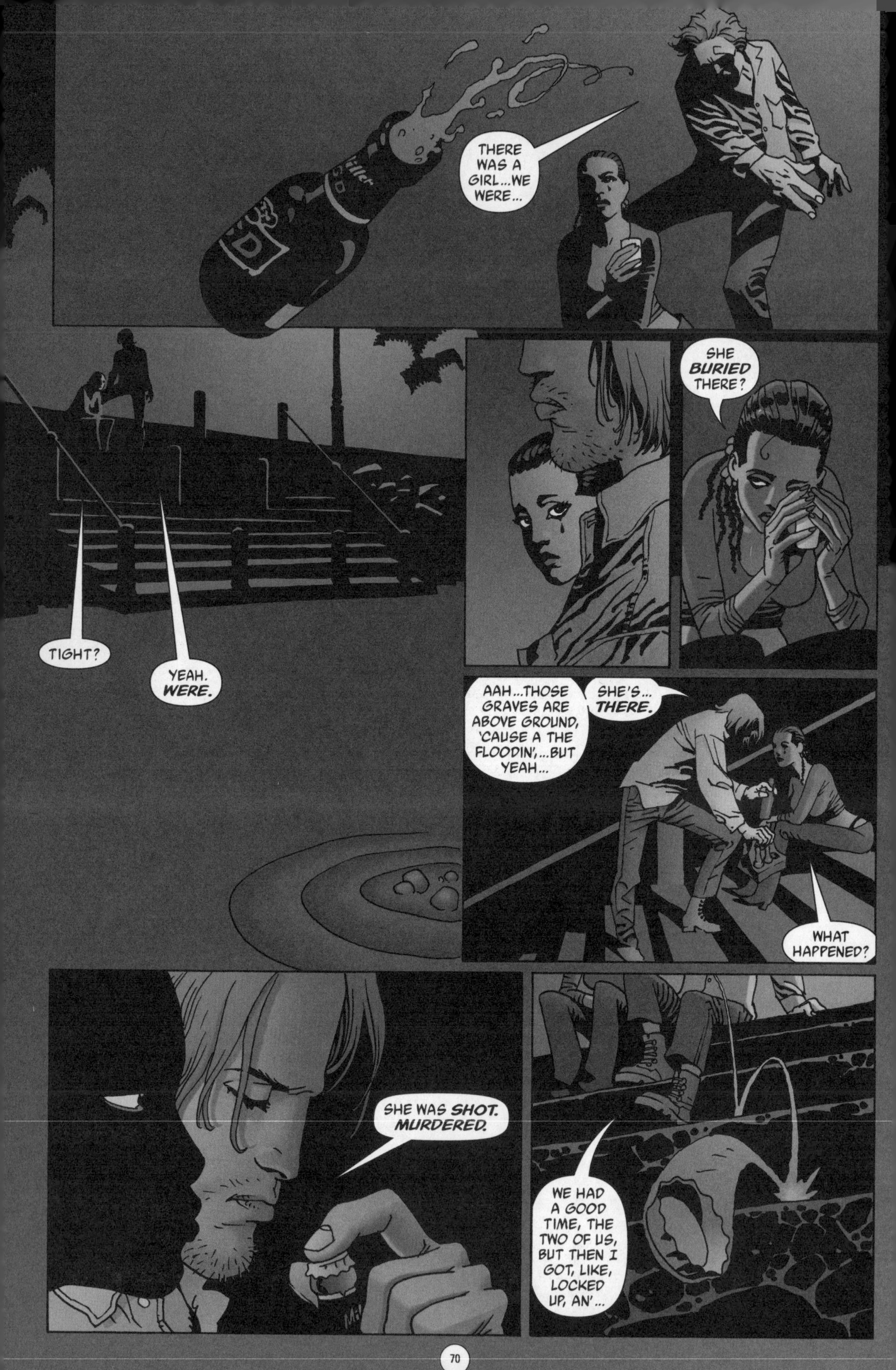
THERE WAS A GIRL...WE WERE...
TIGHT?
YEAH. WERE.
SHE BURIED THERE?
AAH...THOSE GRAVES ARE ABOVE GROUND, 'CAUSE A THE FLOODIN',...BUT YEAH...
SHE'S... THERE.
WHAT HAPPENED?
SHE WAS SHOT. MURDERED.
WE HAD A GOOD TIME, THE TWO OF US, BUT THEN I GOT, LIKE, LOCKED UP, AN'...

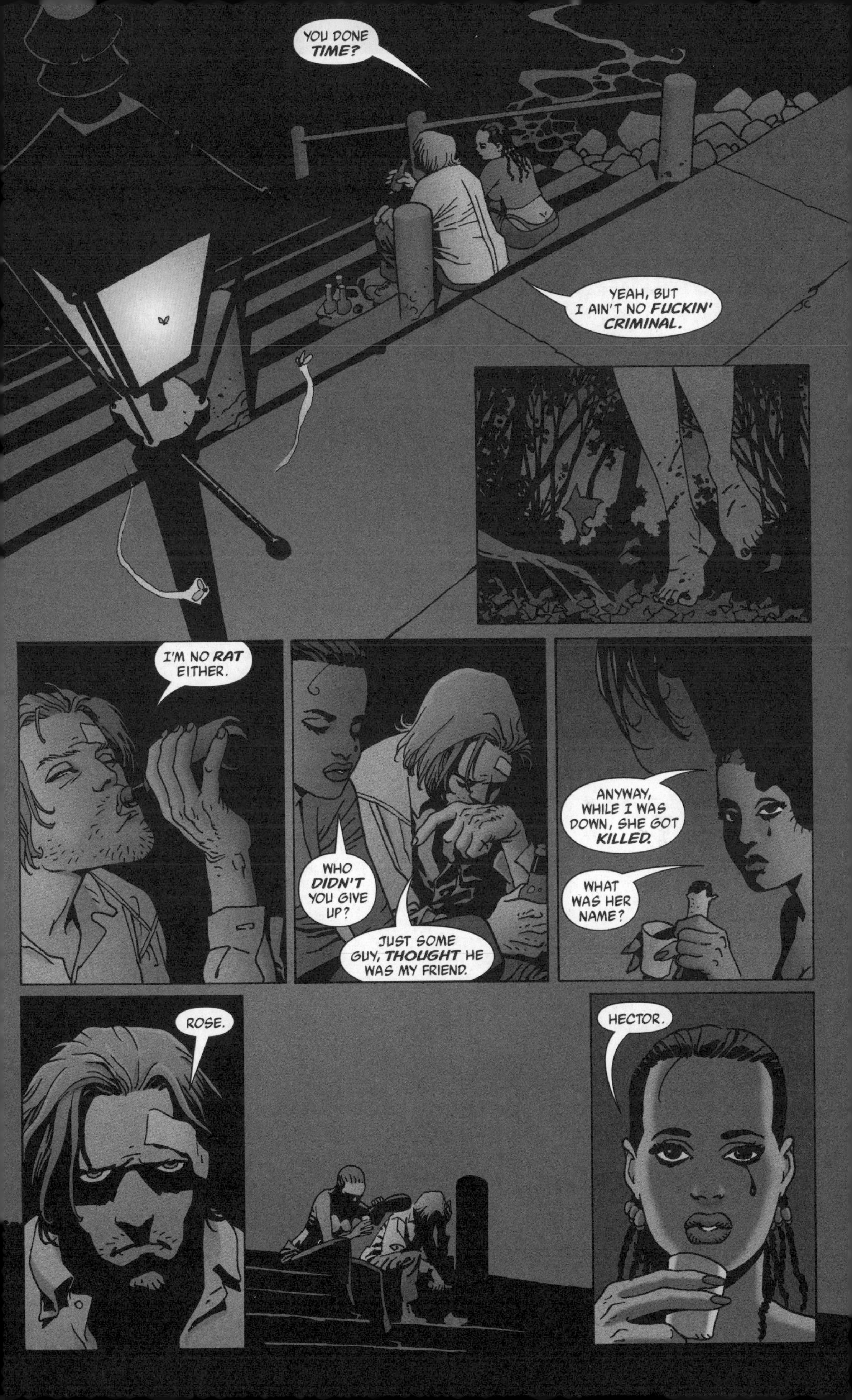
YOU DONE TIME?
YEAH, BUT I AIN'T NO FUCKIN' CRIMINAL.
I'M NO RAT EITHER.
WHO DIDN'T YOU GIVE UP?
JUST SOME GUY, THOUGHT HE WAS MY FRIEND.
ANYWAY, WHILE I WAS DOWN, SHE GOT KILLED.
WHAT WAS HER NAME?
ROSE.
HECTOR.

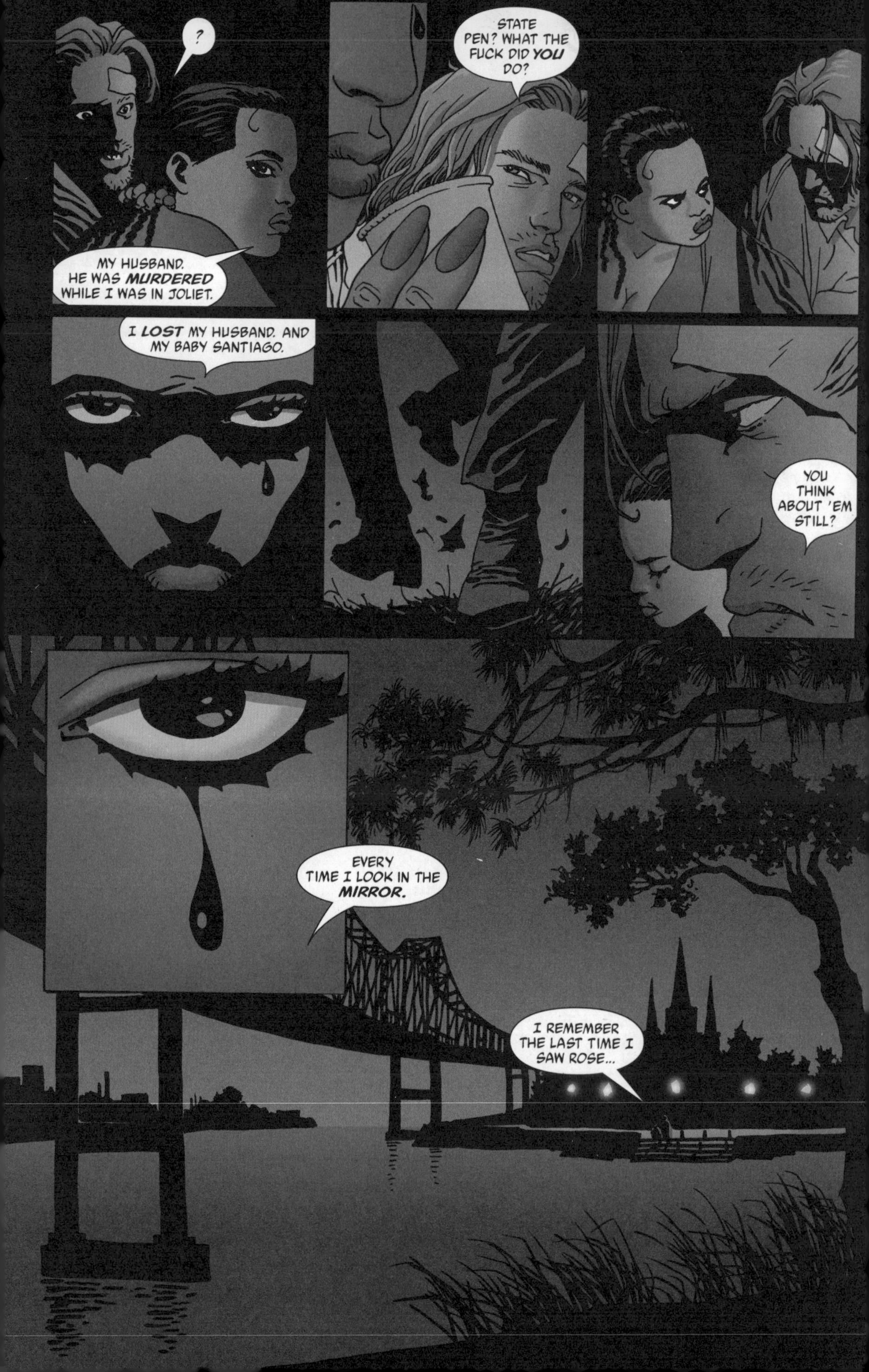
?
MY HUSBAND. HE WAS MURDERED WHILE I WAS IN JOLIET.
STATE PEN? WHAT THE FUCK DID YOU DO?
I LOST MY HUSBAND. AND MY BABY SANTIAGO.
YOU THINK ABOUT 'EM STILL?
EVERY TIME I LOOK IN THE MIRROR.
I REMEMBER THE LAST TIME I SAW ROSE...

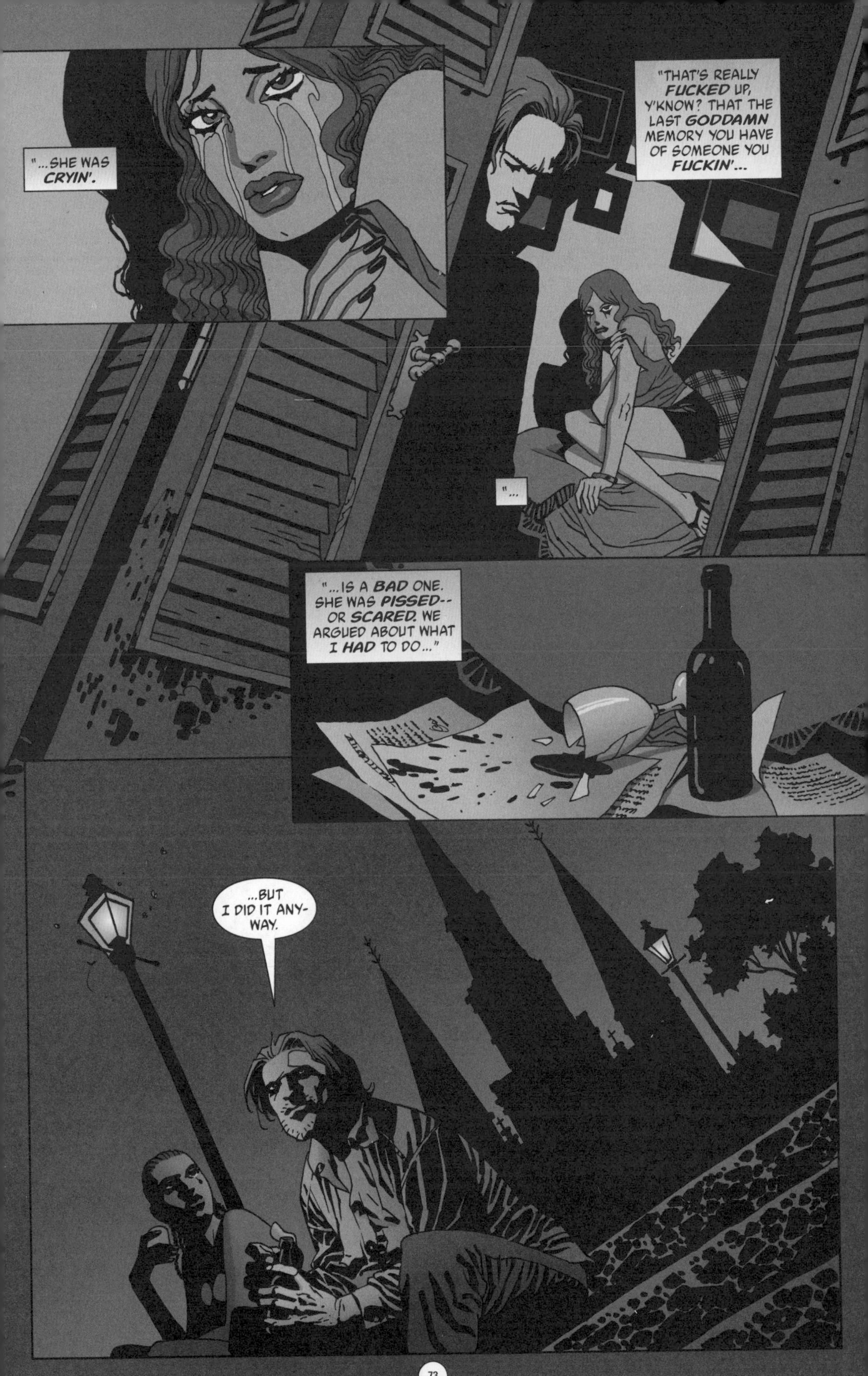
"...SHE WAS CRYIN'.
"THAT'S REALLY FUCKED UP, Y'KNOW? THAT THE LAST GODDAMN MEMORY YOU HAVE OF SOMEONE YOU FUCKIN'...
"...
"...IS A BAD ONE. SHE WAS PISSED-- OR SCARED. WE ARGUED ABOUT WHAT I HAD TO DO..."
...BUT I DID IT ANY- WAY.

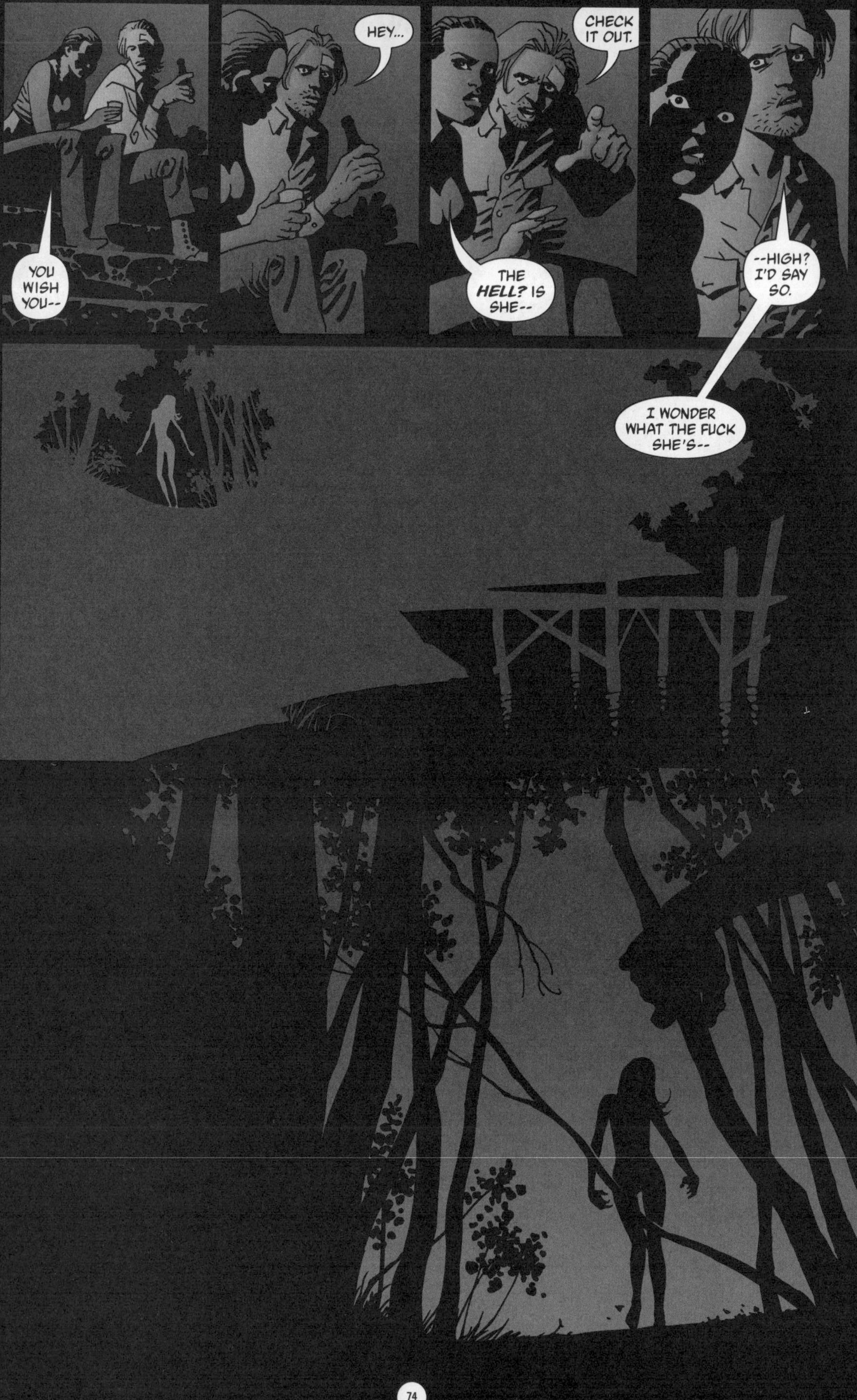
YOU WISH YOU--
HEY...
CHECK IT OUT.
THE HELL? IS SHE--
--HIGH? I'D SAY SO.
I WONDER WHAT THE FUCK SHE'S--

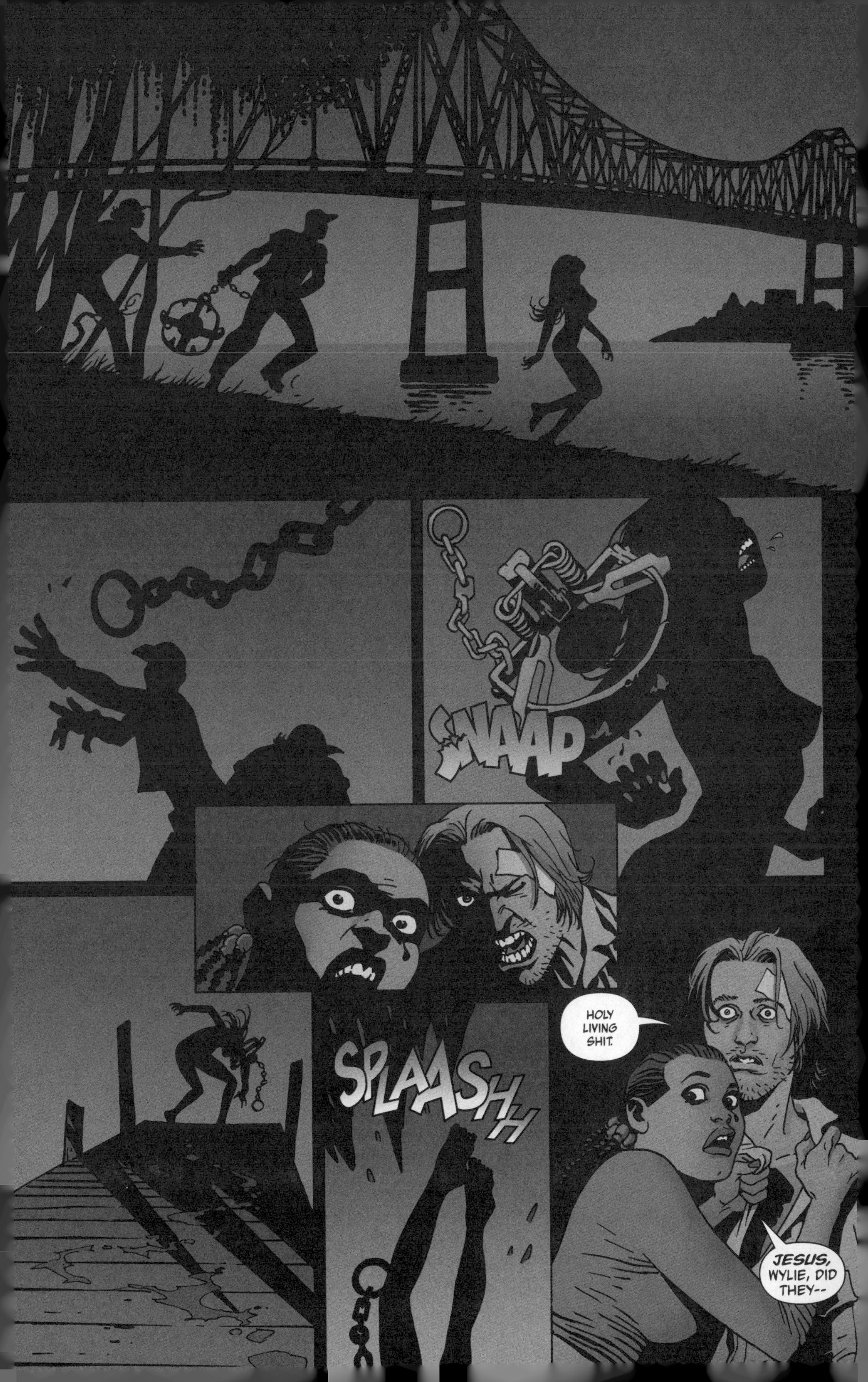
SNAAP
SPLAASHH
HOLY LIVING SHIT.
JESUS, WYLIE, DID THEY--

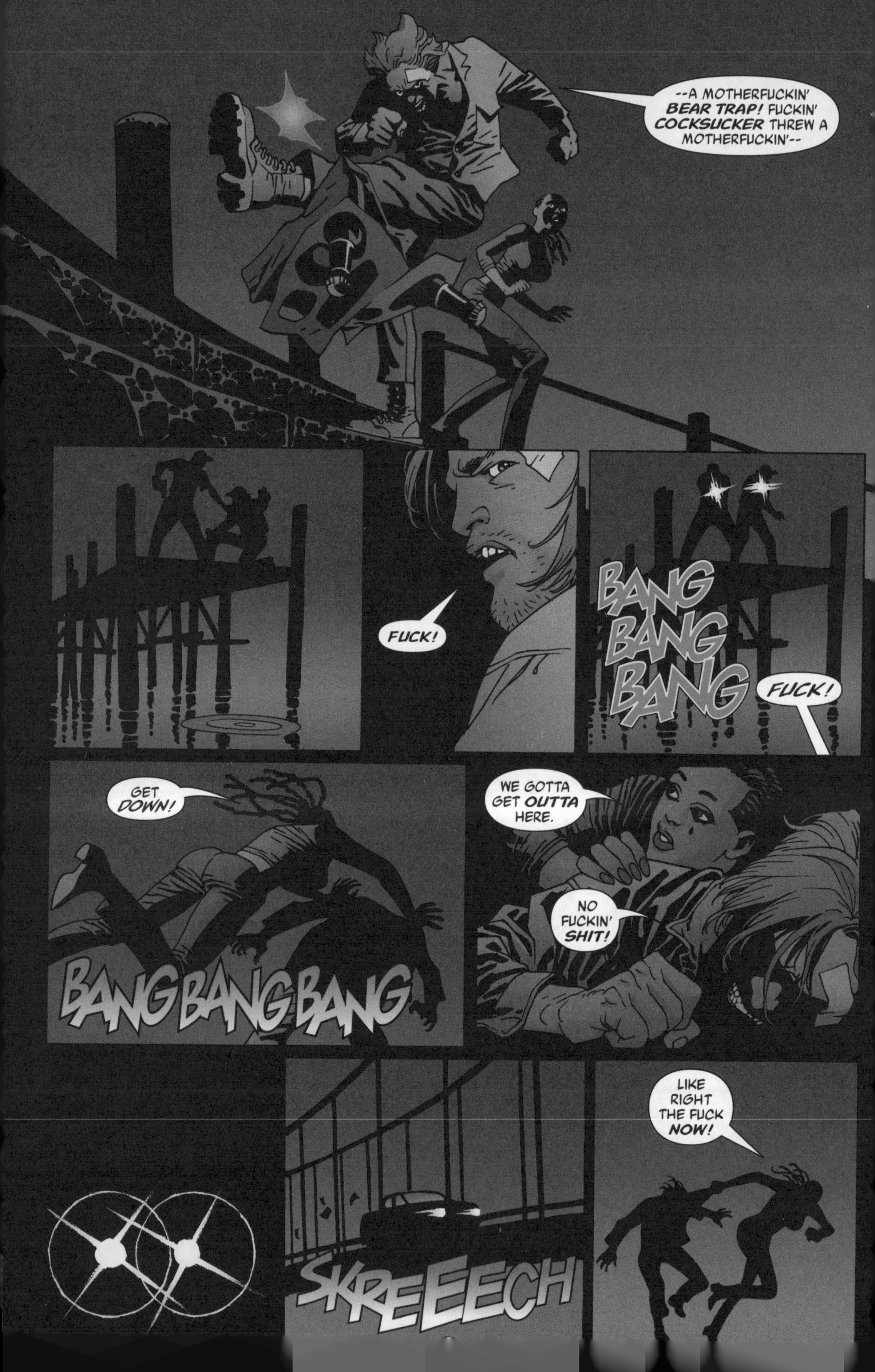
--A MOTHERFUCKIN' BEAR TRAP! FUCKIN' COCKSUCKER THREW A MOTHERFUCKIN'--
FUCK!
BANG BANG BANG
FUCK!
GET DOWN!
BANG BANG BANG
WE GOTTA GET OUTTA HERE.
NO FUCKIN' SHIT!
SKREEECH
LIKE RIGHT THE FUCK NOW!

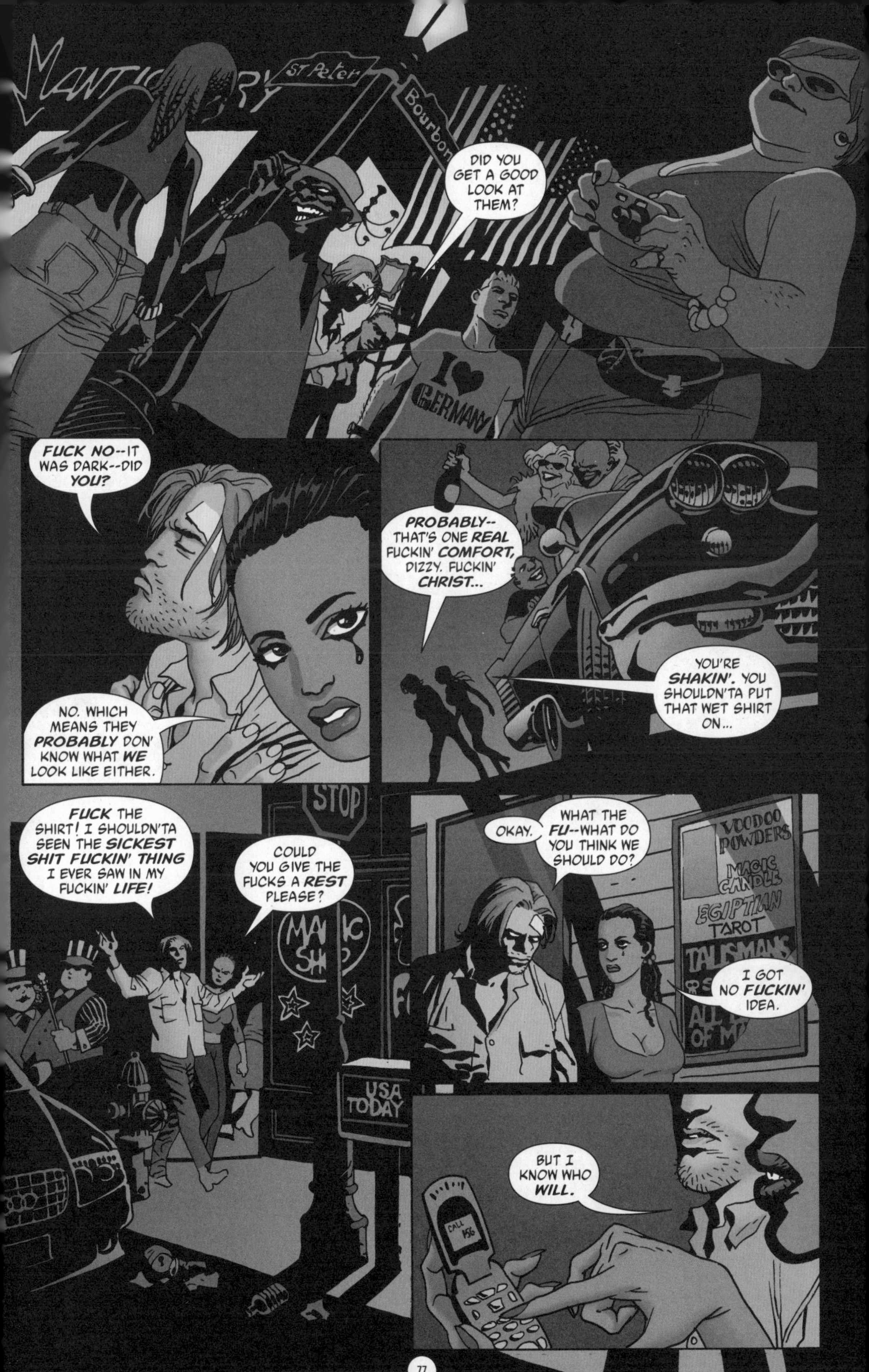

MANTICORY
ST. PETER
BOURBON
DID YOU GET A GOOD LOOK AT THEM?
I ♥ GERMANY
FUCK NO--IT WAS DARK--DID YOU?
NO. WHICH MEANS THEY PROBABLY DON' KNOW WHAT WE LOOK LIKE EITHER.
PROBABLY-- THAT'S ONE REAL FUCKIN' COMFORT, DIZZY. FUCKIN' CHRIST...
YOU'RE SHAKIN'. YOU SHOULDN'TA PUT THAT WET SHIRT ON...
STOP
FUCK THE SHIRT! I SHOULDN'TA SEEN THE SICKEST SHIT FUCKIN' THING I EVER SAW IN MY FUCKIN' LIFE!
COULD YOU GIVE THE FUCKS A REST PLEASE?
USA TODAY
WHAT THE FU--WHAT DO YOU THINK WE SHOULD DO?
OKAY.
VOODOO POWDERS
MAGIC CANDLE
EGIPTIAN TAROT
TALISMANS
I GOT NO FUCKIN' IDEA.
BUT I KNOW WHO WILL.
CALL 156

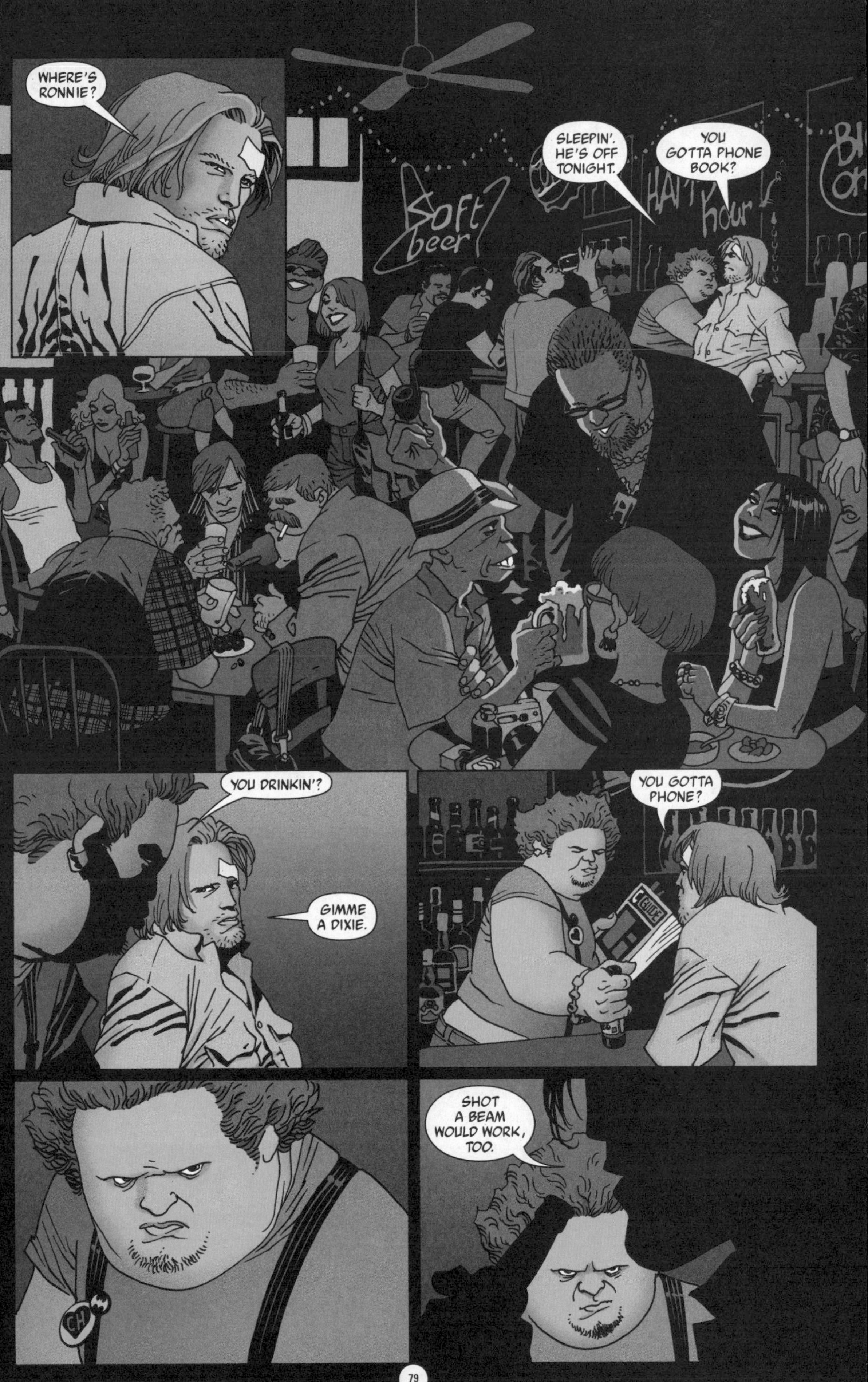
WHERE'S RONNIE?
SLEEPIN'. HE'S OFF TONIGHT.
YOU GOTTA PHONE BOOK?
Soft beer
HAPPY hour
YOU DRINKIN'?
GIMME A DIXIE.
YOU GOTTA PHONE?
GUIDE
SHOT A BEAM WOULD WORK, TOO.

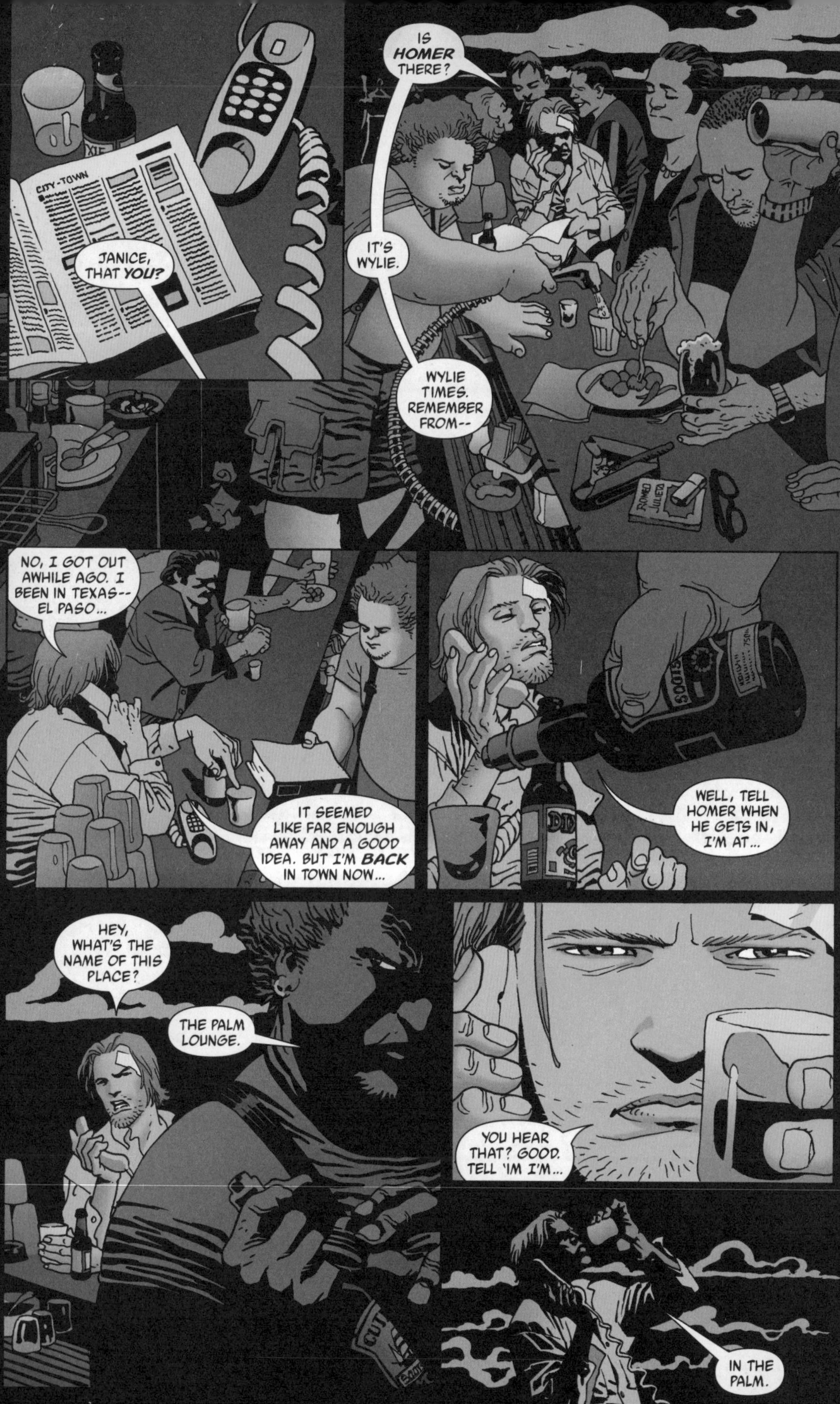
CITY-TOWN
JANICE, THAT YOU?
IS HOMER THERE?
IT'S WYLIE.
WYLIE TIMES. REMEMBER FROM--
ROMEO JULIETA
NO, I GOT OUT AWHILE AGO. I BEEN IN TEXAS-- EL PASO...
IT SEEMED LIKE FAR ENOUGH AWAY AND A GOOD IDEA. BUT I'M BACK IN TOWN NOW...
WELL, TELL HOMER WHEN HE GETS IN, I'M AT...
HEY, WHAT'S THE NAME OF THIS PLACE?
THE PALM LOUNGE.
YOU HEAR THAT? GOOD. TELL 'IM I'M...
IN THE PALM.

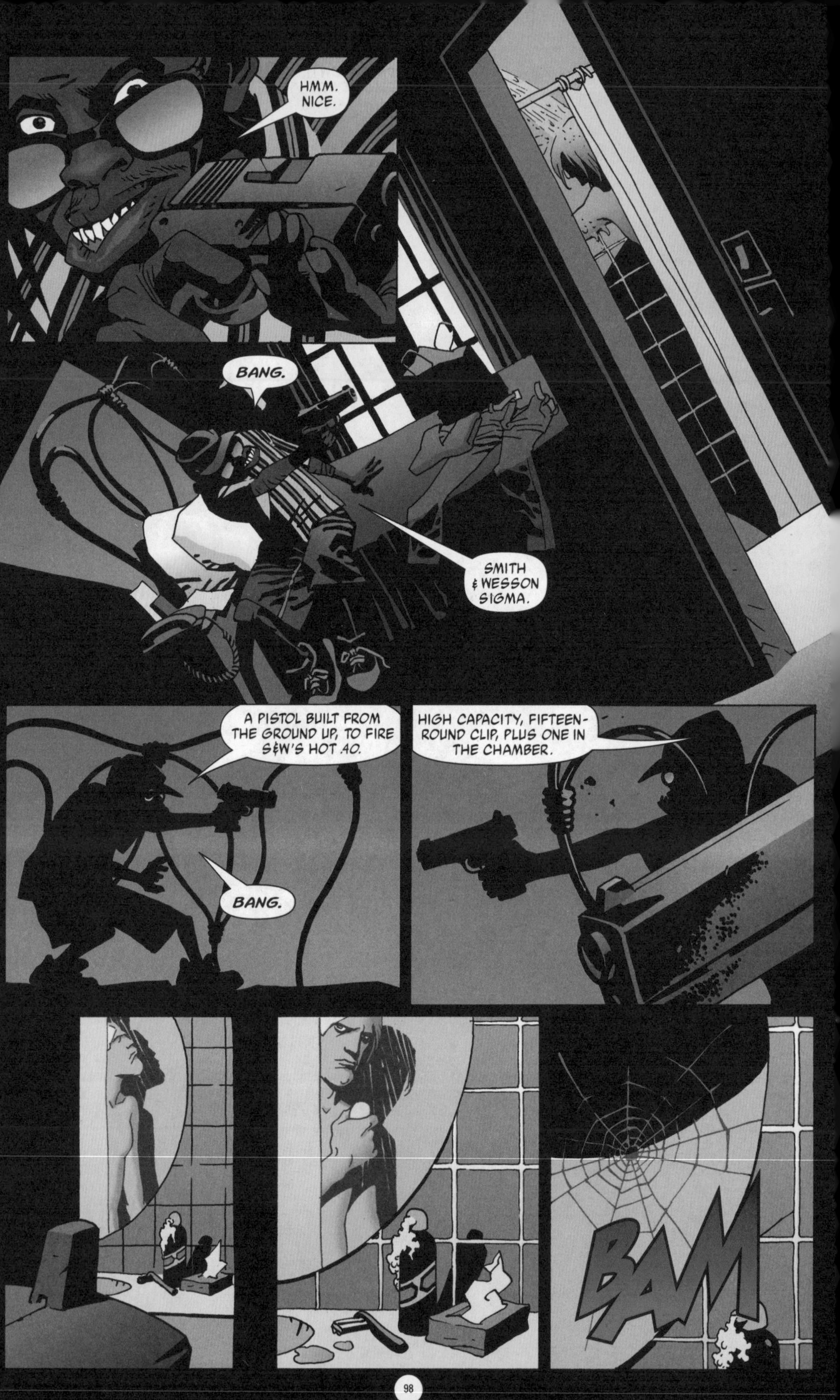
HMM. NICE.
BANG.
SMITH & WESSON SIGMA.
A PISTOL BUILT FROM THE GROUND UP, TO FIRE S&W'S HOT .40.
BANG.
HIGH CAPACITY, FIFTEEN-ROUND CLIP, PLUS ONE IN THE CHAMBER.
BAM

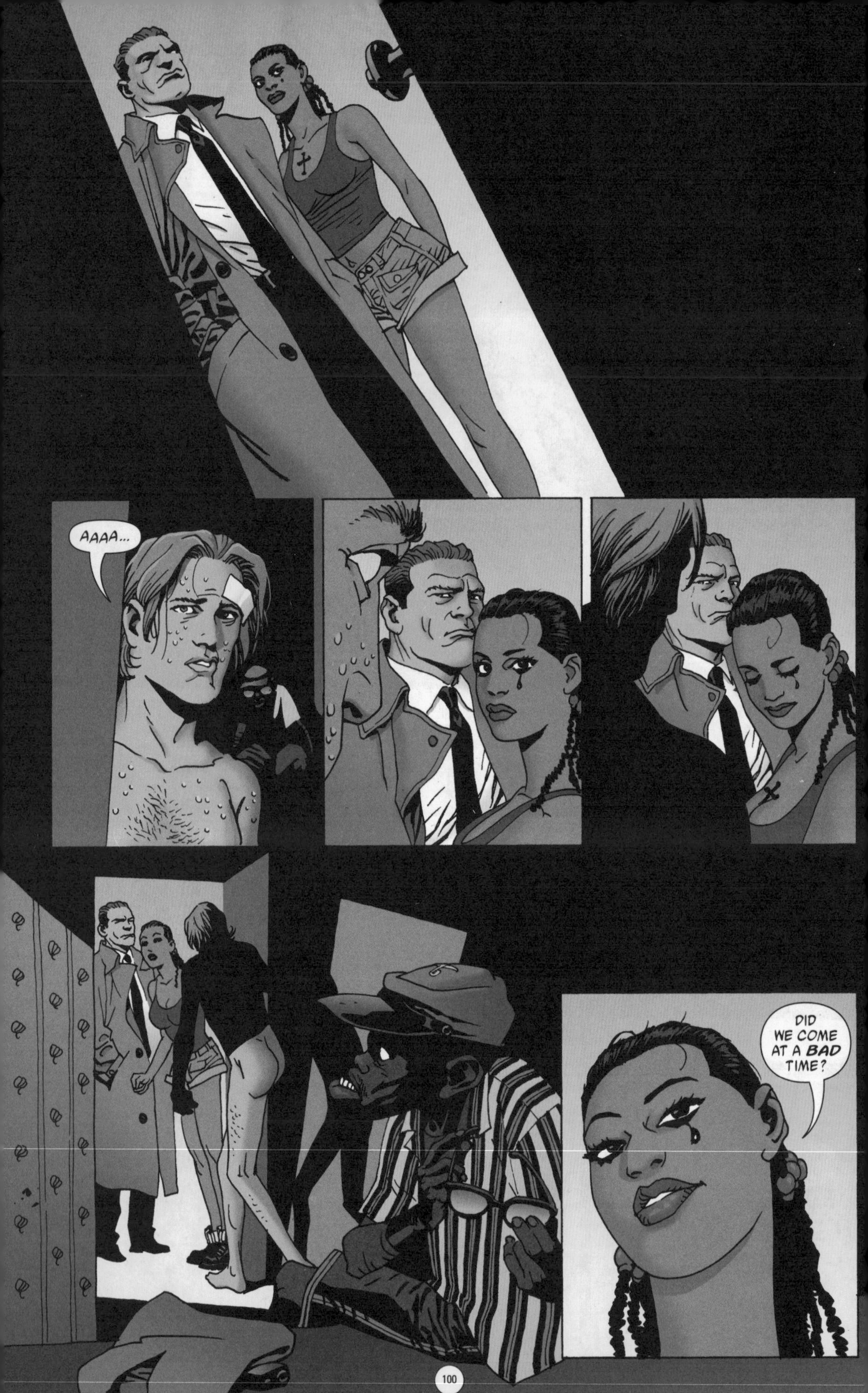

AAAA...
DID WE COME AT A BAD TIME?

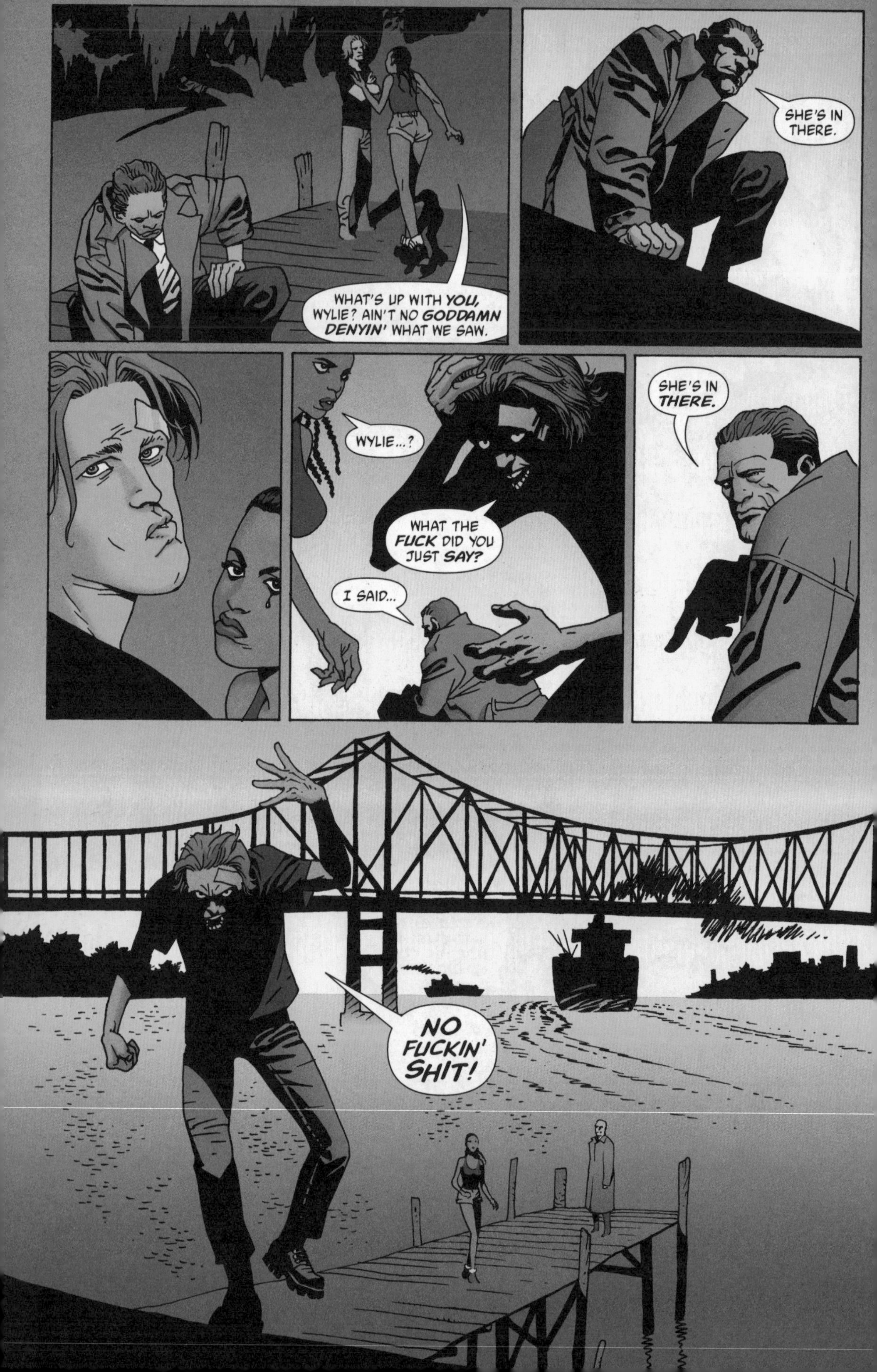
WHAT'S UP WITH YOU, WYLIE? AIN'T NO GODDAMN DENYIN' WHAT WE SAW.
SHE'S IN THERE.
WYLIE...?
WHAT THE FUCK DID YOU JUST SAY?
I SAID...
SHE'S IN THERE.
NO FUCKIN' SHIT!

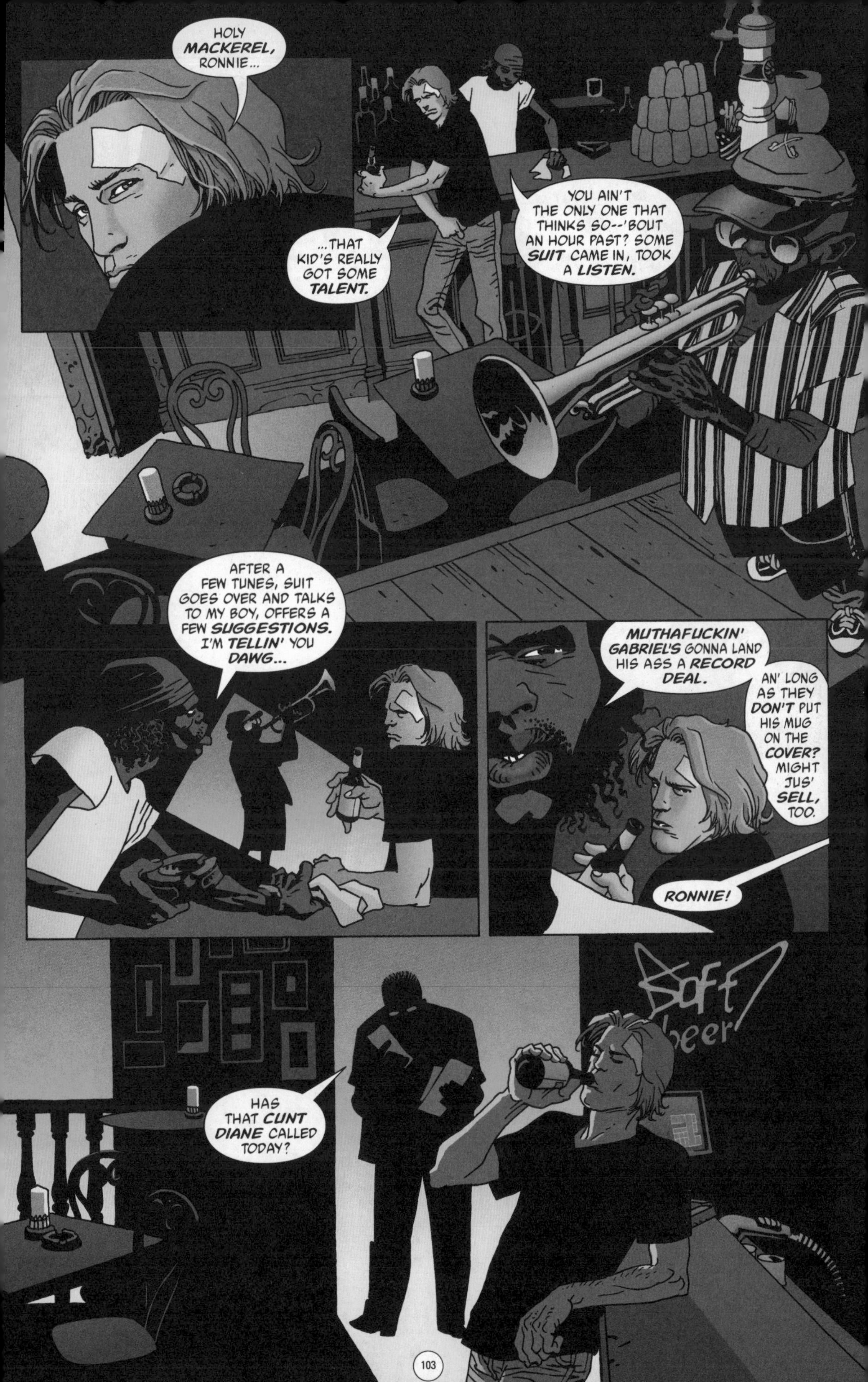
HOLY MACKEREL, RONNIE...
...THAT KID'S REALLY GOT SOME TALENT.
YOU AIN'T THE ONLY ONE THAT THINKS SO--'BOUT AN HOUR PAST? SOME SUIT CAME IN, TOOK A LISTEN.
AFTER A FEW TUNES, SUIT GOES OVER AND TALKS TO MY BOY, OFFERS A FEW SUGGESTIONS. I'M TELLIN' YOU DAWG...
MUTHAFUCKIN' GABRIEL'S GONNA LAND HIS ASS A RECORD DEAL.
AN' LONG AS THEY DON'T PUT HIS MUG ON THE COVER? MIGHT JUS' SELL, TOO.
RONNIE!
Soft beer
HAS THAT CUNT DIANE CALLED TODAY?

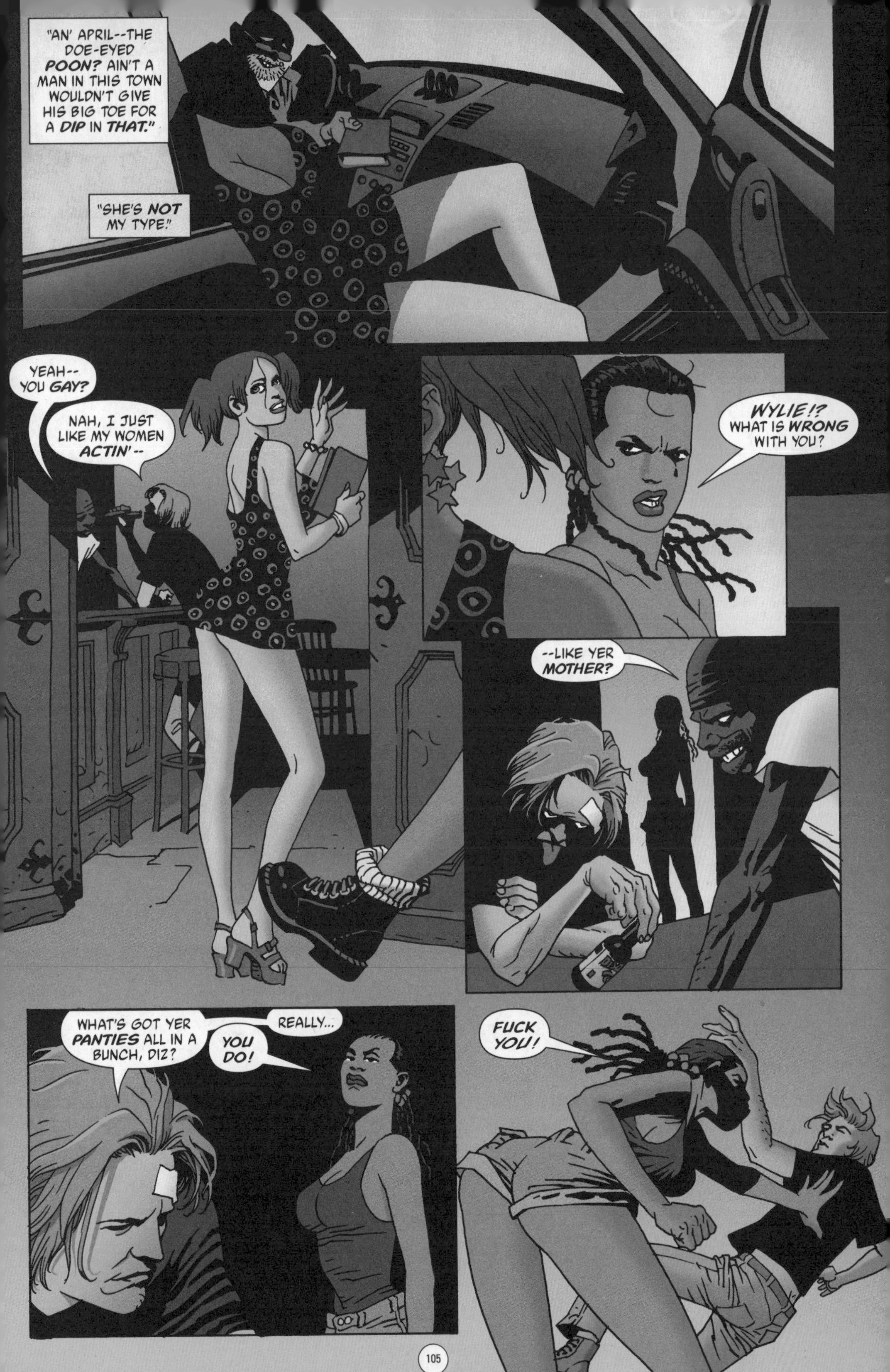
"AN' APRIL--THE DOE-EYED POON? AIN'T A MAN IN THIS TOWN WOULDN'T GIVE HIS BIG TOE FOR A DIP IN THAT."
"SHE'S NOT MY TYPE."
YEAH-- YOU GAY?
NAH, I JUST LIKE MY WOMEN ACTIN'--
WYLIE!? WHAT IS WRONG WITH YOU?
--LIKE YER MOTHER?
WHAT'S GOT YER PANTIES ALL IN A BUNCH, DIZ?
REALLY... YOU DO!
FUCK YOU!

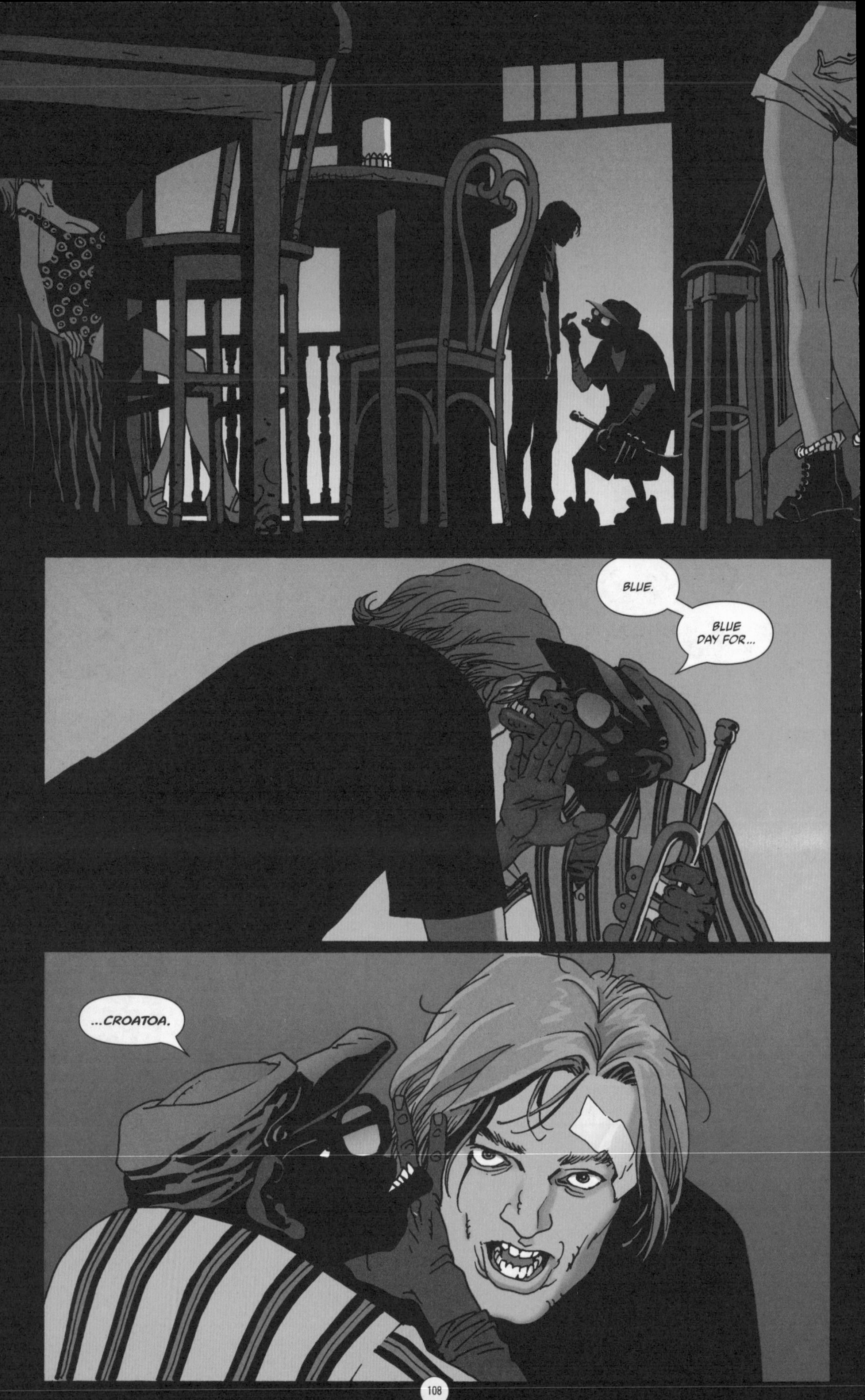
BLUE.
BLUE DAY FOR...
...CROATOA.

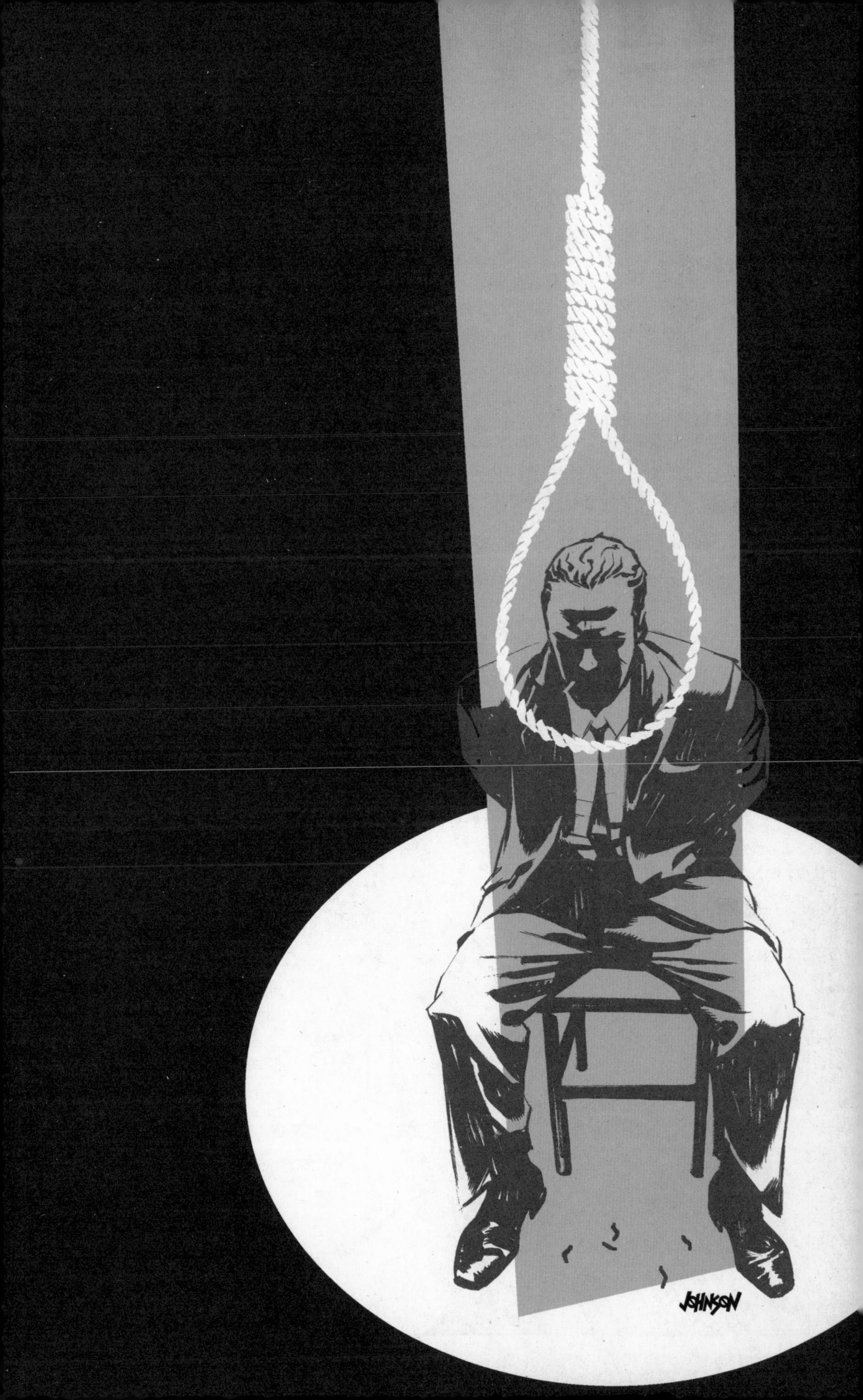
JOHNSON

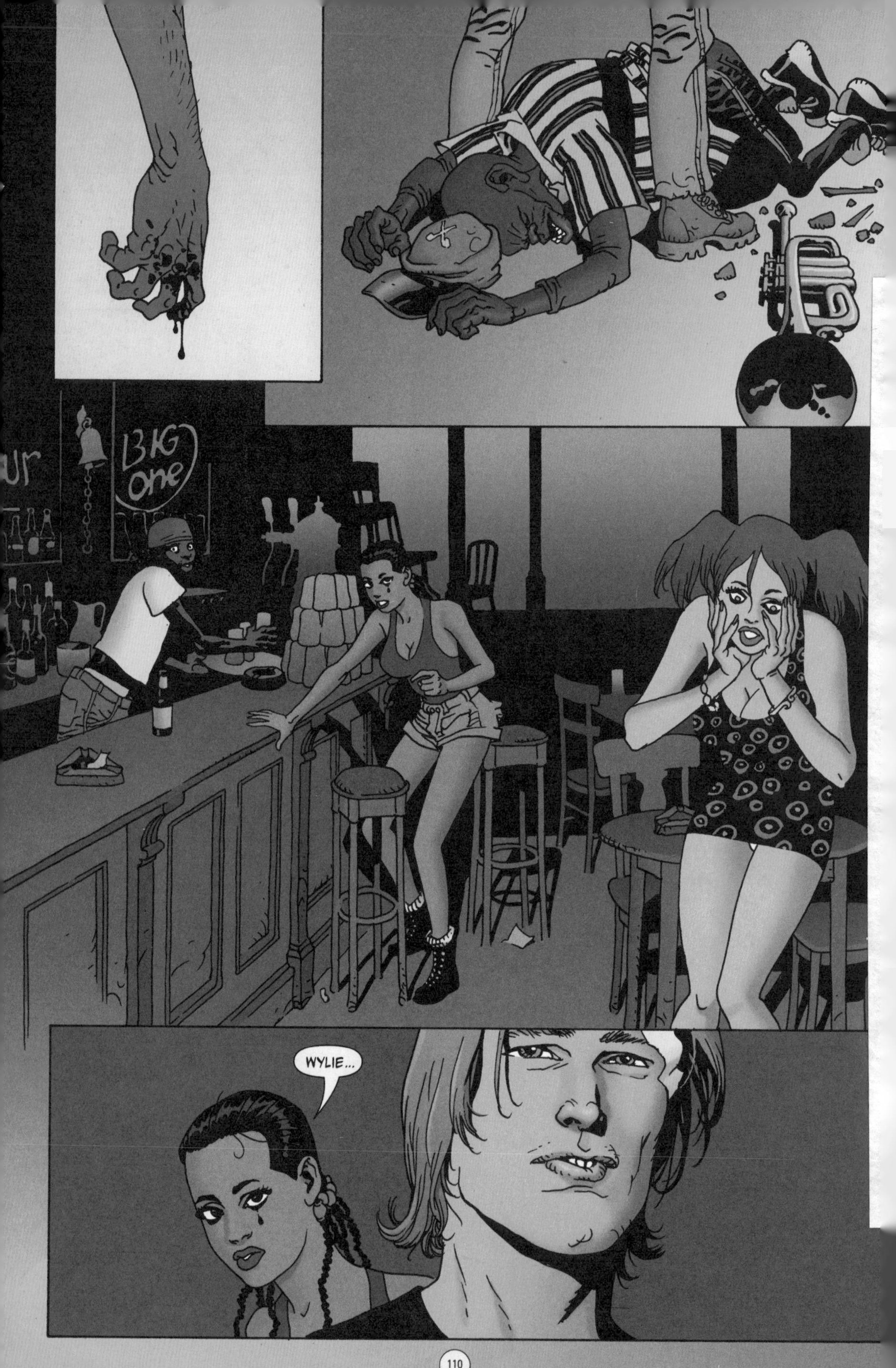
BIG one
WYLIE...

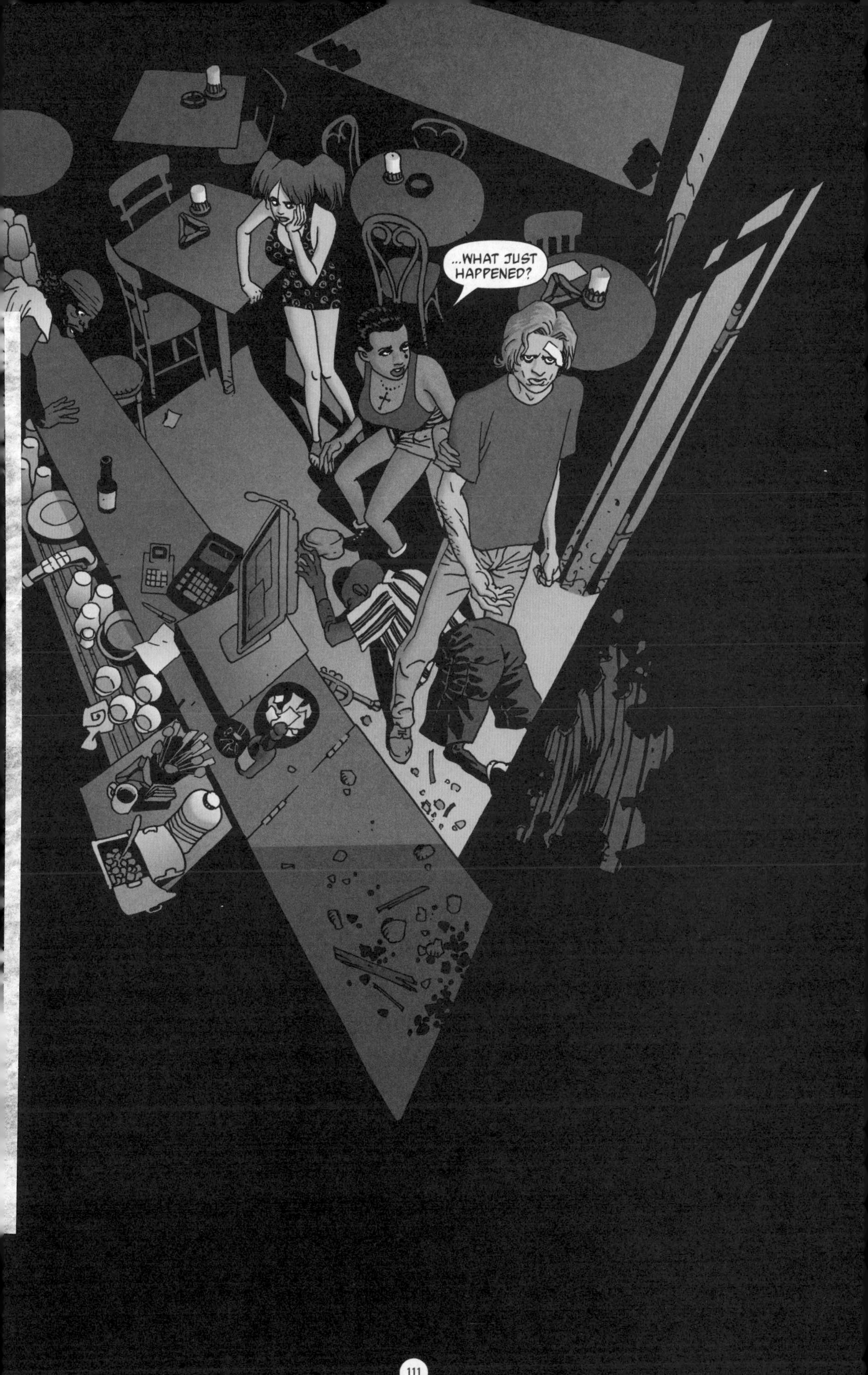
...WHAT JUST HAPPENED?

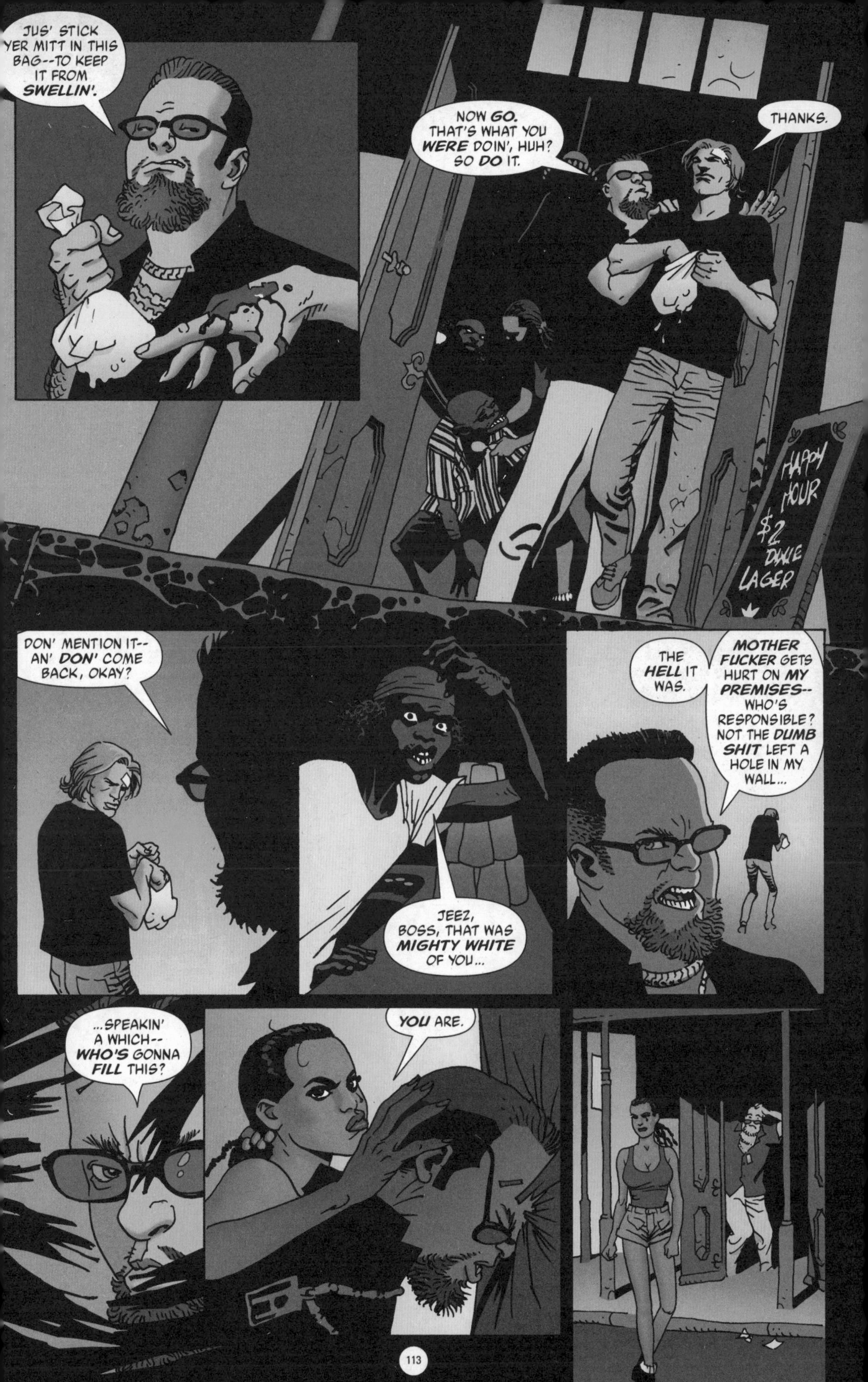
JUS' STICK YER MITT IN THIS BAG--TO KEEP IT FROM SWELLIN'.
NOW GO. THAT'S WHAT YOU WERE DOIN', HUH? SO DO IT.
THANKS.
HAPPY HOUR $2 DIXIE LAGER
DON' MENTION IT--AN' DON' COME BACK, OKAY?
JEEZ, BOSS, THAT WAS MIGHTY WHITE OF YOU...
THE HELL IT WAS.
MOTHER FUCKER GETS HURT ON MY PREMISES--WHO'S RESPONSIBLE? NOT THE DUMB SHIT LEFT A HOLE IN MY WALL...
...SPEAKIN' A WHICH--WHO'S GONNA FILL THIS?
YOU ARE.

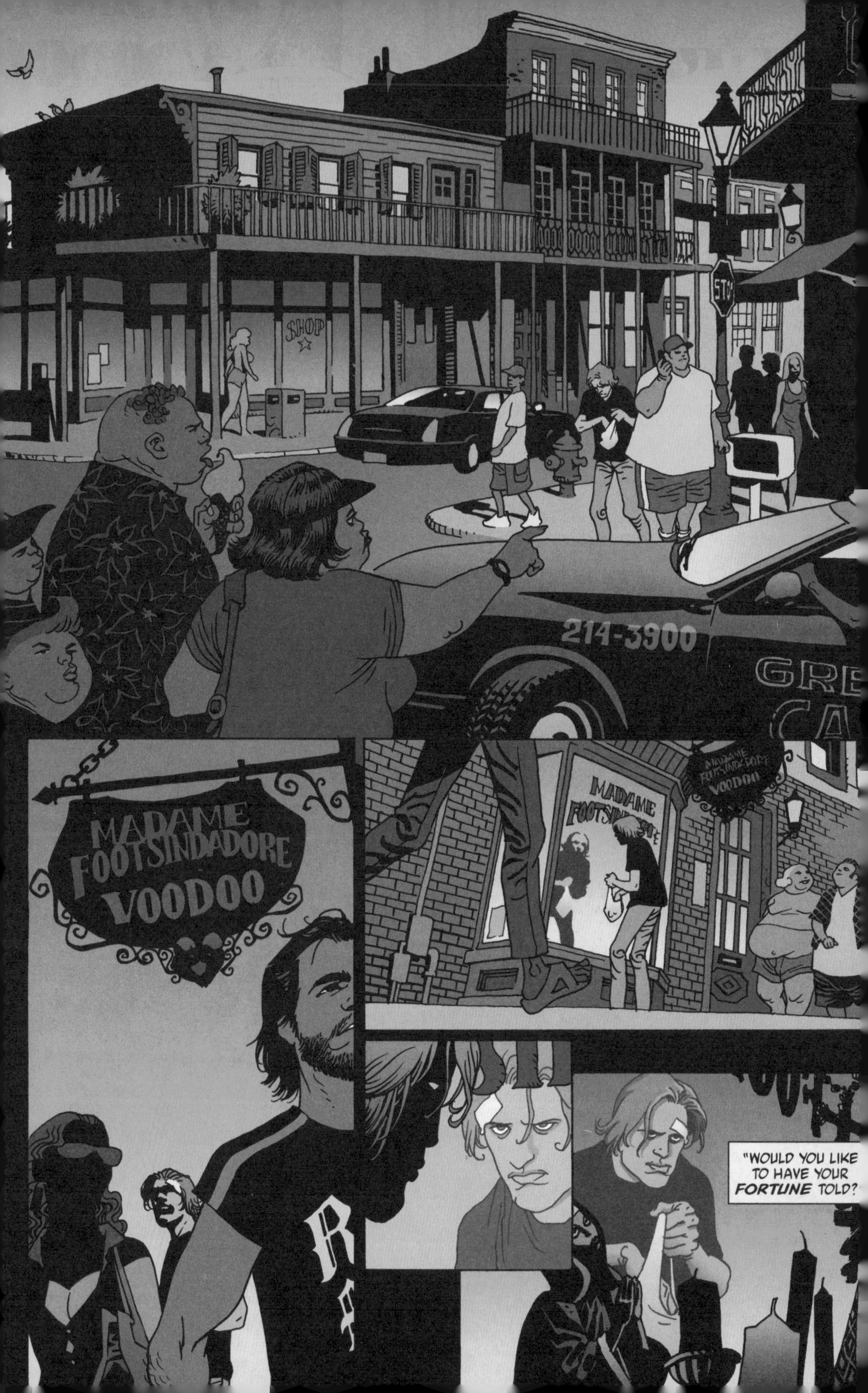
SHOP
STOP
214-3900
MADAME FOOTSINDADORE VOODOO
"WOULD YOU LIKE TO HAVE YOUR FORTUNE TOLD?

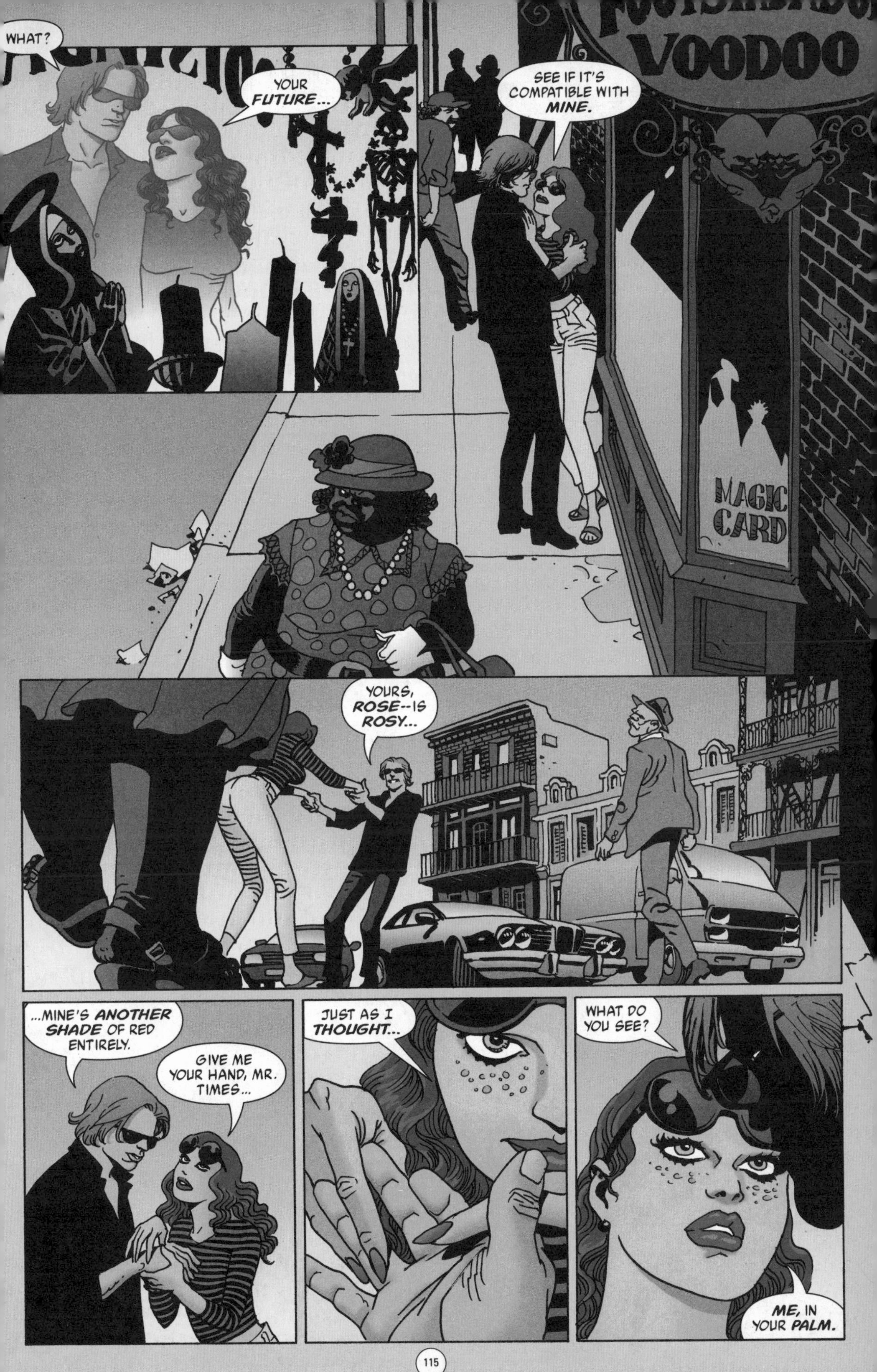

WHAT?
YOUR FUTURE...
SEE IF IT'S COMPATIBLE WITH MINE.
VOODOO
MAGIC CARD
YOURS, ROSE--IS ROSY...
...MINE'S ANOTHER SHADE OF RED ENTIRELY.
GIVE ME YOUR HAND, MR. TIMES...
JUST AS I THOUGHT...
WHAT DO YOU SEE?
ME, IN YOUR PALM.

116

YOU GOTTA *TALK* TO HIM, WYLIE. FIND OUT--

--WHAT I GOTTA *DO*, DIZ, IS *MY BIZ*.

SO IT'LL BE SOMETHING *STUPID*, RIGHT?

MIGHT. WHO CARES?

I DO.

HAR, HAR, HARDY, HAR *HAR*. YOU *HARDLY* KNOW ME--

--BUT WHAT I *DO* KNOW, I *LIKE*.

AS FOR MR. SHEPHERD. I'M NOT GONNA *STAND BY* AN' LET YOU DO--

'CAUSE I DON' FUCKIN' KNOW WHAT *I'M* GONNA DO, *OKAY!?*

WHAT?

TELL ME!

GAY FORCE

SHIT... DIZZY... YOU WANNA WATCH THE GAME?

GAYS IN THE ARMY

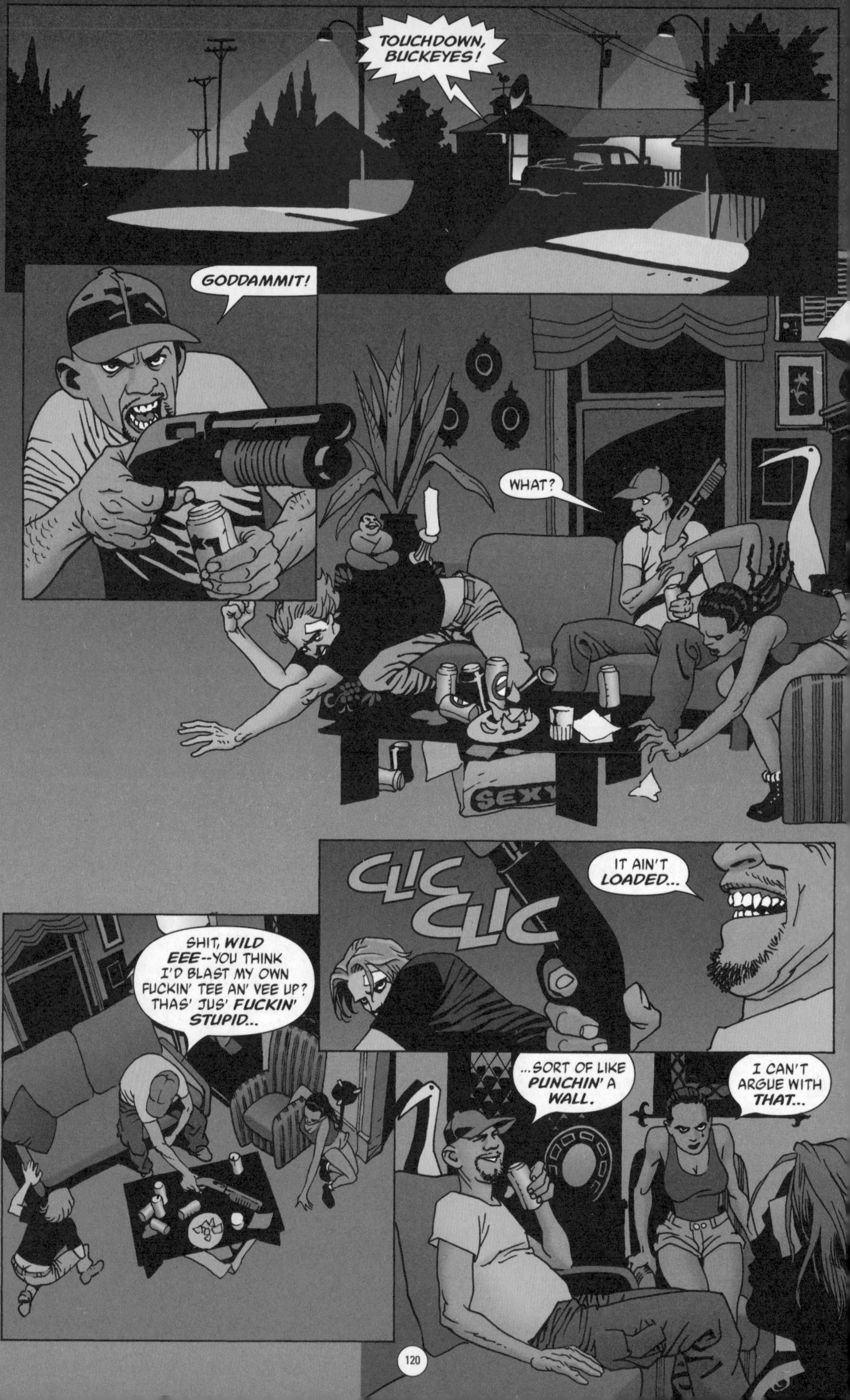
TOUCHDOWN, BUCKEYES!
GODDAMMIT!
WHAT?
SEXY
CLIC CLIC
IT AIN'T LOADED...
SHIT, WILD EEE--YOU THINK I'D BLAST MY OWN FUCKIN' TEE AN' VEE UP? THAS' JUS' FUCKIN' STUPID...
...SORT OF LIKE PUNCHIN' A WALL.
I CAN'T ARGUE WITH THAT...

HELL NO YOU *CAN'T*, HONEY. YOU GO FIGHTIN' A *BUILDIN'*, BUILDIN'S GONNA WIN NINE TIMES OUTTA TEN.

SHIIIT...MAYBE. FUCK. GOTTA FIGURE IT IN THOUGH, IF YOU PLAY THE *ODDS*. SURE THING AIN'T NO SUCH, 'CAUSE *EVERY FUCKER* GITS A *LUCKY DAY*.

JANICE-- BRING US A *BEER*, HUH!?

SO ONE TIME OUTTA TEN, THE BUILDING GOES *DOWN*?

WE OUT!

GODDAMMIT! WARREN SAID HE'D BRING A TWO-FOUR AN' THE MOTHERFUCKER'S *DRAGGIN'* HIS *SORRY ASS*.

WE GOT *WHISKEY*, RIGHT?

NOPE. LADIES DRANK IT ALL TODAY. THEY NEEDED TO GET A LITTLE *TIGHT* 'FORE THEY OPENED UP THEIR POCKET-BOOKS FOR A *LOOSE TIME* IN THE *BOUDOIR*.

YOU WANT SOMETHIN' FER THAT HAND, WYLIE?

A BEER WOULD BE NICE.

SAYS *YOU*...

THERE'S 'CUROCHROME IN THE MED'CINE CABINET. YOU DON' WANNA GIT *INFECTED*.

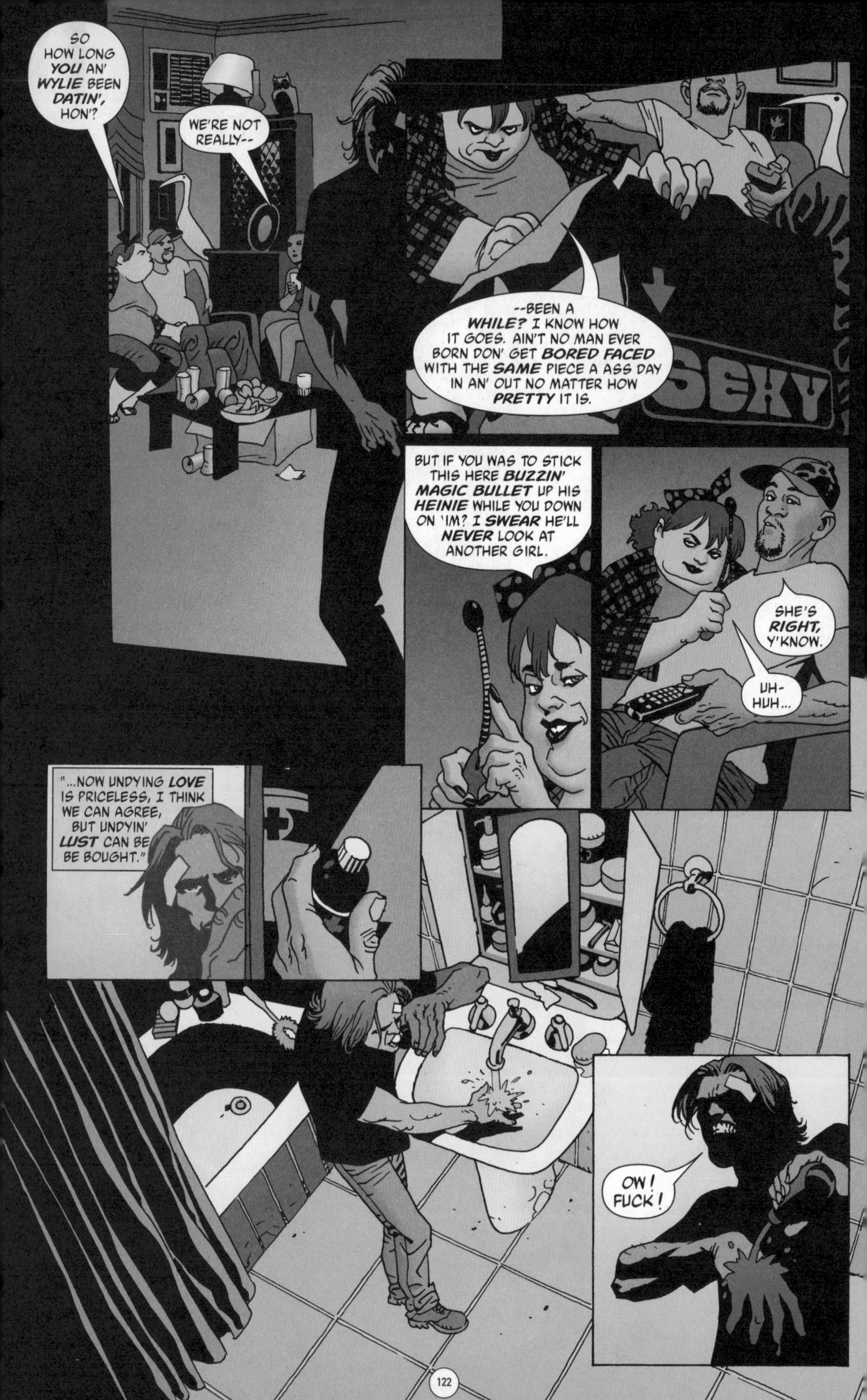
SO HOW LONG YOU AN' WYLIE BEEN DATIN', HON'?
WE'RE NOT REALLY--
--BEEN A WHILE? I KNOW HOW IT GOES. AIN'T NO MAN EVER BORN DON' GET BORED FACED WITH THE SAME PIECE A ASS DAY IN AN' OUT NO MATTER HOW PRETTY IT IS.
SEXY
BUT IF YOU WAS TO STICK THIS HERE BUZZIN' MAGIC BULLET UP HIS HEINIE WHILE YOU DOWN ON 'IM? I SWEAR HE'LL NEVER LOOK AT ANOTHER GIRL.
SHE'S RIGHT, Y'KNOW.
UH-HUH...
"...NOW UNDYING LOVE IS PRICELESS, I THINK WE CAN AGREE, BUT UNDYIN' LUST CAN BE BE BOUGHT."
OW! FUCK!

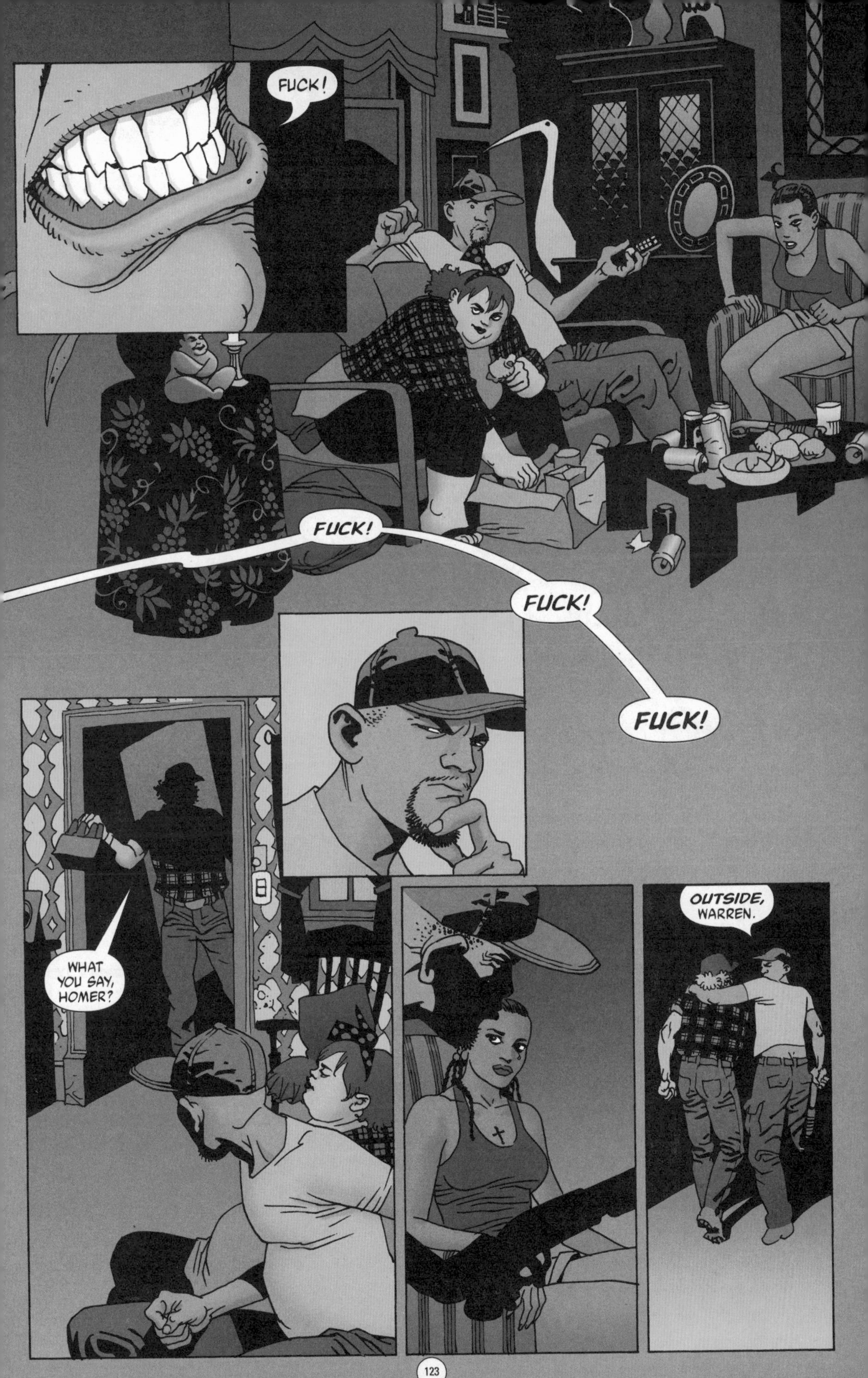
FUCK!
FUCK!
FUCK!
FUCK!
WHAT YOU SAY, HOMER?
OUTSIDE, WARREN.

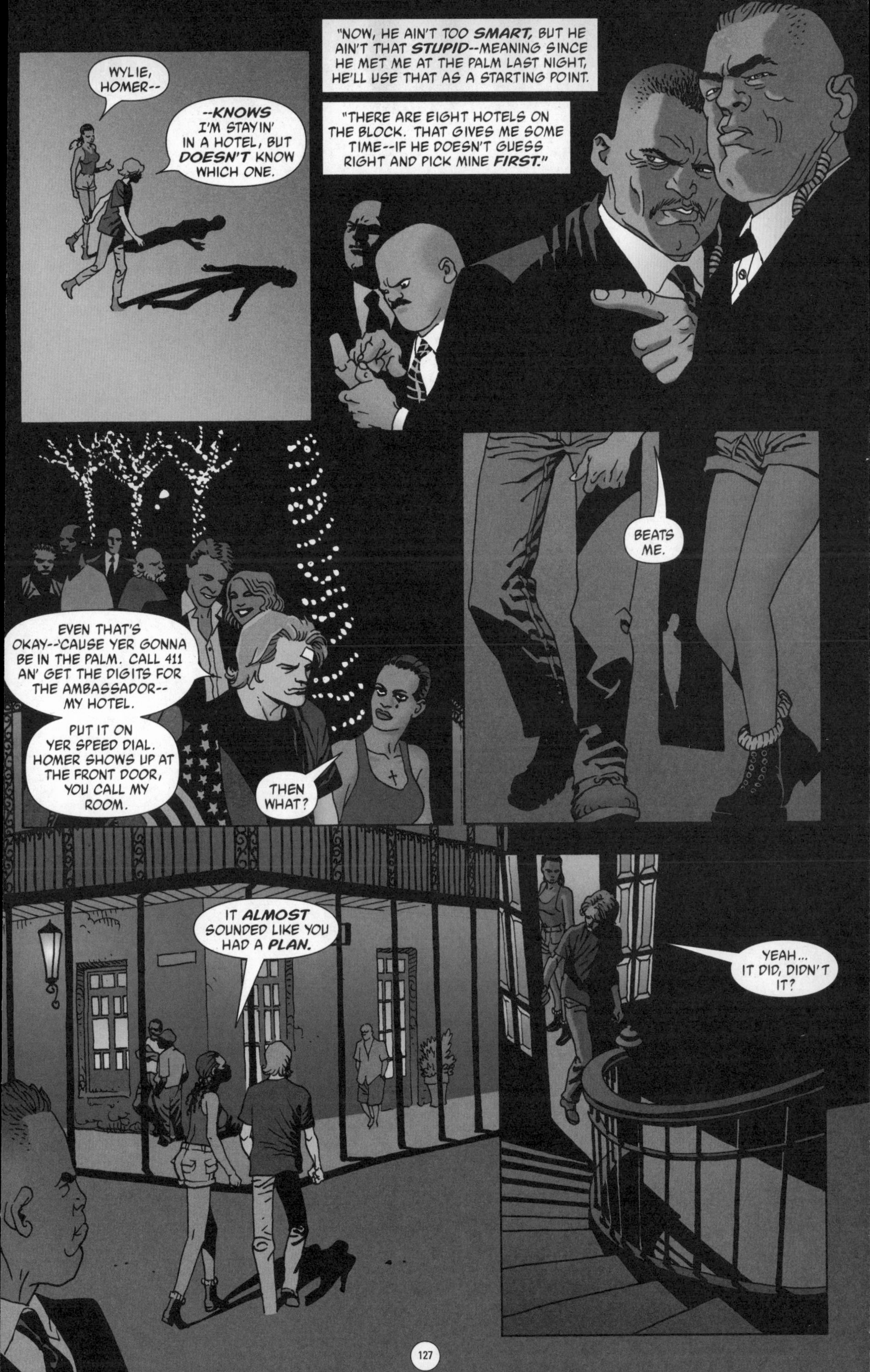
WYLIE, HOMER--
--KNOWS I'M STAYIN' IN A HOTEL, BUT DOESN'T KNOW WHICH ONE.
"NOW, HE AIN'T TOO SMART, BUT HE AIN'T THAT STUPID--MEANING SINCE HE MET ME AT THE PALM LAST NIGHT, HE'LL USE THAT AS A STARTING POINT.
"THERE ARE EIGHT HOTELS ON THE BLOCK. THAT GIVES ME SOME TIME--IF HE DOESN'T GUESS RIGHT AND PICK MINE FIRST."
EVEN THAT'S OKAY--'CAUSE YER GONNA BE IN THE PALM. CALL 411 AN' GET THE DIGITS FOR THE AMBASSADOR--MY HOTEL.
PUT IT ON YER SPEED DIAL. HOMER SHOWS UP AT THE FRONT DOOR, YOU CALL MY ROOM.
THEN WHAT?
BEATS ME.
IT ALMOST SOUNDED LIKE YOU HAD A PLAN.
YEAH... IT DID, DIDN'T IT?

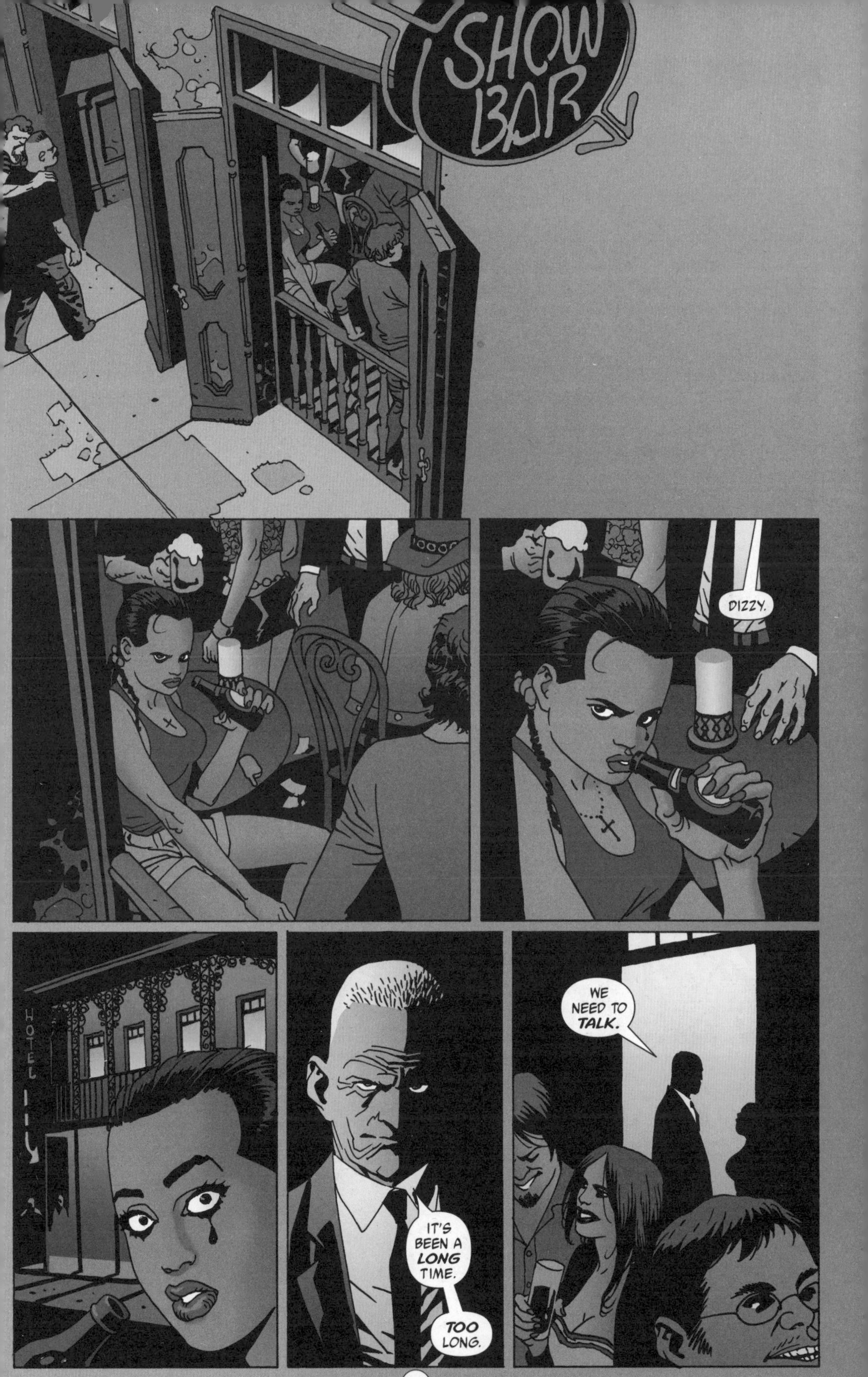
SHOW BAR
DIZZY.
HOTEL
IT'S BEEN A LONG TIME.
TOO LONG.
WE NEED TO TALK.

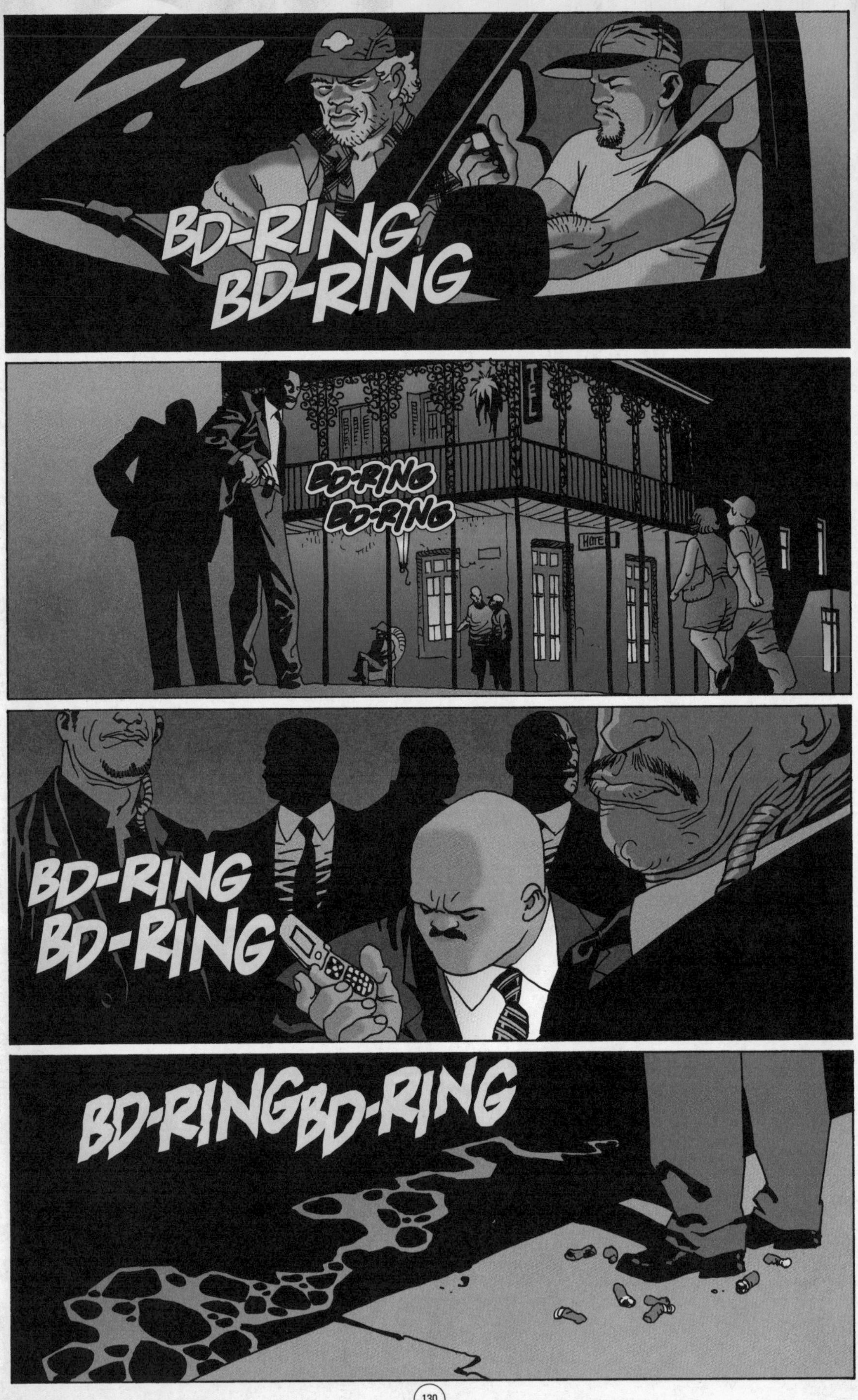
BD-RING
BD-RING
BD-RING
BD-RING
HOTE
BD-RING
BD-RING
BD-RINGBD-RING

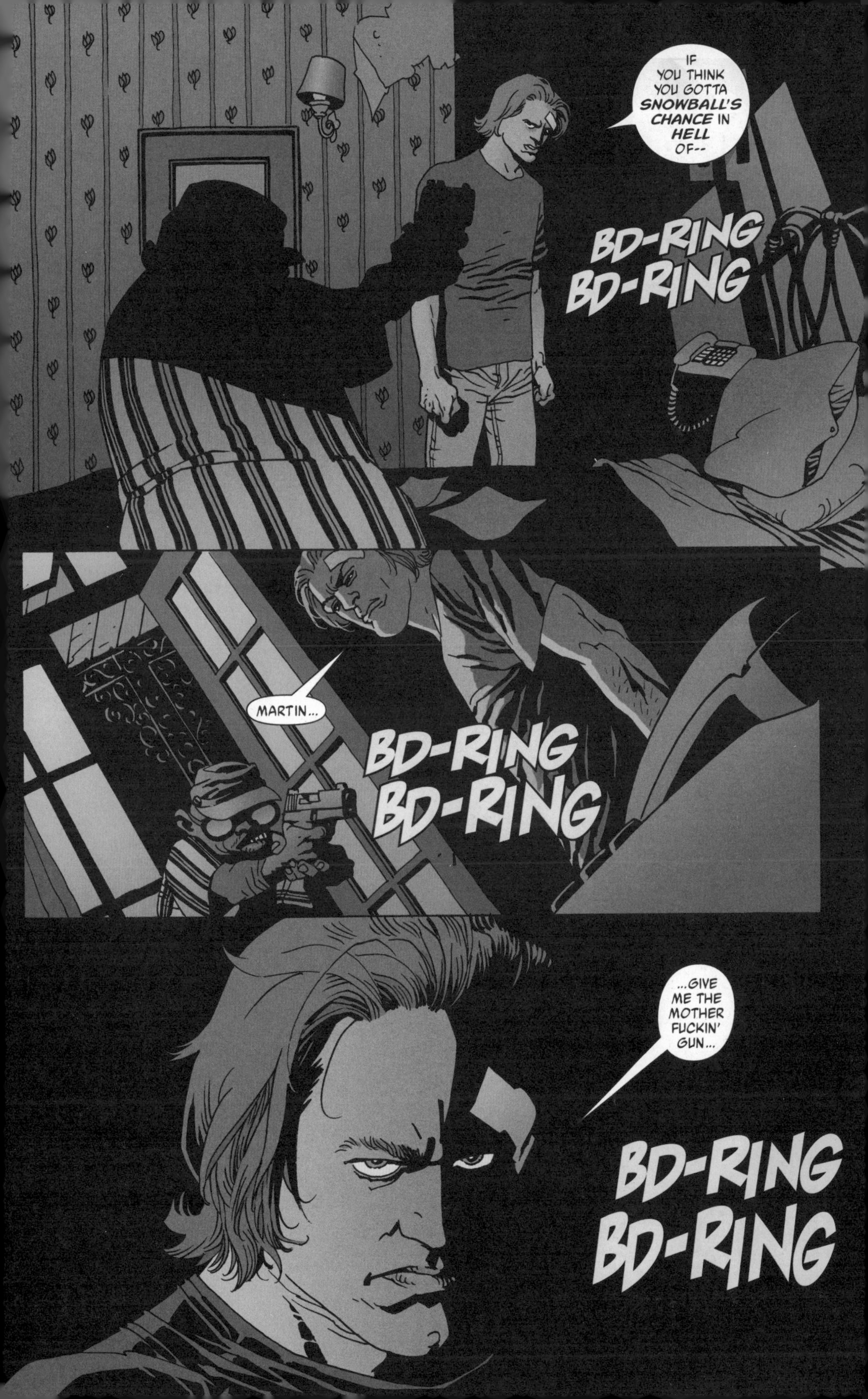
IF YOU THINK YOU GOTTA SNOWBALL'S CHANCE IN HELL OF--
BD-RING BD-RING
MARTIN...
BD-RING BD-RING
...GIVE ME THE MOTHER FUCKIN' GUN...
BD-RING BD-RING

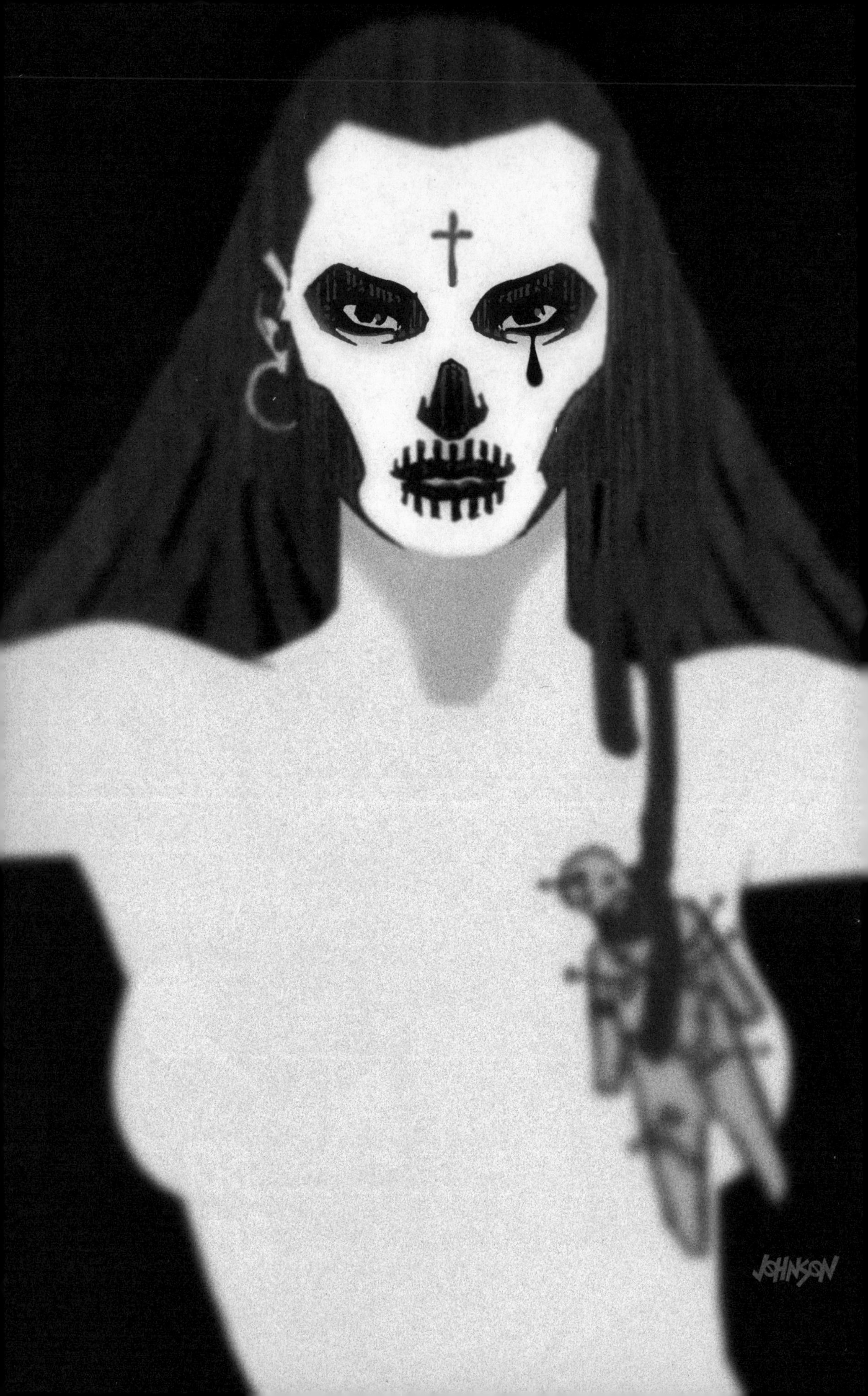
JOHNSON

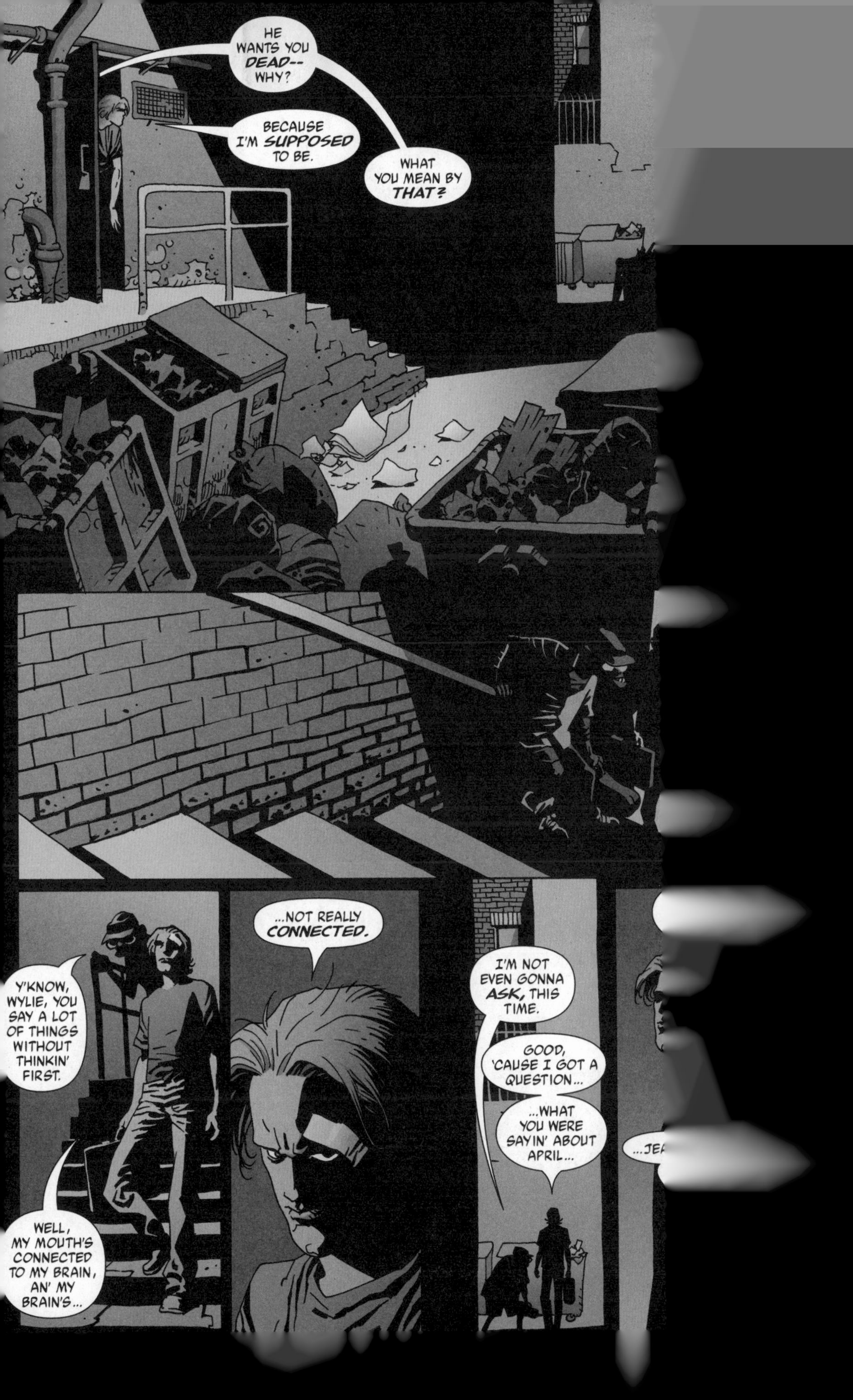

HE WANTS YOU DEAD-- WHY?
BECAUSE I'M SUPPOSED TO BE.
WHAT YOU MEAN BY THAT?
Y'KNOW, WYLIE, YOU SAY A LOT OF THINGS WITHOUT THINKIN' FIRST.
WELL, MY MOUTH'S CONNECTED TO MY BRAIN, AN' MY BRAIN'S...
...NOT REALLY CONNECTED.
I'M NOT EVEN GONNA ASK, THIS TIME.
GOOD, 'CAUSE I GOT A QUESTION...
...WHAT YOU WERE SAYIN' ABOUT APRIL...

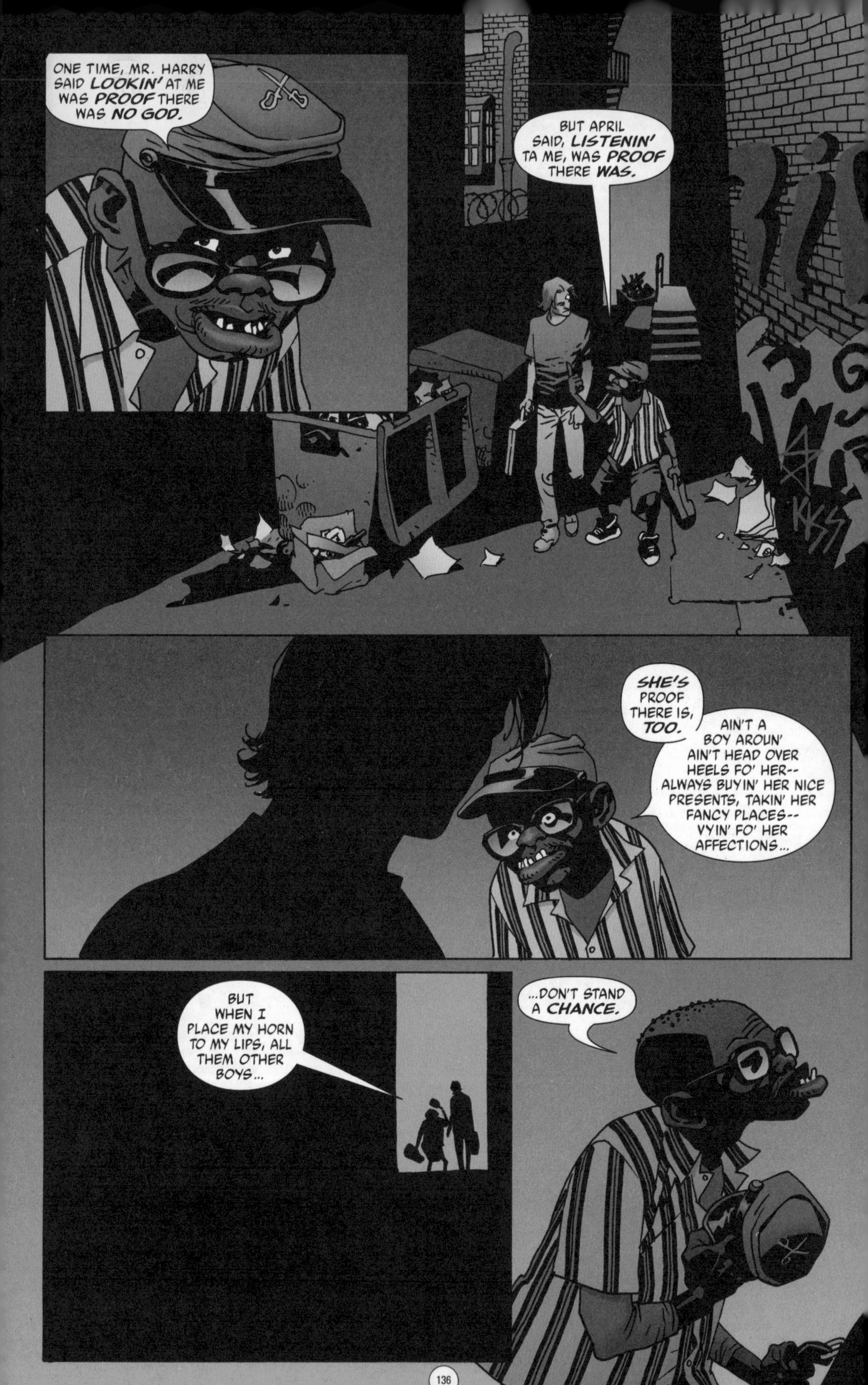
ONE TIME, MR. HARRY SAID LOOKIN' AT ME WAS PROOF THERE WAS NO GOD.
BUT APRIL SAID, LISTENIN' TA ME, WAS PROOF THERE WAS.
SHE'S PROOF THERE IS, TOO.
AIN'T A BOY AROUN' AIN'T HEAD OVER HEELS FO' HER-- ALWAYS BUYIN' HER NICE PRESENTS, TAKIN' HER FANCY PLACES-- VYIN' FO' HER AFFECTIONS...
BUT WHEN I PLACE MY HORN TO MY LIPS, ALL THEM OTHER BOYS...
...DON'T STAND A CHANCE.

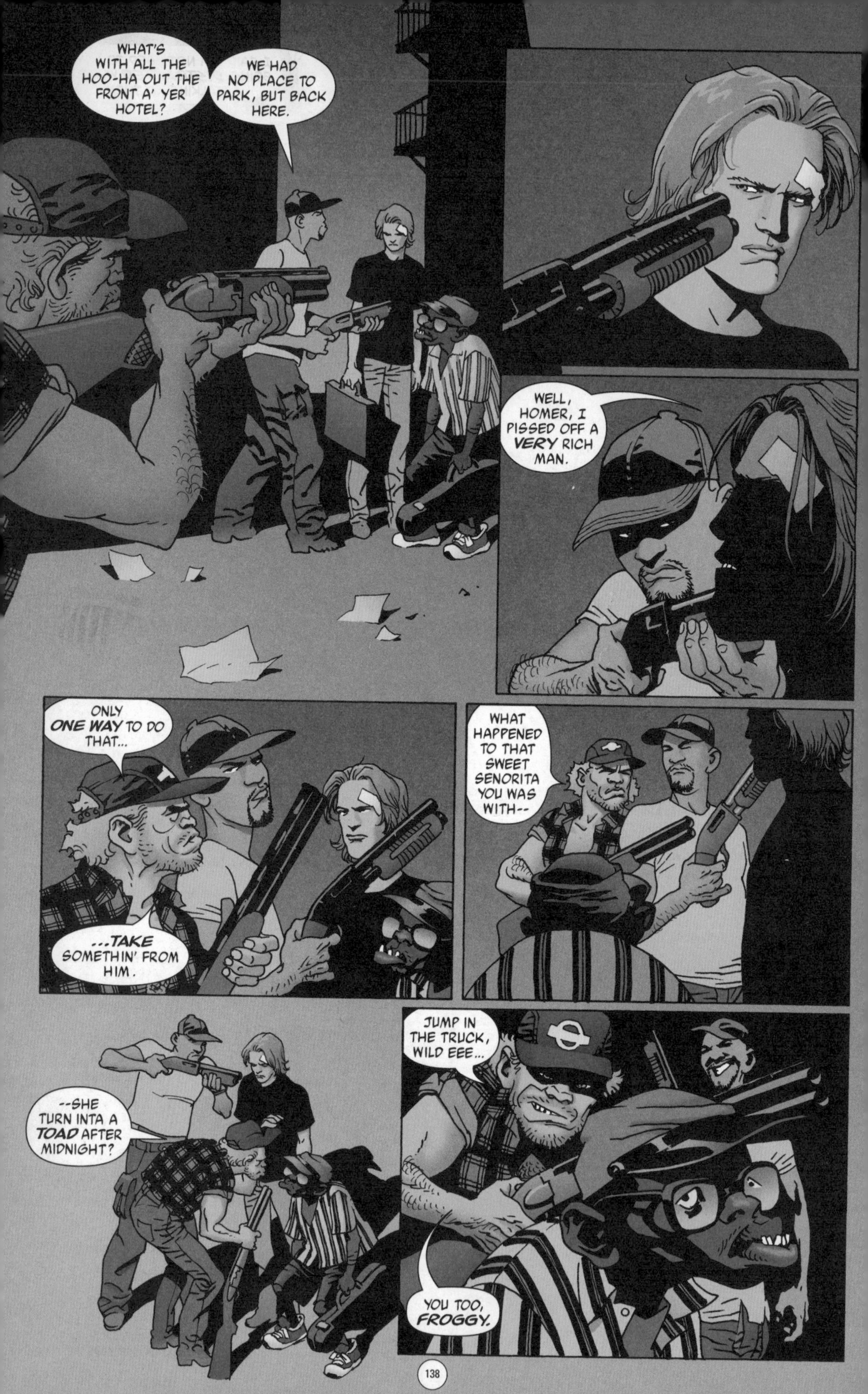
WHAT'S WITH ALL THE HOO-HA OUT THE FRONT A' YER HOTEL?
WE HAD NO PLACE TO PARK, BUT BACK HERE.
WELL, HOMER, I PISSED OFF A VERY RICH MAN.
ONLY ONE WAY TO DO THAT...
...TAKE SOMETHIN' FROM HIM.
WHAT HAPPENED TO THAT SWEET SENORITA YOU WAS WITH--
--SHE TURN INTA A TOAD AFTER MIDNIGHT?
JUMP IN THE TRUCK, WILD EEE...
YOU TOO, FROGGY.

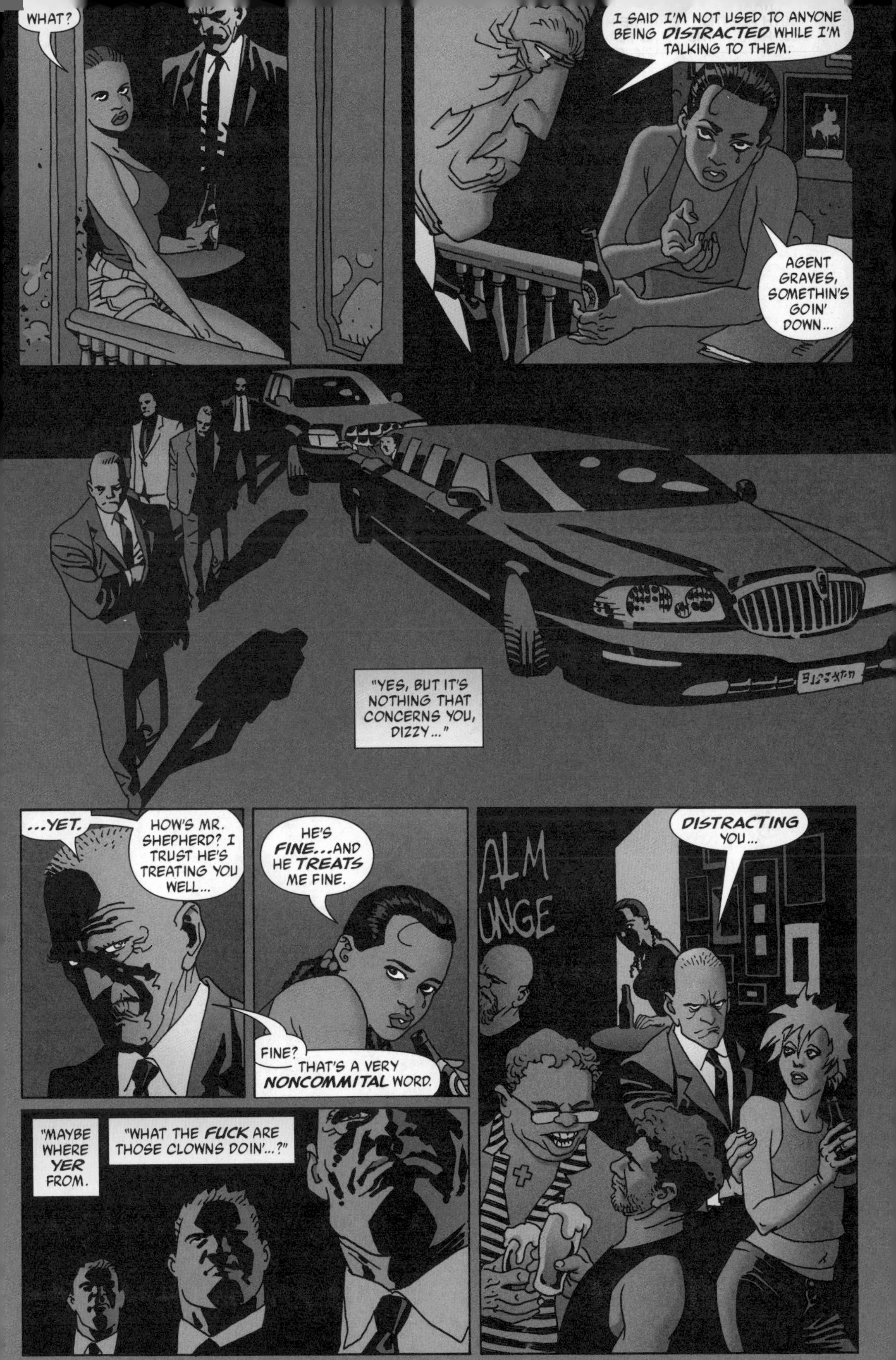
WHAT?
I SAID I'M NOT USED TO ANYONE BEING DISTRACTED WHILE I'M TALKING TO THEM.
AGENT GRAVES, SOMETHIN'S GOIN' DOWN...
"YES, BUT IT'S NOTHING THAT CONCERNS YOU, DIZZY..."
...YET.
HOW'S MR. SHEPHERD? I TRUST HE'S TREATING YOU WELL...
HE'S FINE...AND HE TREATS ME FINE.
FINE? THAT'S A VERY NONCOMMITAL WORD.
DISTRACTING YOU...
"MAYBE WHERE YER FROM.
"WHAT THE FUCK ARE THOSE CLOWNS DOIN'...?"

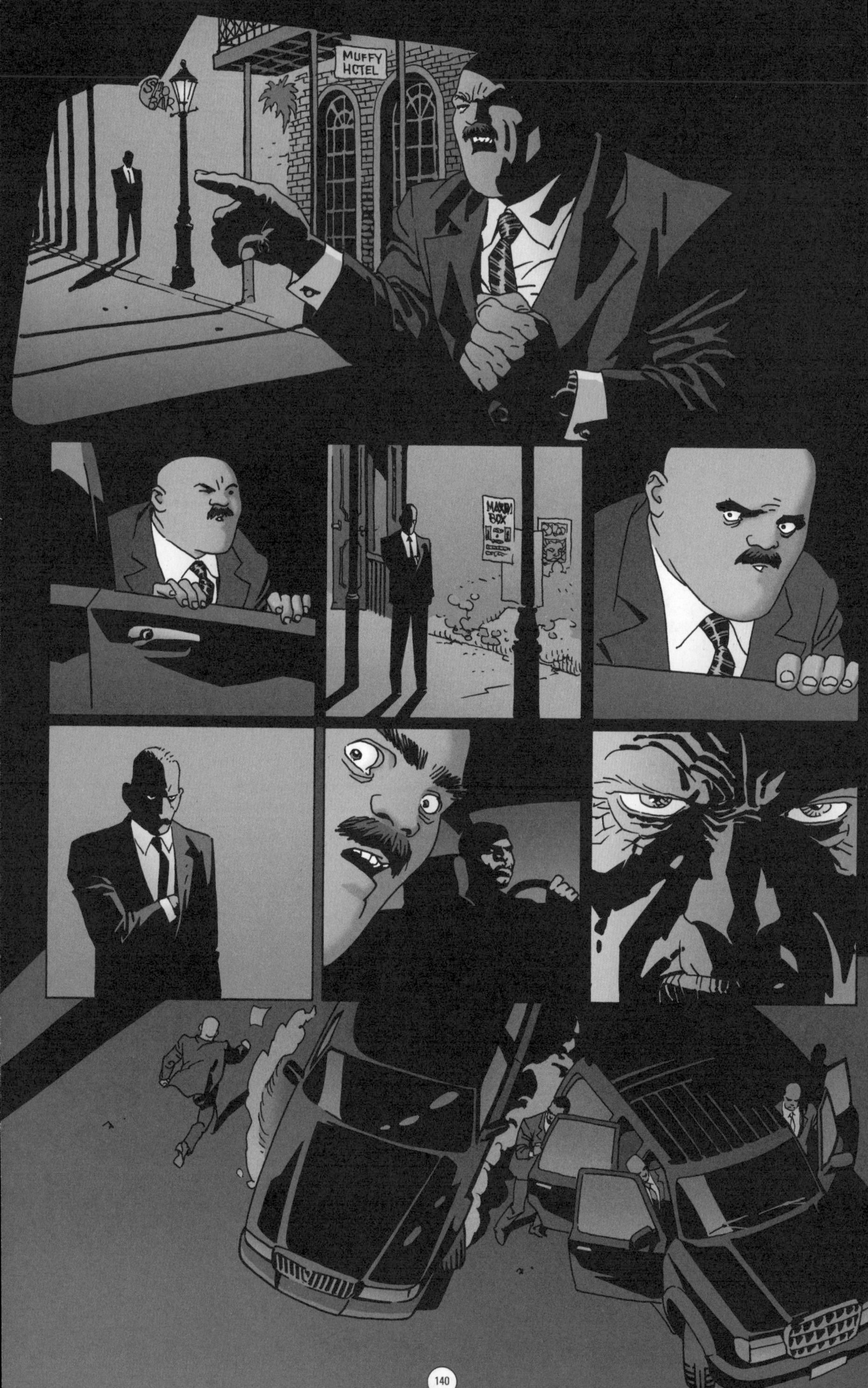
MUFFY
HOTEL

141

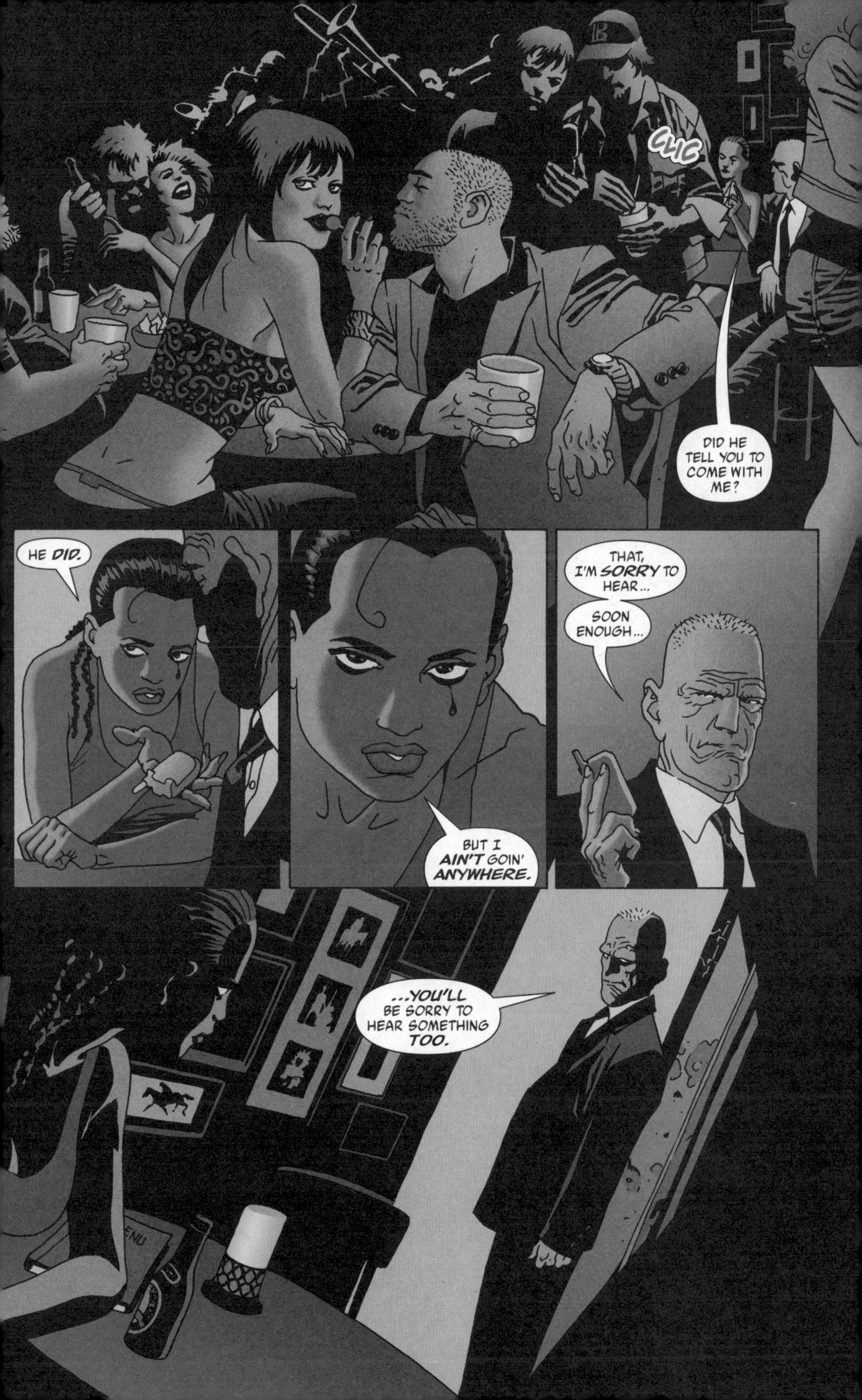
CLIC
DID HE TELL YOU TO COME WITH ME?
HE DID.
BUT I AIN'T GOIN' ANYWHERE.
THAT, I'M SORRY TO HEAR...
SOON ENOUGH...
...YOU'LL BE SORRY TO HEAR SOMETHING TOO.

I WANT TO *DIE* LIKE A *MAN.*

THAT'S *RIGHTEOUS.* GOOD FER YOU.

BUT I'D LIKE TA KNOW SOMETHIN' FIRST...

LAST REQUEST, OKAY?

THAT WOMAN YOU MURDERDED-- *WHO* WAS SHE?

NO ONE. AIN'T THAT *FUCKED?* JUS' SOME CRACKHEAD, WORKIN' HER OL' MAN'S NERVE.

I AM TRULY SORRY YOU WITNESSED SUCH A *NOTHIN'* THING, WILD EEE.

NOW, WHAT YOU TAKE FROM DADDY WARBUCKS?

IT'S DADDY *MADRID*--AND IT'S NOTHING YOU CAN *SPEND,* HOMER.

SEE, THE TRUTH IS, ALL I WAS LOOKIN' FOR YOU TO DO WAS GET ME OUT OF THAT *FRYING* PAN, AND INTO THE...

YOU LET *US* BE THE JUDGE A THAT.

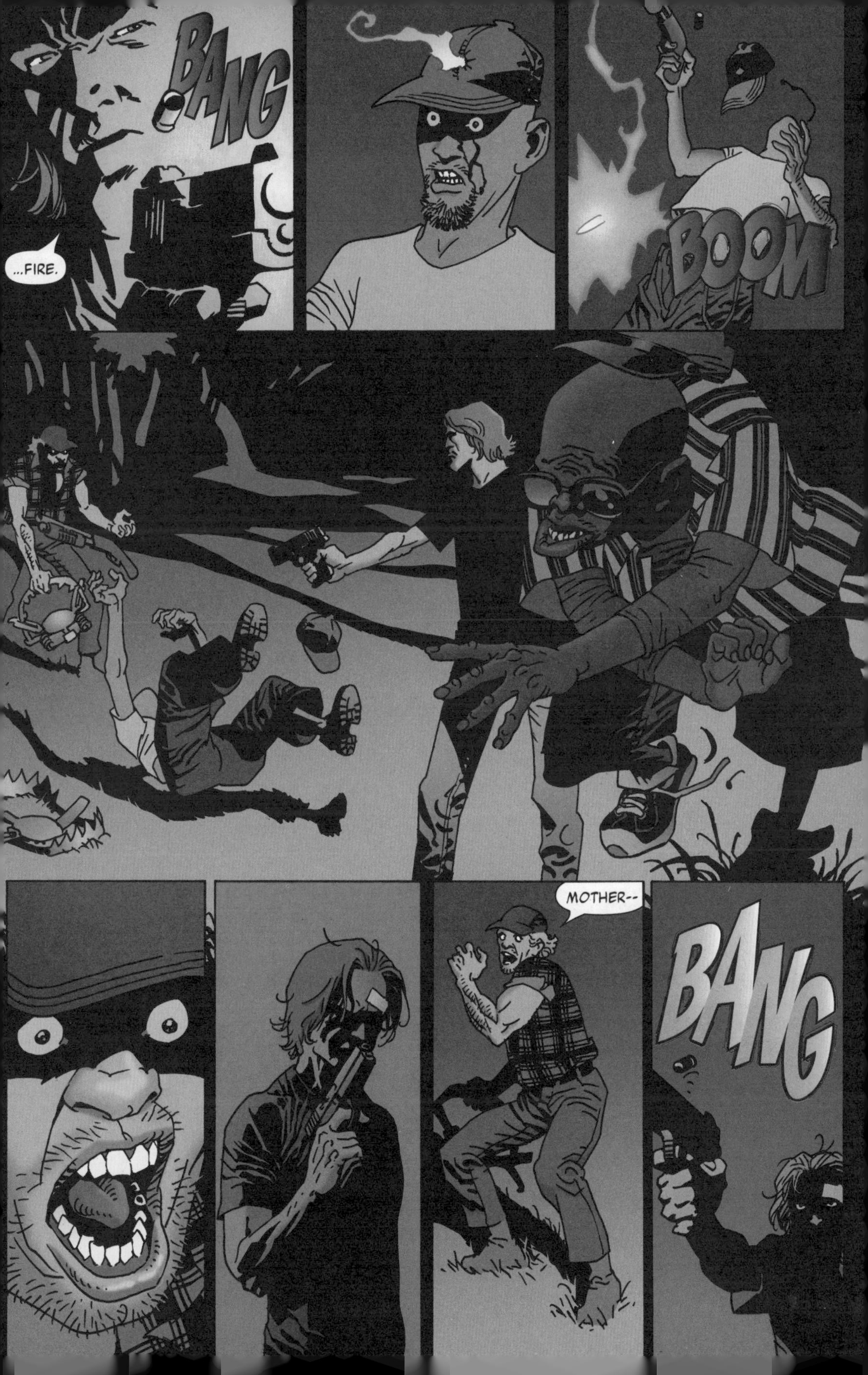
BANG
...FIRE.
BOOM
MOTHER--
BANG

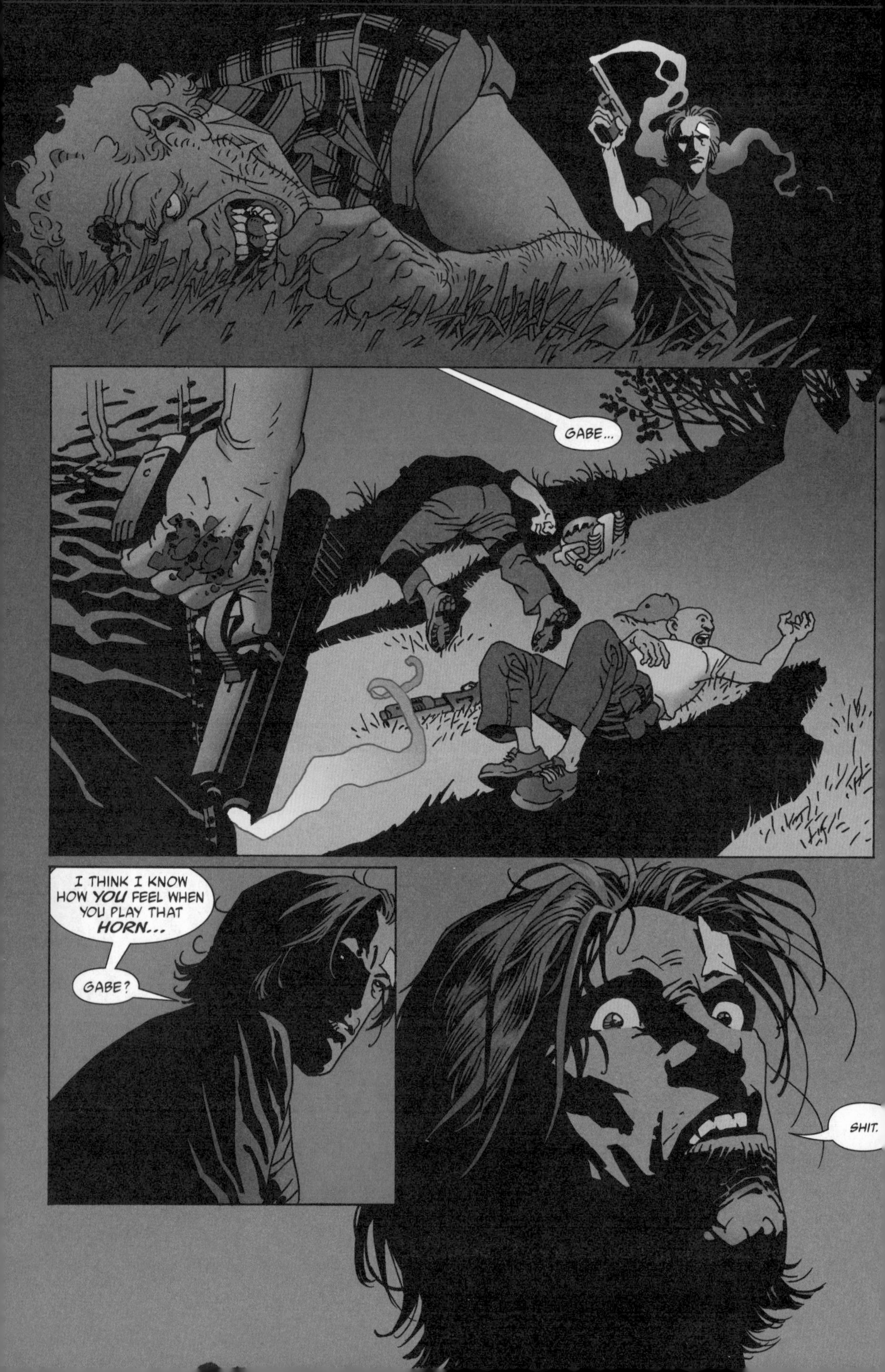
GABE...
I THINK I KNOW HOW *YOU* FEEL WHEN YOU PLAY THAT *HORN...*
GABE?
SHIT.

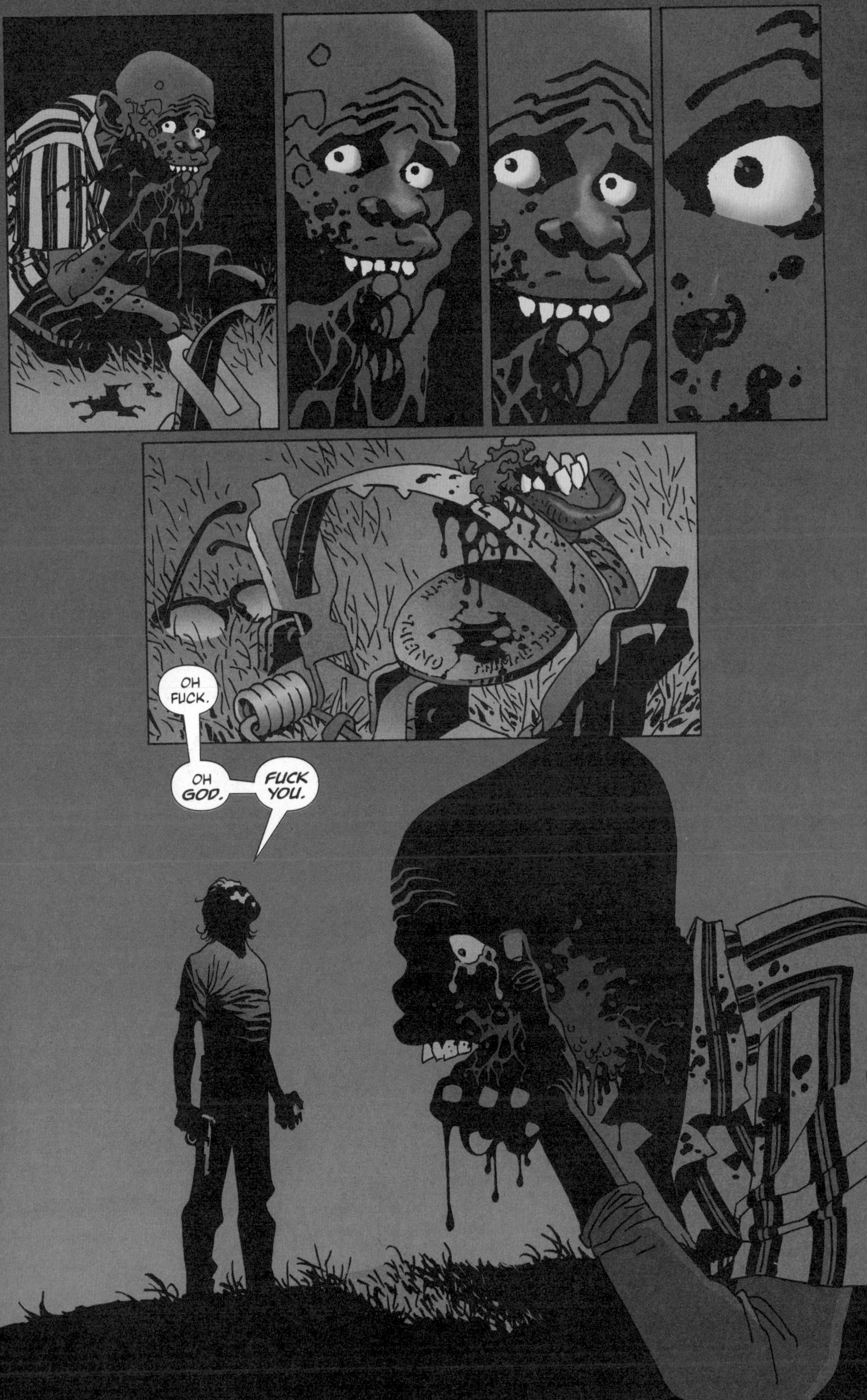
OH FUCK.
OH GOD.
FUCK YOU.

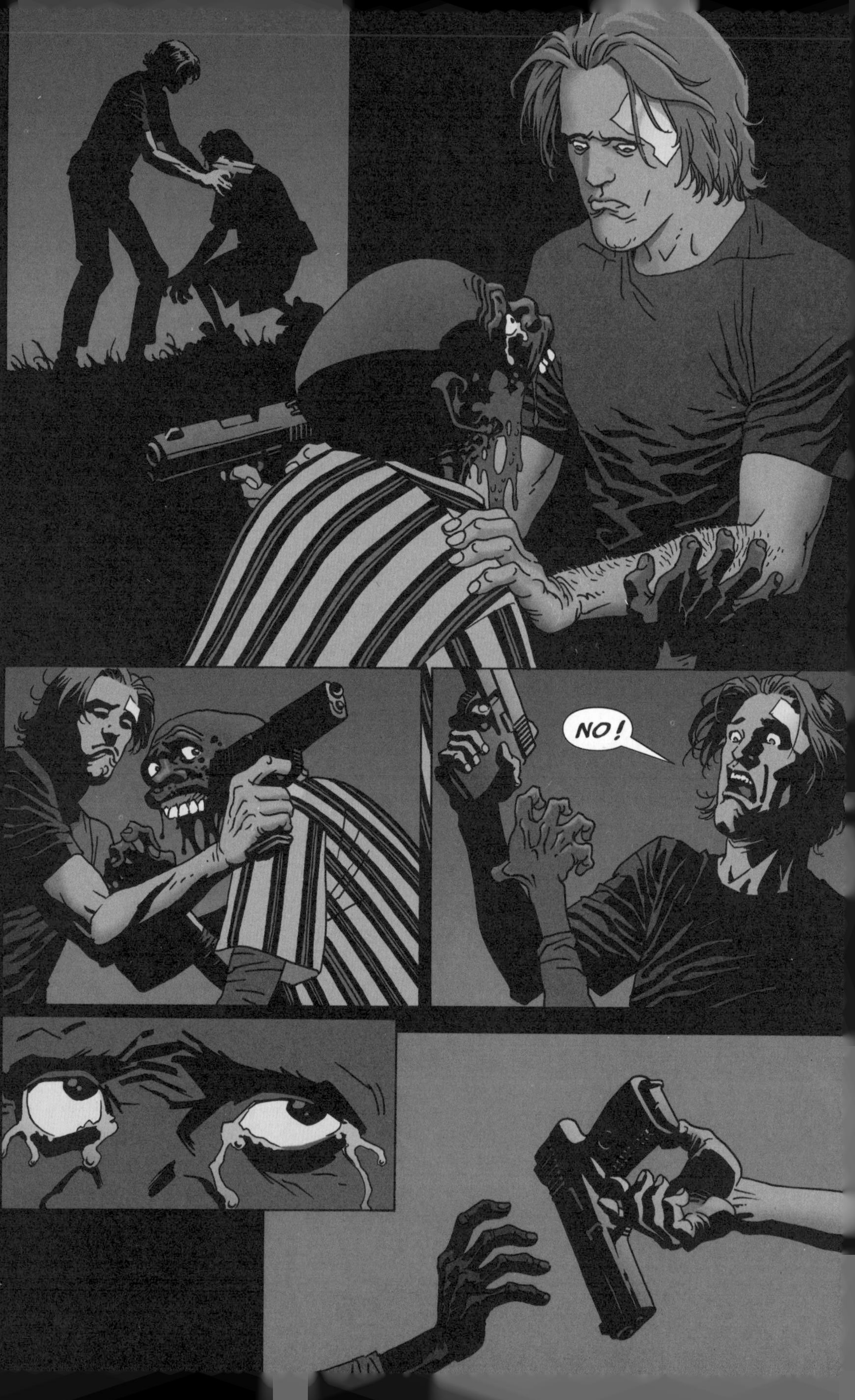
NO!

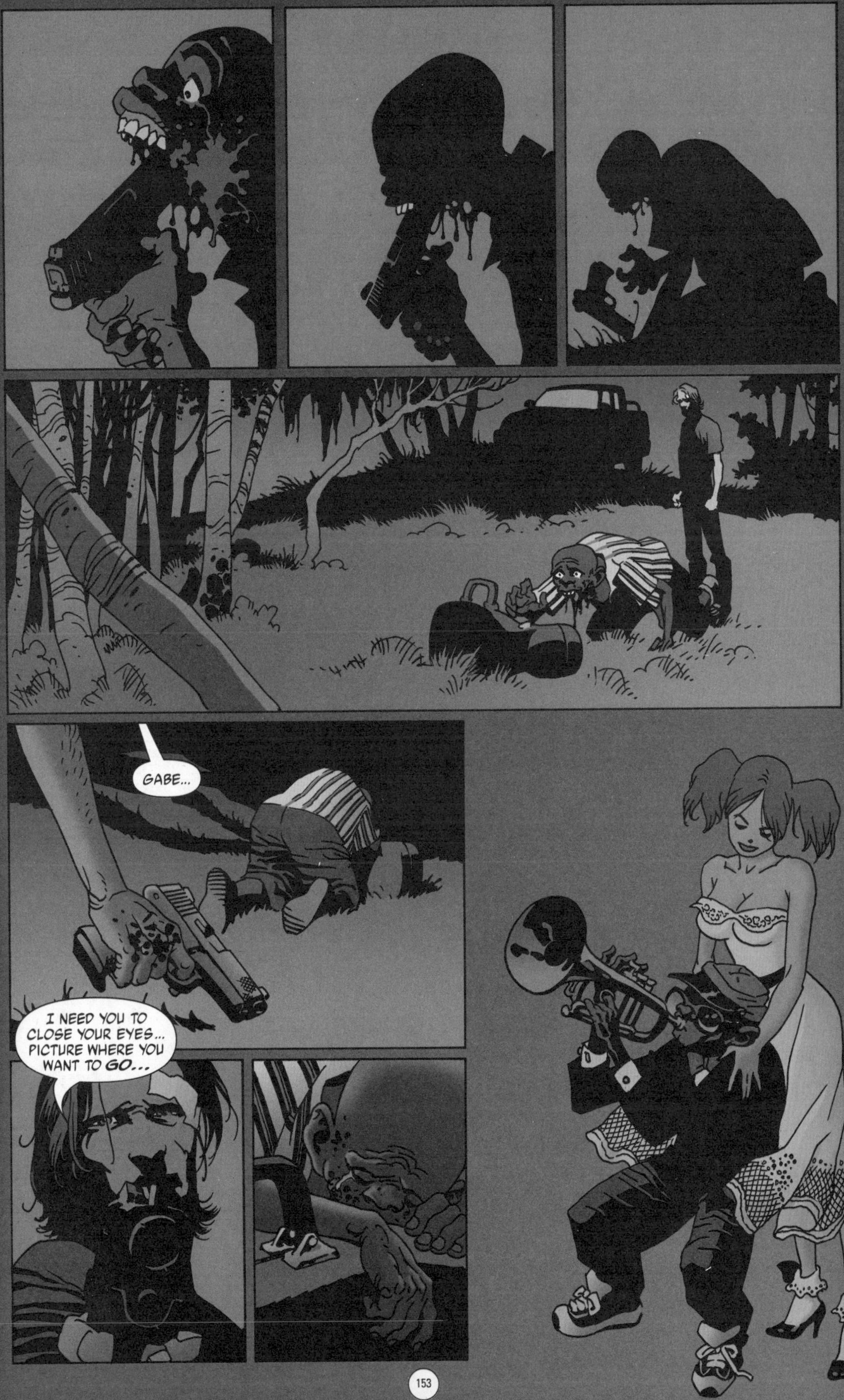
GABE...
I NEED YOU TO CLOSE YOUR EYES... PICTURE WHERE YOU WANT TO GO...

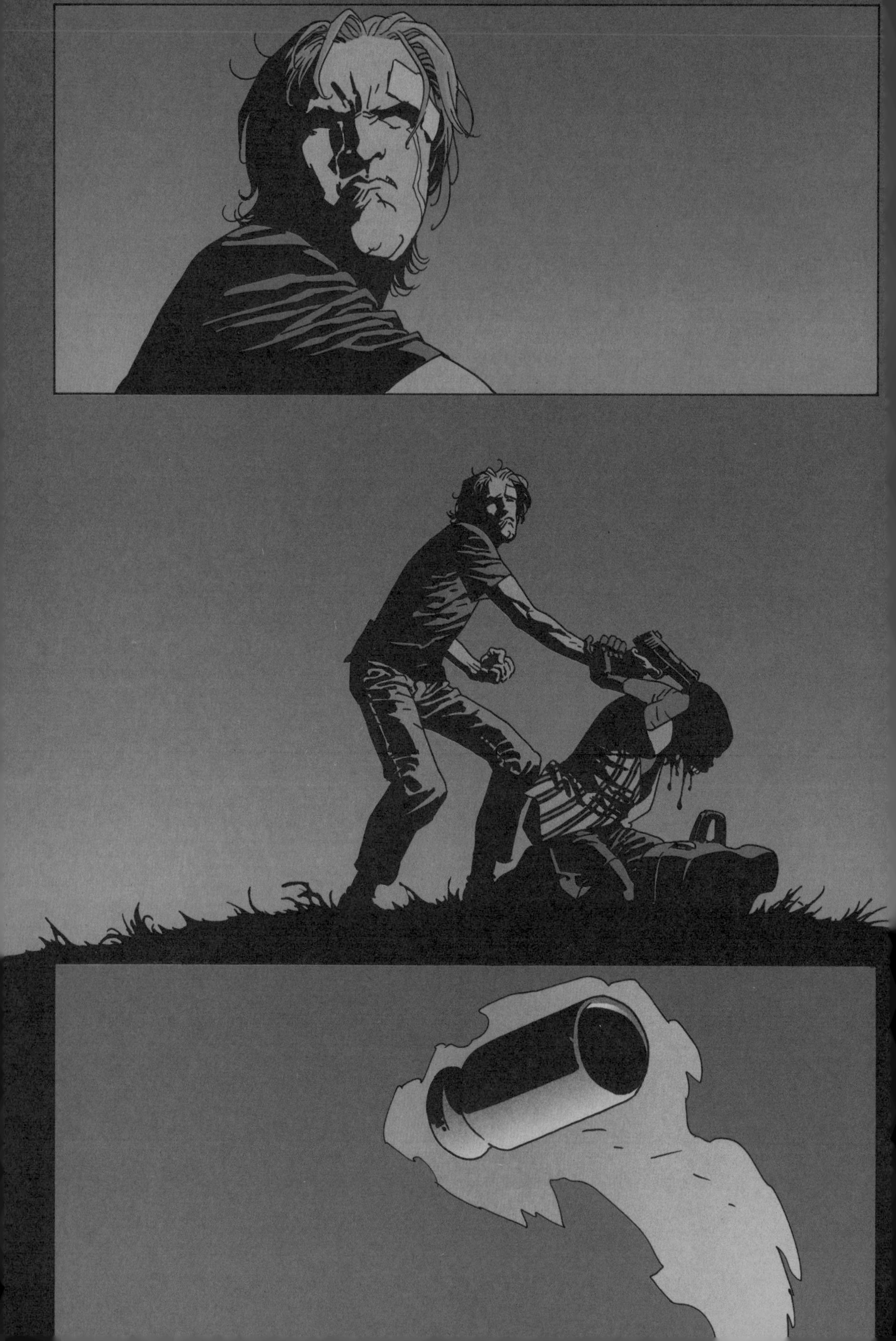

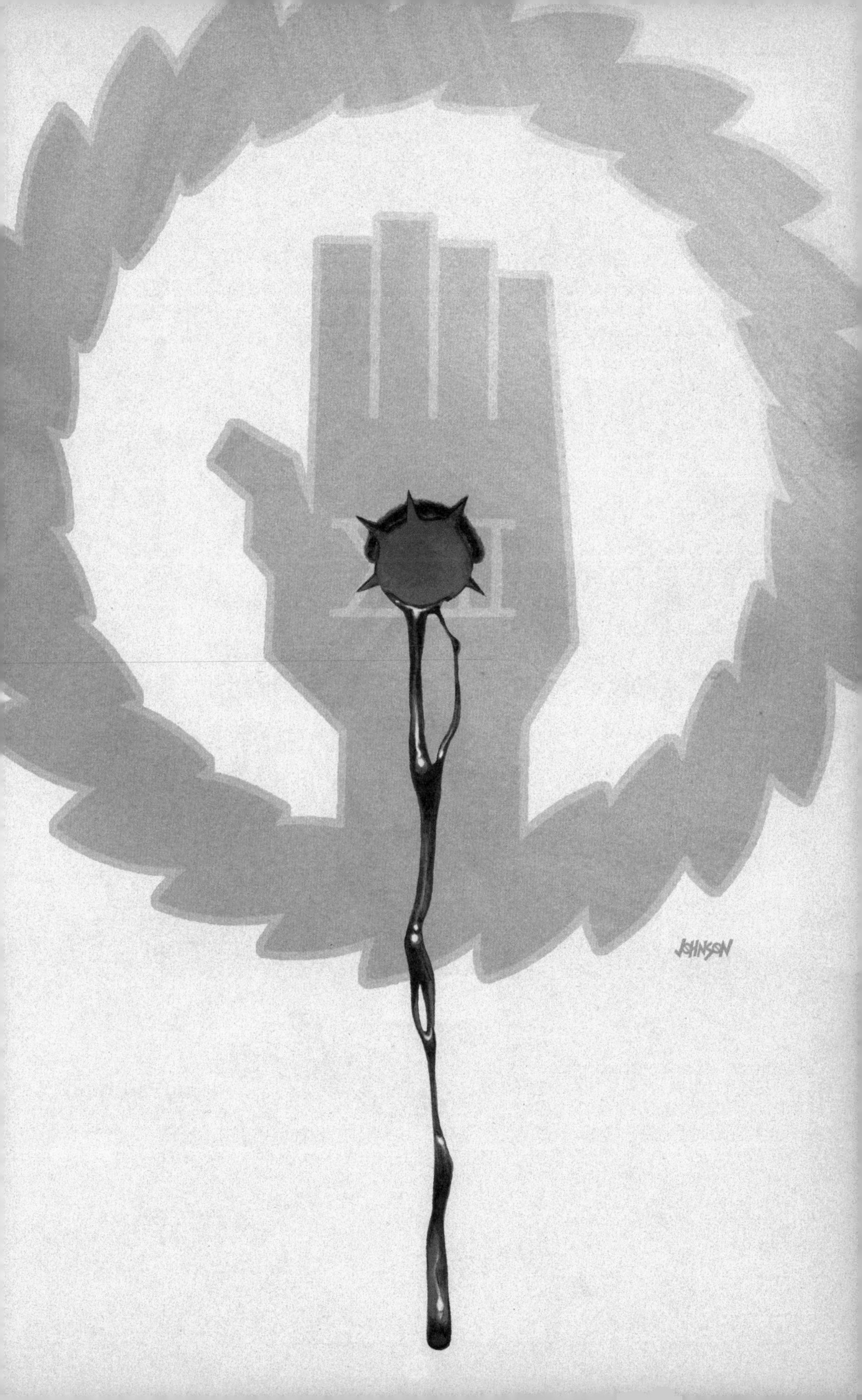
JOHNSON

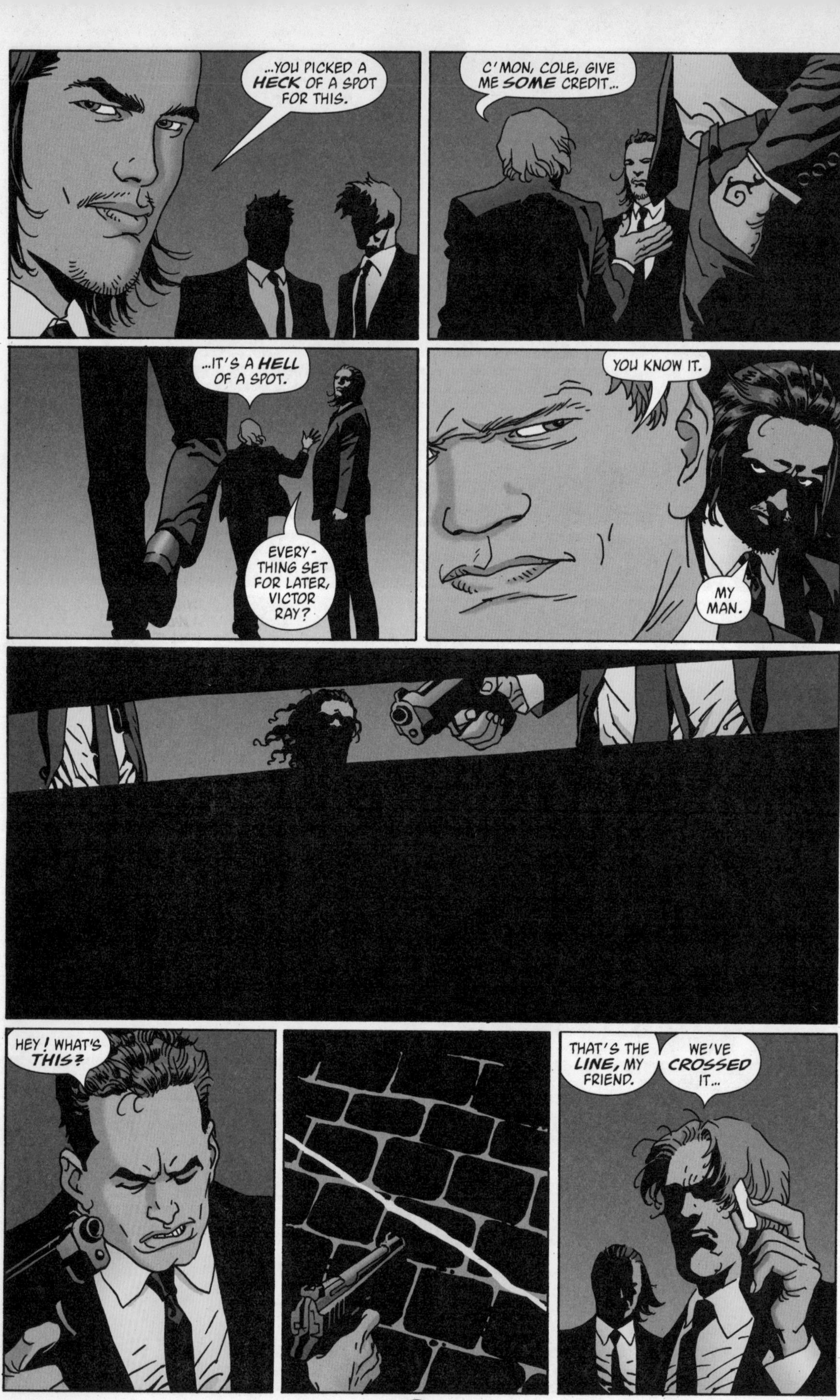

...YOU PICKED A HECK OF A SPOT FOR THIS.
C'MON, COLE, GIVE ME SOME CREDIT...
...IT'S A HELL OF A SPOT.
EVERY-THING SET FOR LATER, VICTOR RAY?
YOU KNOW IT.
MY MAN.
HEY! WHAT'S THIS?
THAT'S THE LINE, MY FRIEND.
WE'VE CROSSED IT...

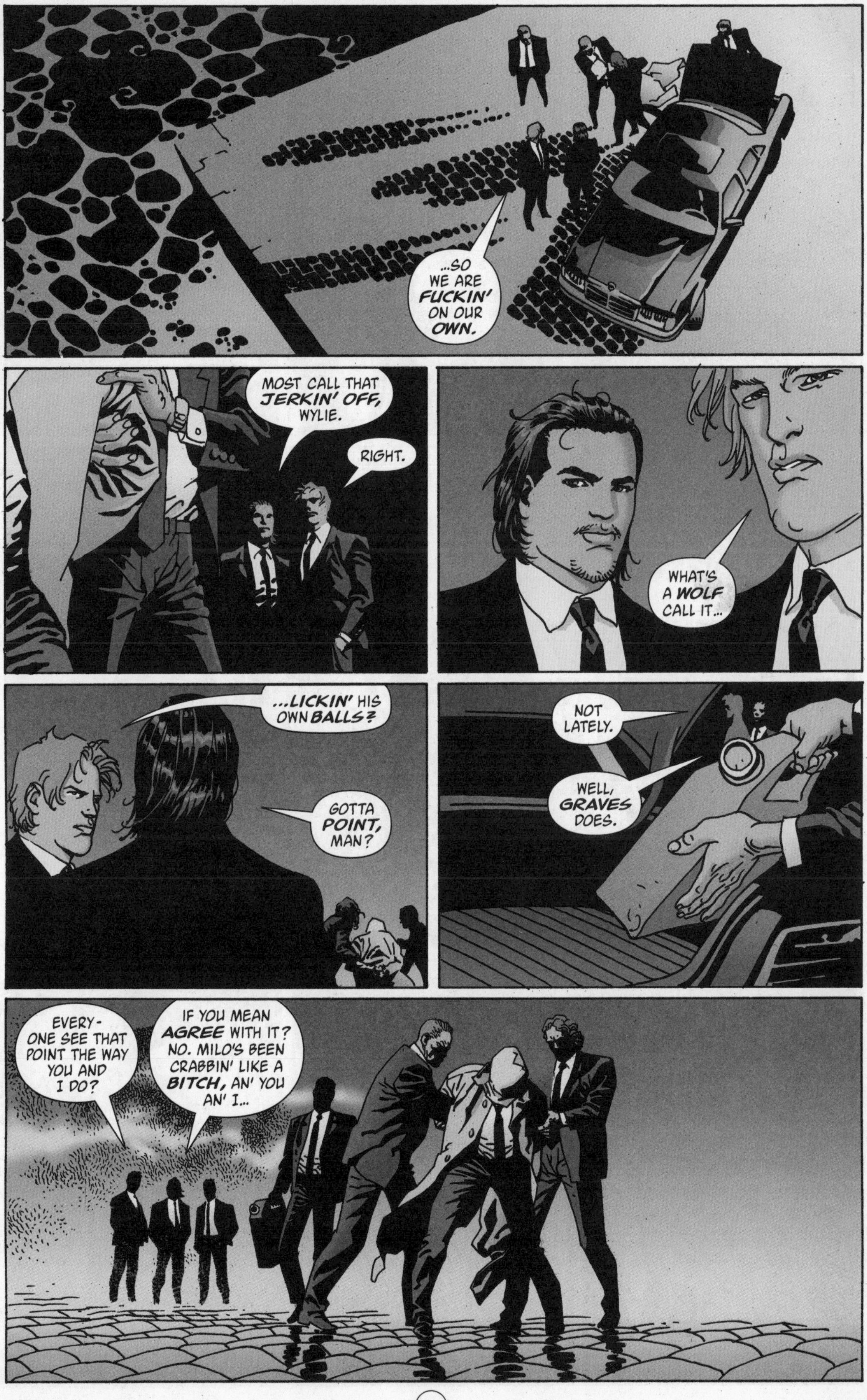
...SO WE ARE FUCKIN' ON OUR OWN.
MOST CALL THAT JERKIN' OFF, WYLIE.
RIGHT.
WHAT'S A WOLF CALL IT...
...LICKIN' HIS OWN BALLS?
GOTTA POINT, MAN?
NOT LATELY.
WELL, GRAVES DOES.
EVERY-ONE SEE THAT POINT THE WAY YOU AND I DO?
IF YOU MEAN AGREE WITH IT? NO. MILO'S BEEN CRABBIN' LIKE A BITCH, AN' YOU AN' I...

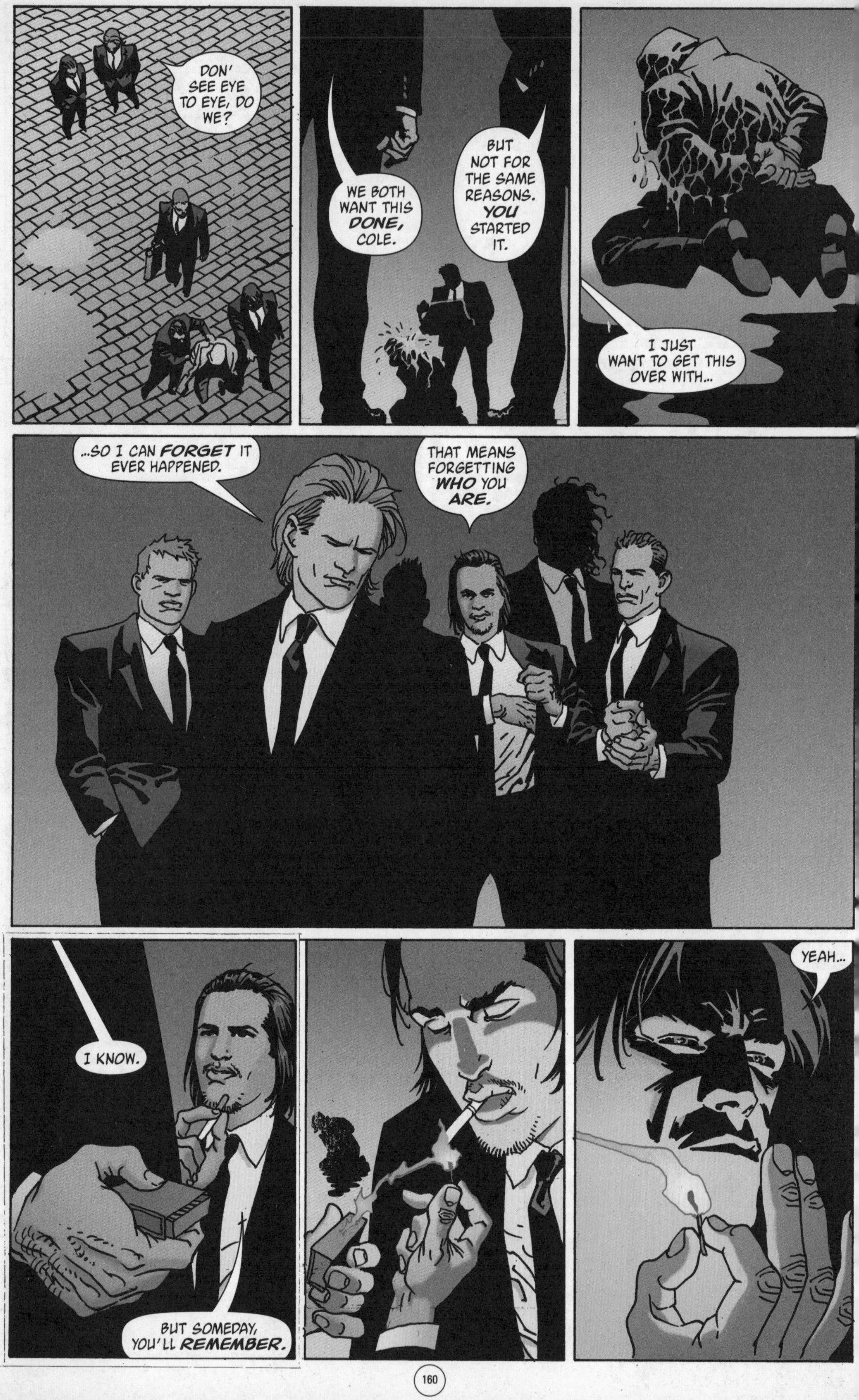
DON' SEE EYE TO EYE, DO WE?
WE BOTH WANT THIS DONE, COLE.
BUT NOT FOR THE SAME REASONS. YOU STARTED IT.
I JUST WANT TO GET THIS OVER WITH...
...SO I CAN FORGET IT EVER HAPPENED.
THAT MEANS FORGETTING WHO YOU ARE.
I KNOW.
BUT SOMEDAY, YOU'LL REMEMBER.
YEAH...

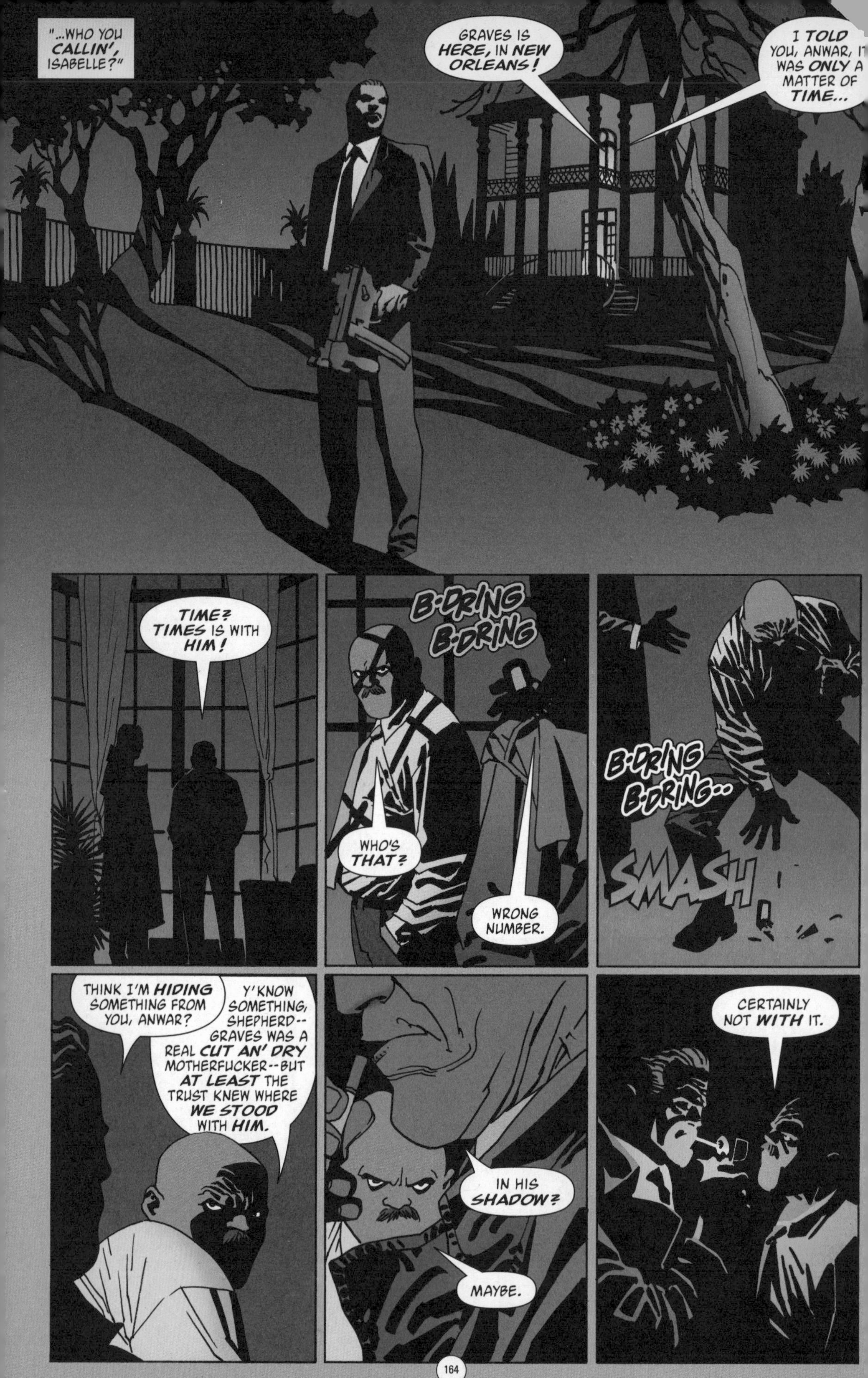
"...WHO YOU CALLIN', ISABELLE?"
GRAVES IS HERE, IN NEW ORLEANS!
I TOLD YOU, ANWAR, IT WAS ONLY A MATTER OF TIME...
TIME? TIMES IS WITH HIM!
B-DRING B-DRING
WHO'S THAT?
WRONG NUMBER.
B-DRING B-DRING..
SMASH
THINK I'M HIDING SOMETHING FROM YOU, ANWAR?
Y'KNOW SOMETHING, SHEPHERD-- GRAVES WAS A REAL CUT AN' DRY MOTHERFUCKER--BUT AT LEAST THE TRUST KNEW WHERE WE STOOD WITH HIM.
IN HIS SHADOW?
MAYBE.
CERTAINLY NOT WITH IT.

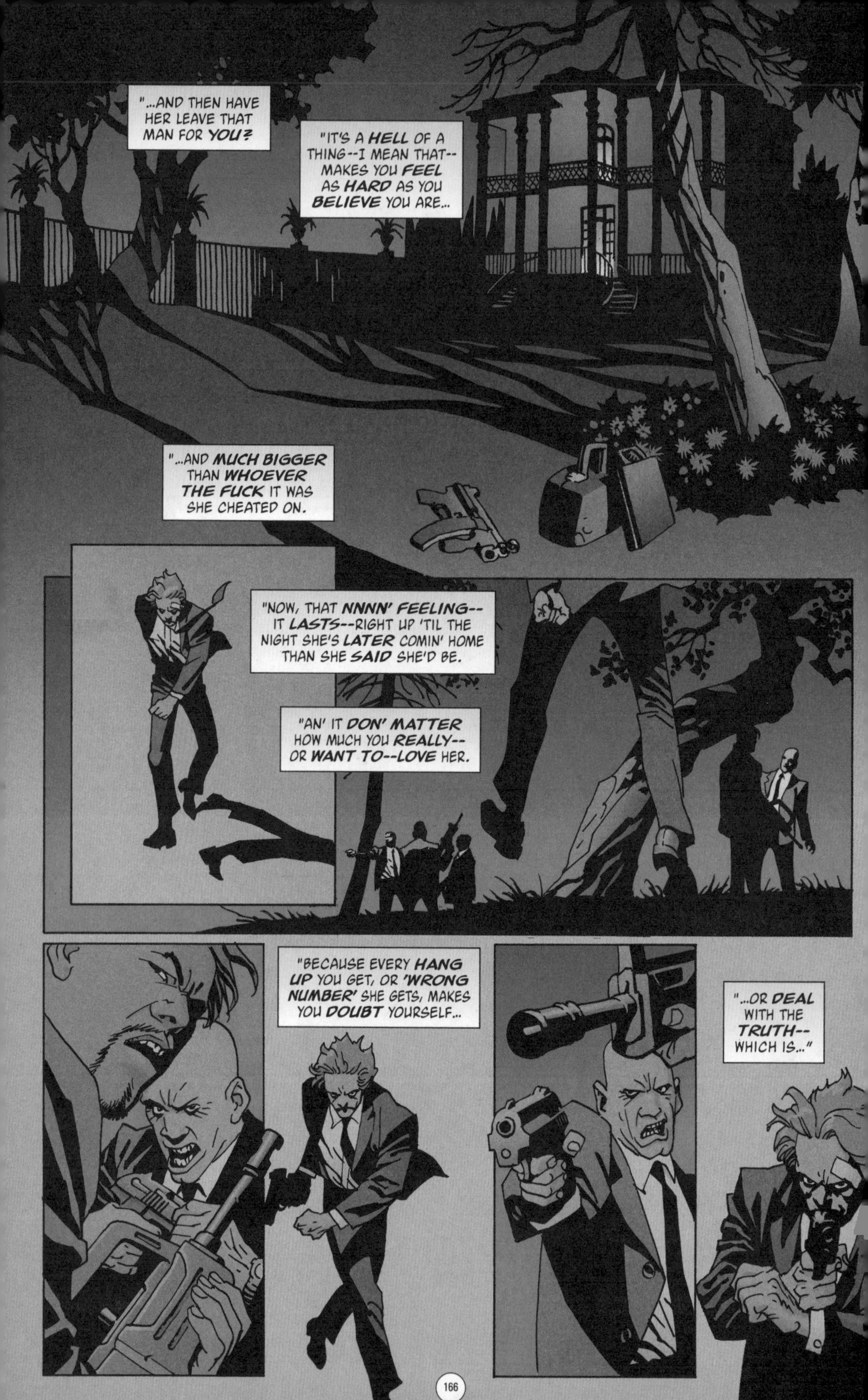
"...AND THEN HAVE HER LEAVE THAT MAN FOR YOU?
"IT'S A HELL OF A THING--I MEAN THAT--MAKES YOU FEEL AS HARD AS YOU BELIEVE YOU ARE...
"...AND MUCH BIGGER THAN WHOEVER THE FUCK IT WAS SHE CHEATED ON.
"NOW, THAT NNNN' FEELING--IT LASTS--RIGHT UP 'TIL THE NIGHT SHE'S LATER COMIN' HOME THAN SHE SAID SHE'D BE.
"AN' IT DON' MATTER HOW MUCH YOU REALLY--OR WANT TO--LOVE HER.
"BECAUSE EVERY HANG UP YOU GET, OR 'WRONG NUMBER' SHE GETS, MAKES YOU DOUBT YOURSELF...
"...OR DEAL WITH THE TRUTH--WHICH IS..."

IF SHE DID IT *ONCE*, SHE CAN DO IT *AGAIN*.

AN' YOU MIGHT BE THE *"WHOEVER THE FUCK IT WAS"* THIS TIME.

GET DOWN.

BAMBAMBAM

BANG

JESUS...

WHAT?

BAM BAMBAM BANG

NOT A WASTED ROUND...

...EVERY *SHOT* HAS A POINT.

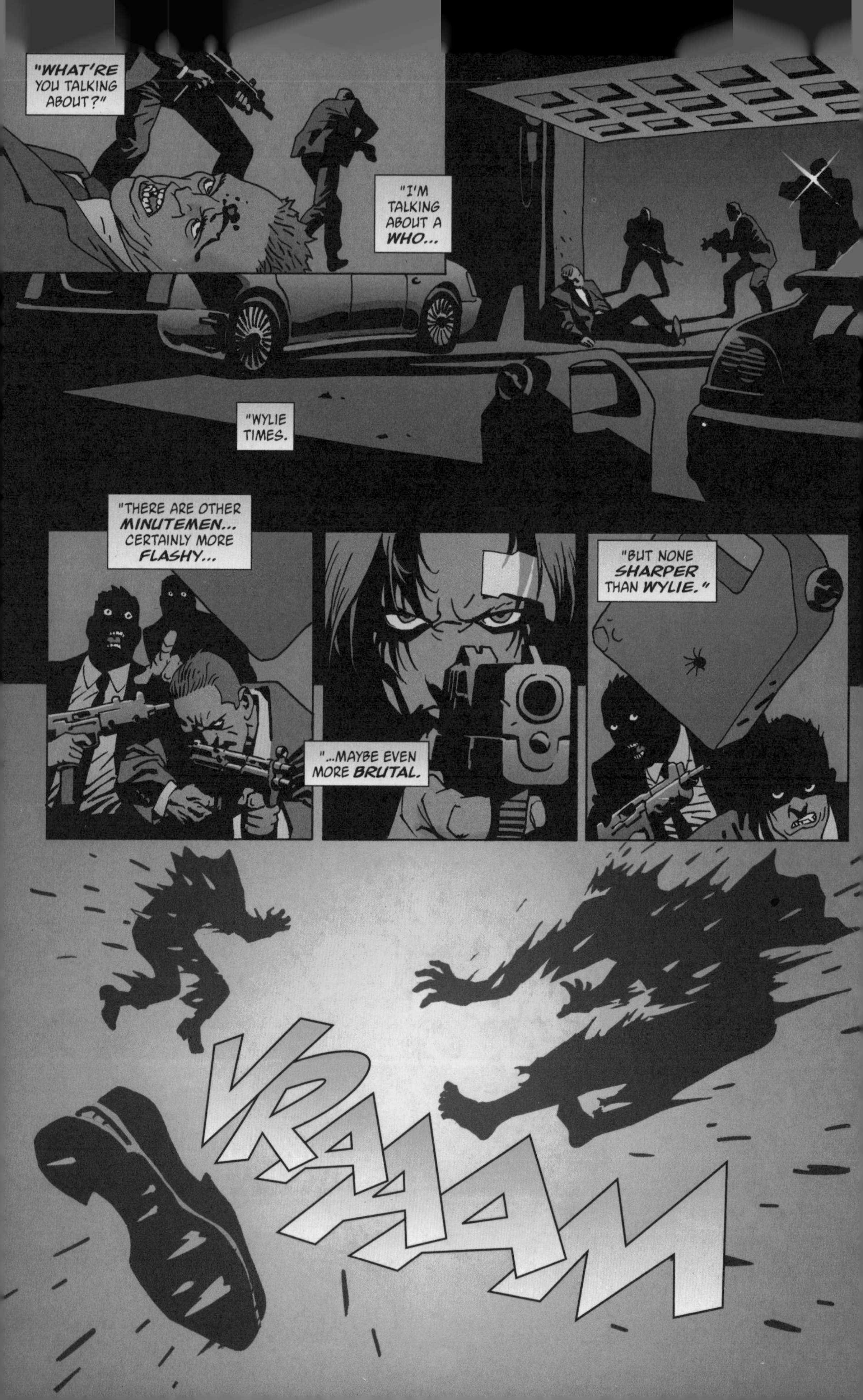
"WHAT'RE YOU TALKING ABOUT?"
"I'M TALKING ABOUT A WHO...
"WYLIE TIMES.
"THERE ARE OTHER MINUTEMEN... CERTAINLY MORE FLASHY...
"...MAYBE EVEN MORE BRUTAL.
"BUT NONE SHARPER THAN WYLIE."
VRAAAM

BANG
BANG

HE'S A MURDERIN' *BASTARD*--

BANG

NO...THE *DOG* MURDERED THE *BASTARD* IN L.A.

MR. MADRID--

BANG

BANG

BUMBUMBUMBUM

SHEPHERD! DO SOMETHING!

I AM.

I'M FINISHING THE *RACE.*

WHAT ARE YOU *WAITING* FOR, WYLIE?

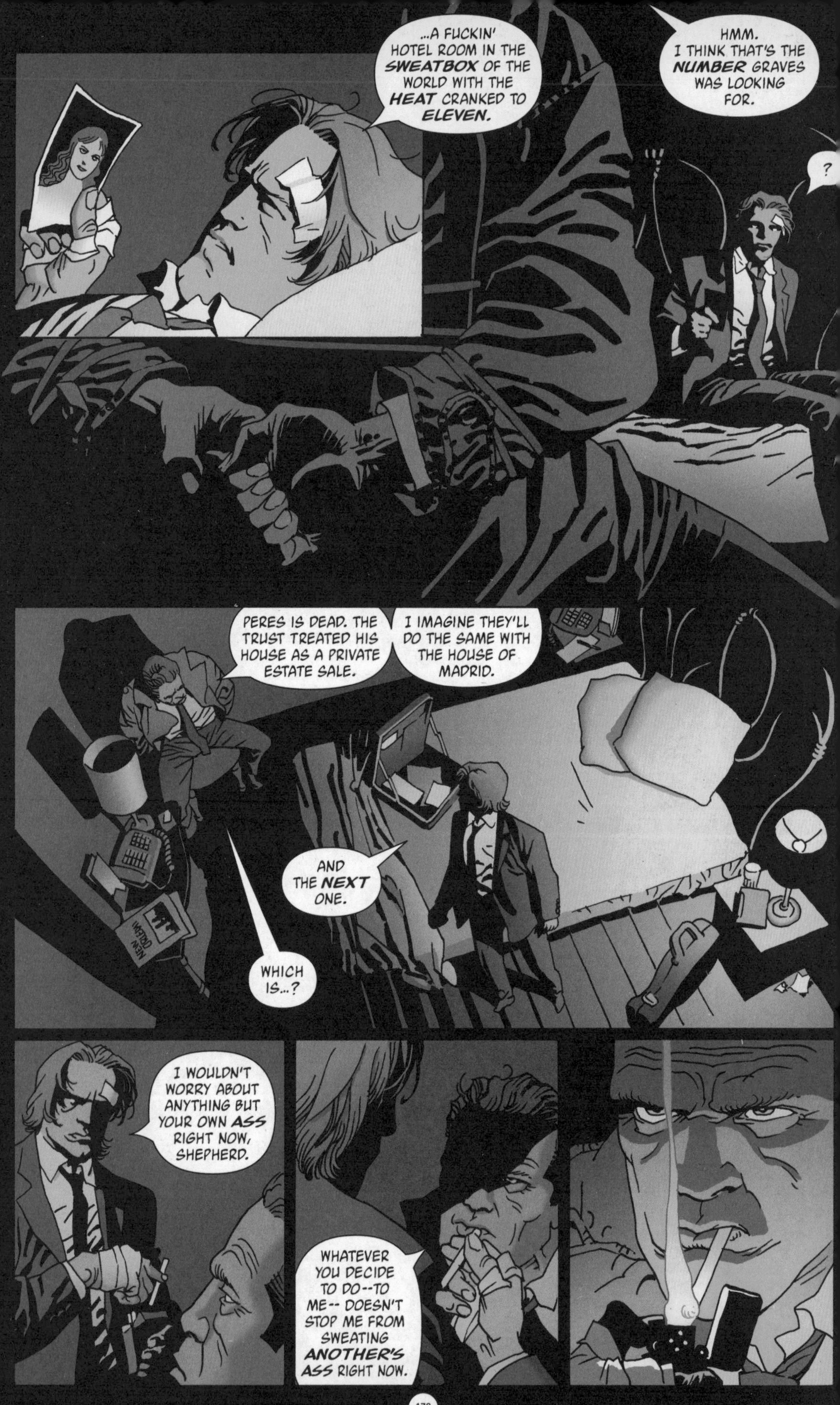
...A FUCKIN' HOTEL ROOM IN THE SWEATBOX OF THE WORLD WITH THE HEAT CRANKED TO ELEVEN.
HMM. I THINK THAT'S THE NUMBER GRAVES WAS LOOKING FOR.
?
PERES IS DEAD. THE TRUST TREATED HIS HOUSE AS A PRIVATE ESTATE SALE.
I IMAGINE THEY'LL DO THE SAME WITH THE HOUSE OF MADRID.
AND THE NEXT ONE.
WHICH IS...?
I WOULDN'T WORRY ABOUT ANYTHING BUT YOUR OWN ASS RIGHT NOW, SHEPHERD.
WHATEVER YOU DECIDE TO DO--TO ME-- DOESN'T STOP ME FROM SWEATING ANOTHER'S ASS RIGHT NOW.

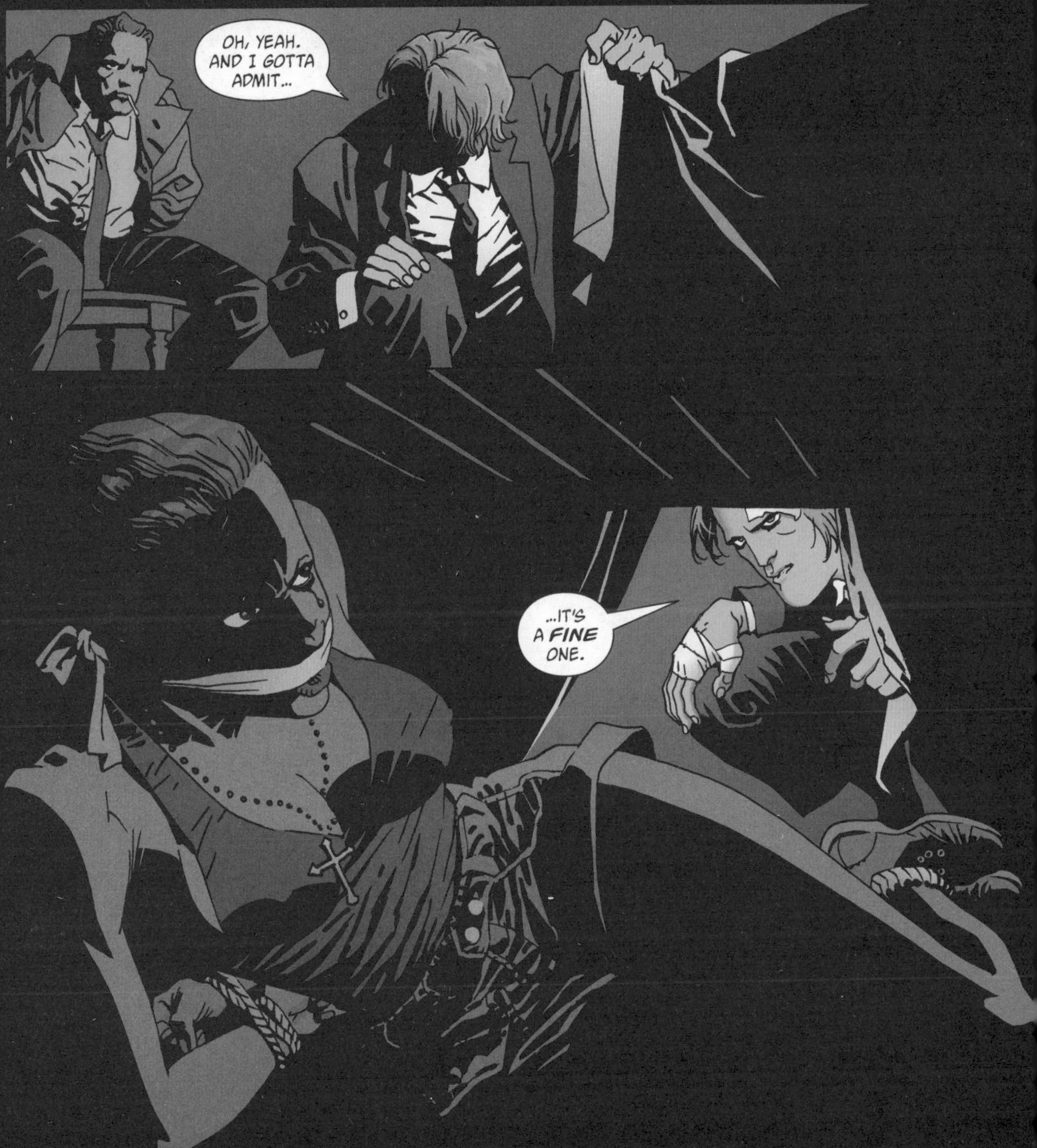
OH, YEAH. AND I GOTTA ADMIT...
...IT'S A FINE ONE.

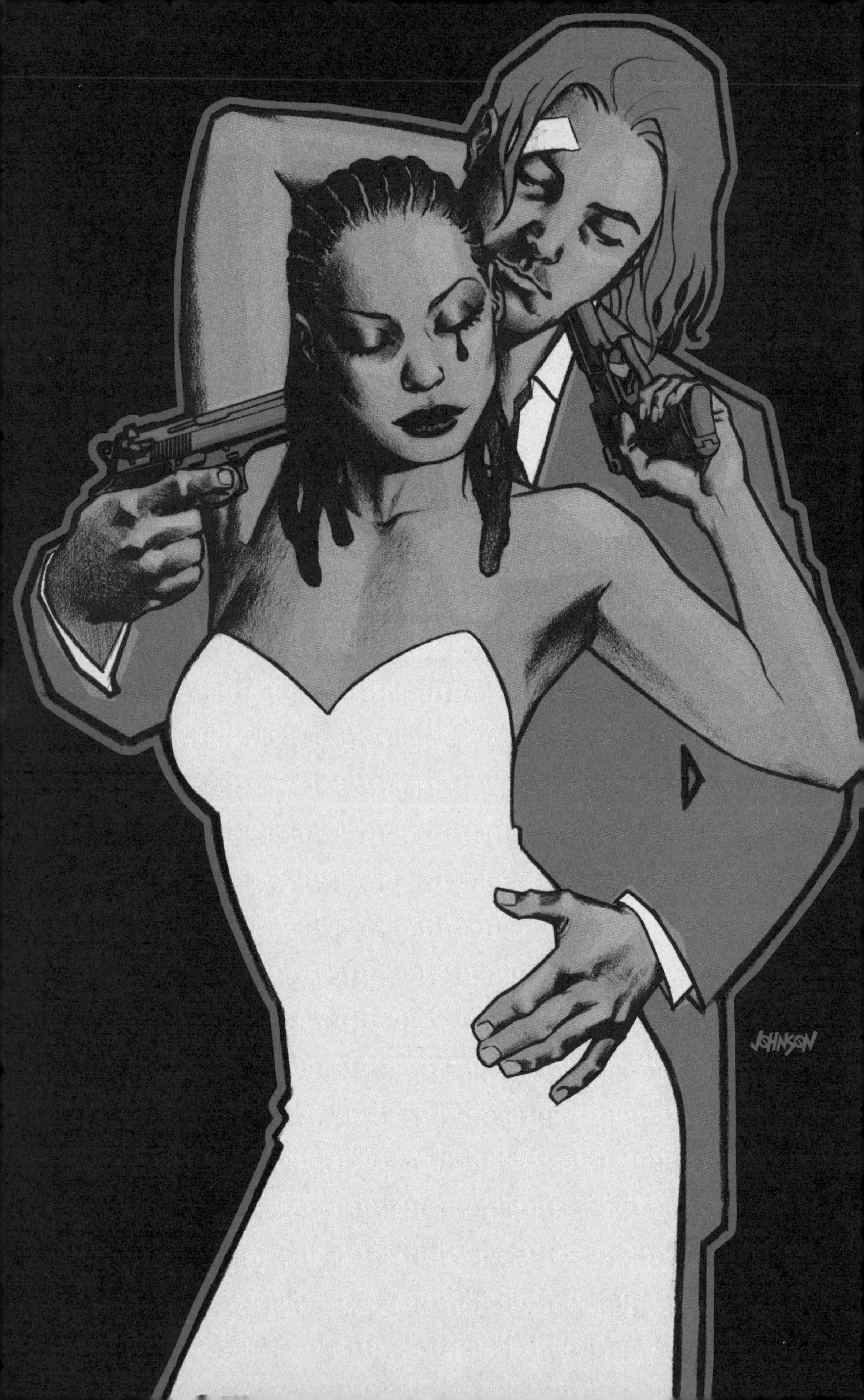
JOHNSON

"TOO MUCH FOR HER OWN GOOD, BUT NOT AT ALL WITH WHAT'S BETWEEN YOU AND ME."

PLEASE CLEAN THIS ROOM

PLEASE

"THAT'D BE TRUE IF SHE'D WAITED IN THE BAR LIKE I TOLD HER."

"HA...I TOLD HER THE SAME."

"AIN'T THAT A BITCH, SHE DIDN'T LISTEN TO EITHER ONE OF US."

"NOR DID SHE LISTEN TO GRAVES. HE CAME FOR HER TONIGHT."

"SHE'S BEEN TRAINED, WYLIE."

"WHY? WHAT'S DIZZY TO GRAVES?"

"FOR?"

"--AS A REPLACEMENT. ONE OF THE SEVEN."

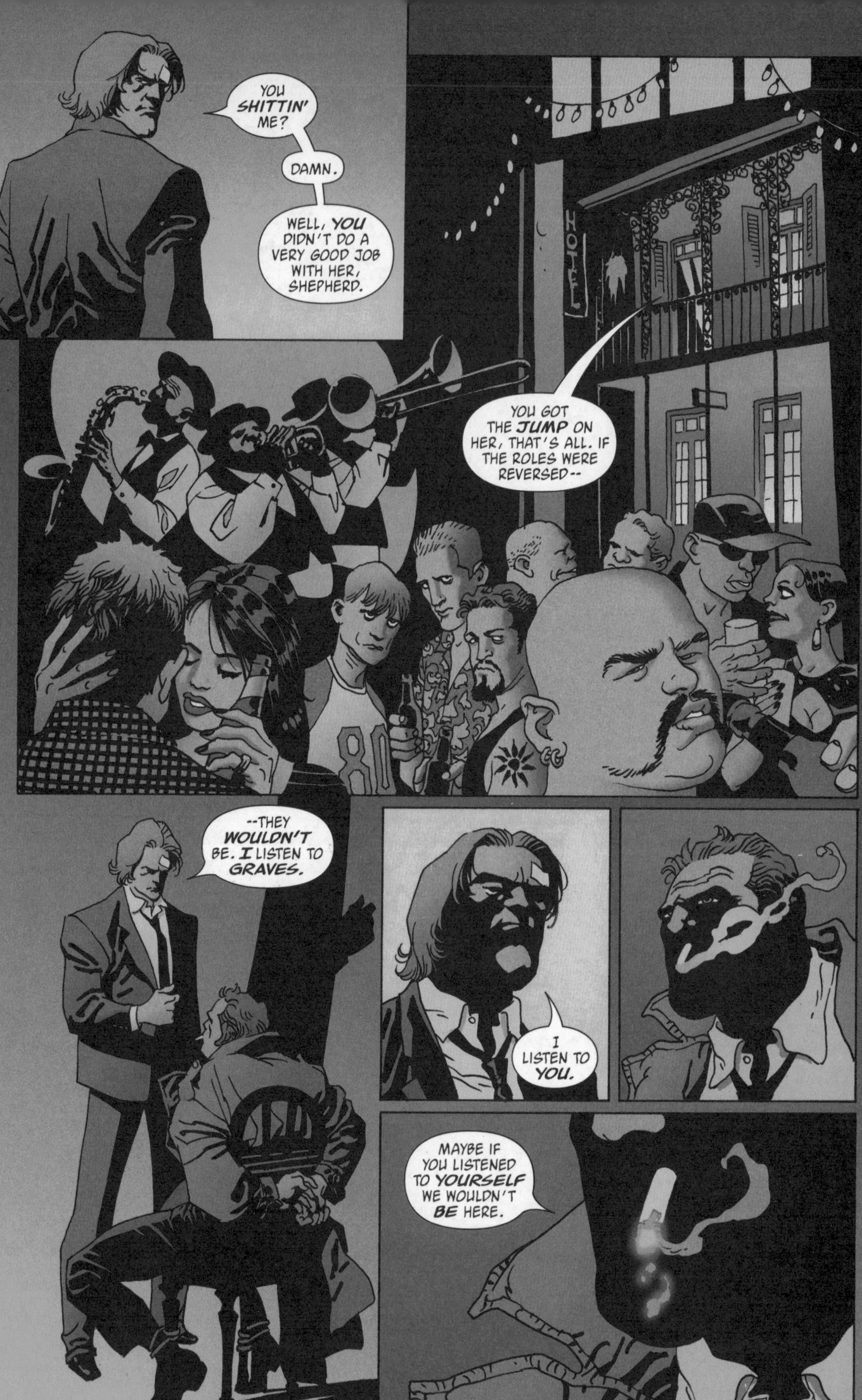
YOU SHITTIN' ME?
DAMN.
WELL, YOU DIDN'T DO A VERY GOOD JOB WITH HER, SHEPHERD.
HOTEL
YOU GOT THE JUMP ON HER, THAT'S ALL. IF THE ROLES WERE REVERSED--
80
--THEY WOULDN'T BE. I LISTEN TO GRAVES.
I LISTEN TO YOU.
MAYBE IF YOU LISTENED TO YOURSELF WE WOULDN'T BE HERE.

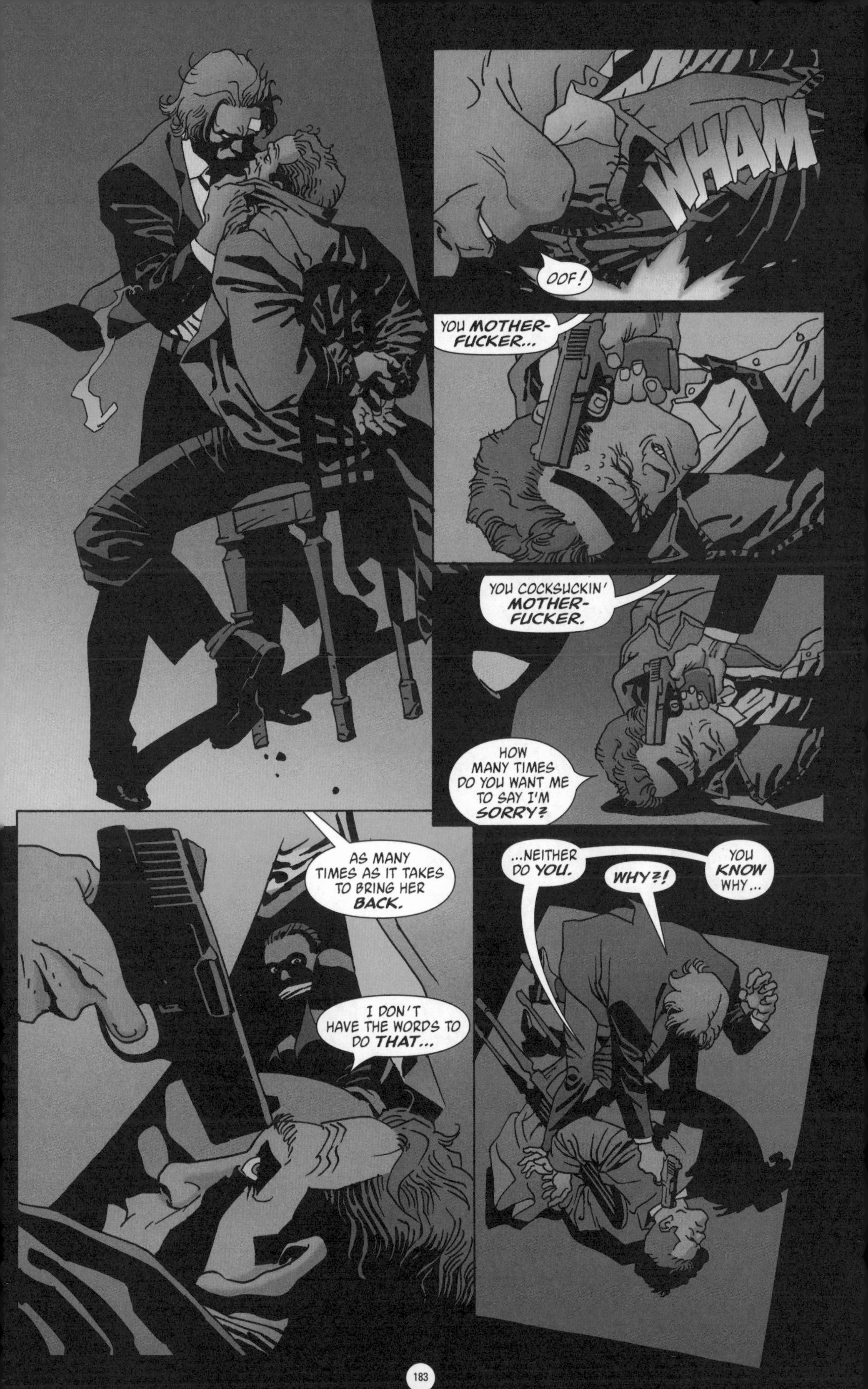
WHAM
OOF!
YOU MOTHER-FUCKER...
YOU COCKSUCKIN' MOTHER-FUCKER.
HOW MANY TIMES DO YOU WANT ME TO SAY I'M SORRY?
AS MANY TIMES AS IT TAKES TO BRING HER BACK.
I DON'T HAVE THE WORDS TO DO THAT...
...NEITHER DO YOU.
WHY?!
YOU KNOW WHY...

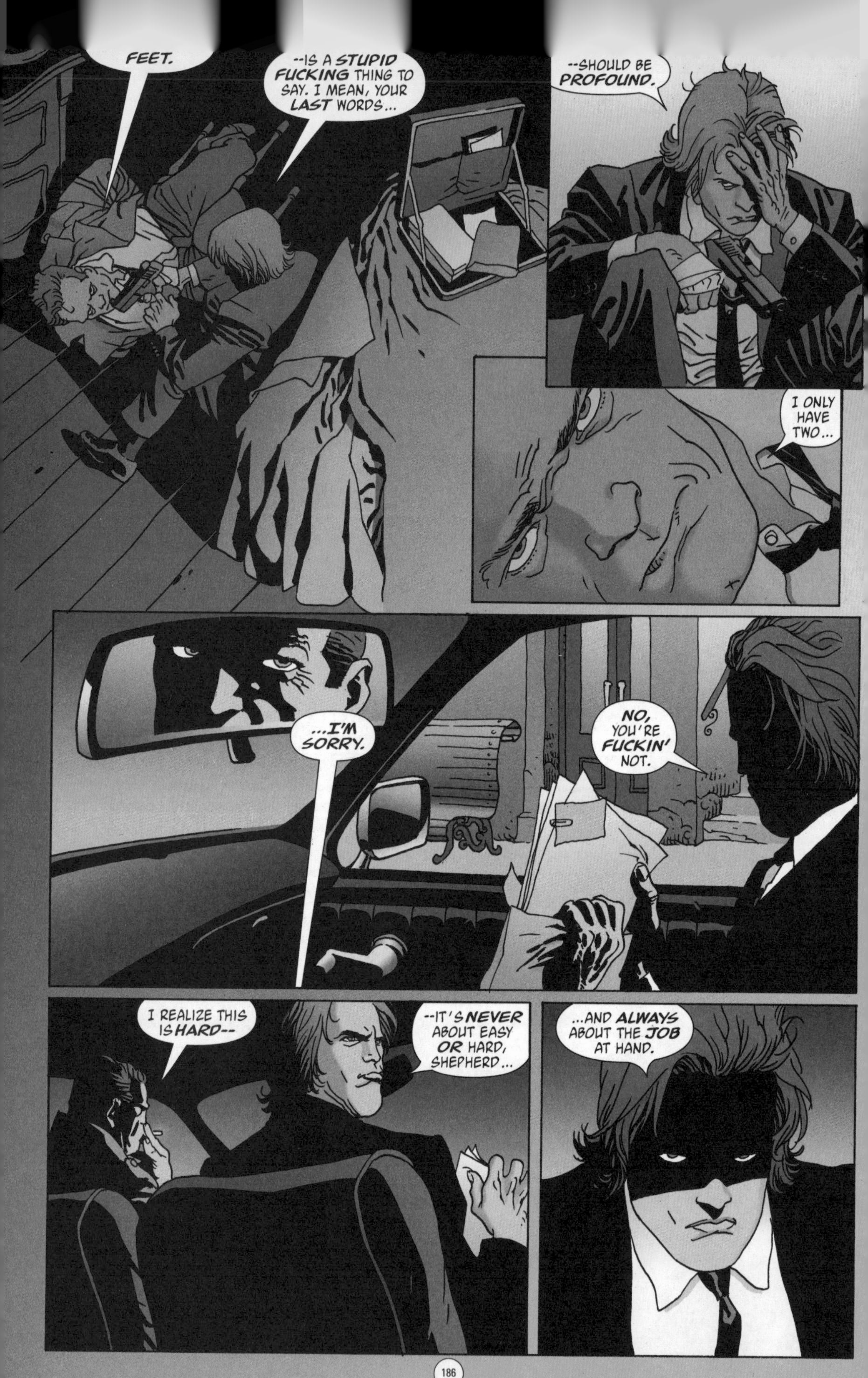

FEET.
--IS A STUPID FUCKING THING TO SAY. I MEAN, YOUR LAST WORDS...
--SHOULD BE PROFOUND.
I ONLY HAVE TWO...
...I'M SORRY.
NO, YOU'RE FUCKIN' NOT.
I REALIZE THIS IS HARD--
--IT'S NEVER ABOUT EASY OR HARD, SHEPHERD...
...AND ALWAYS ABOUT THE JOB AT HAND.

THAT WAS ONE OF THE FIRST THINGS YOU TAUGHT ME. AND RIGHT NOW...

...I FEEL *FUCKED* FOR EVER GOING TO YOUR *SCHOOL.*

ORLEAN HOTEL

SO THIS IS IT, HUH?

WHAT?

GRADUATION DAY.

ORLEANS HOTEL

"WHEN YOU WALKED OUT OF THE CAR, I *WAS* SORRY..."

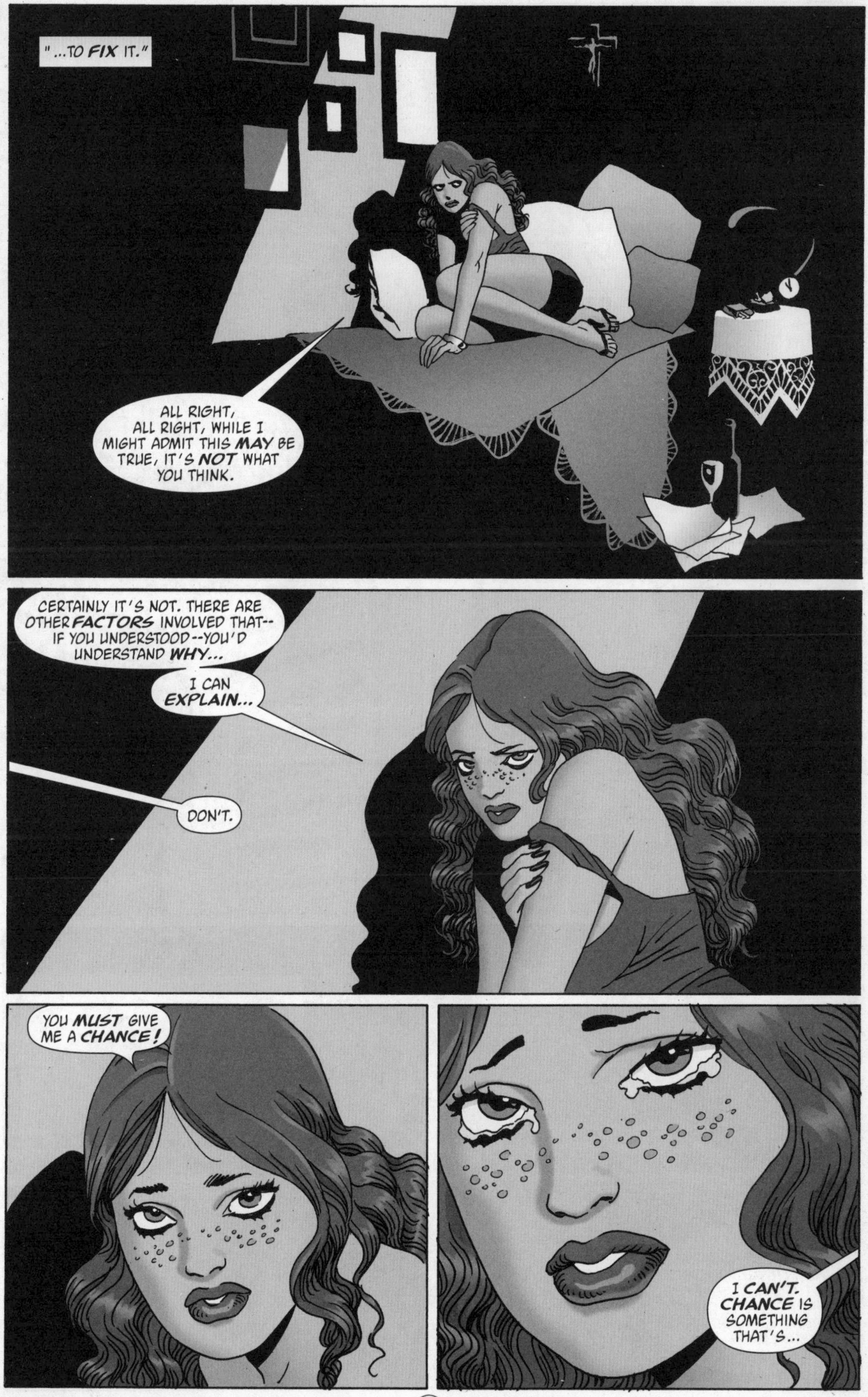
"...TO FIX IT."
ALL RIGHT, ALL RIGHT, WHILE I MIGHT ADMIT THIS MAY BE TRUE, IT'S NOT WHAT YOU THINK.
CERTAINLY IT'S NOT. THERE ARE OTHER FACTORS INVOLVED THAT-- IF YOU UNDERSTOOD--YOU'D UNDERSTAND WHY...
I CAN EXPLAIN...
DON'T.
YOU MUST GIVE ME A CHANCE!
I CAN'T. CHANCE IS SOMETHING THAT'S...

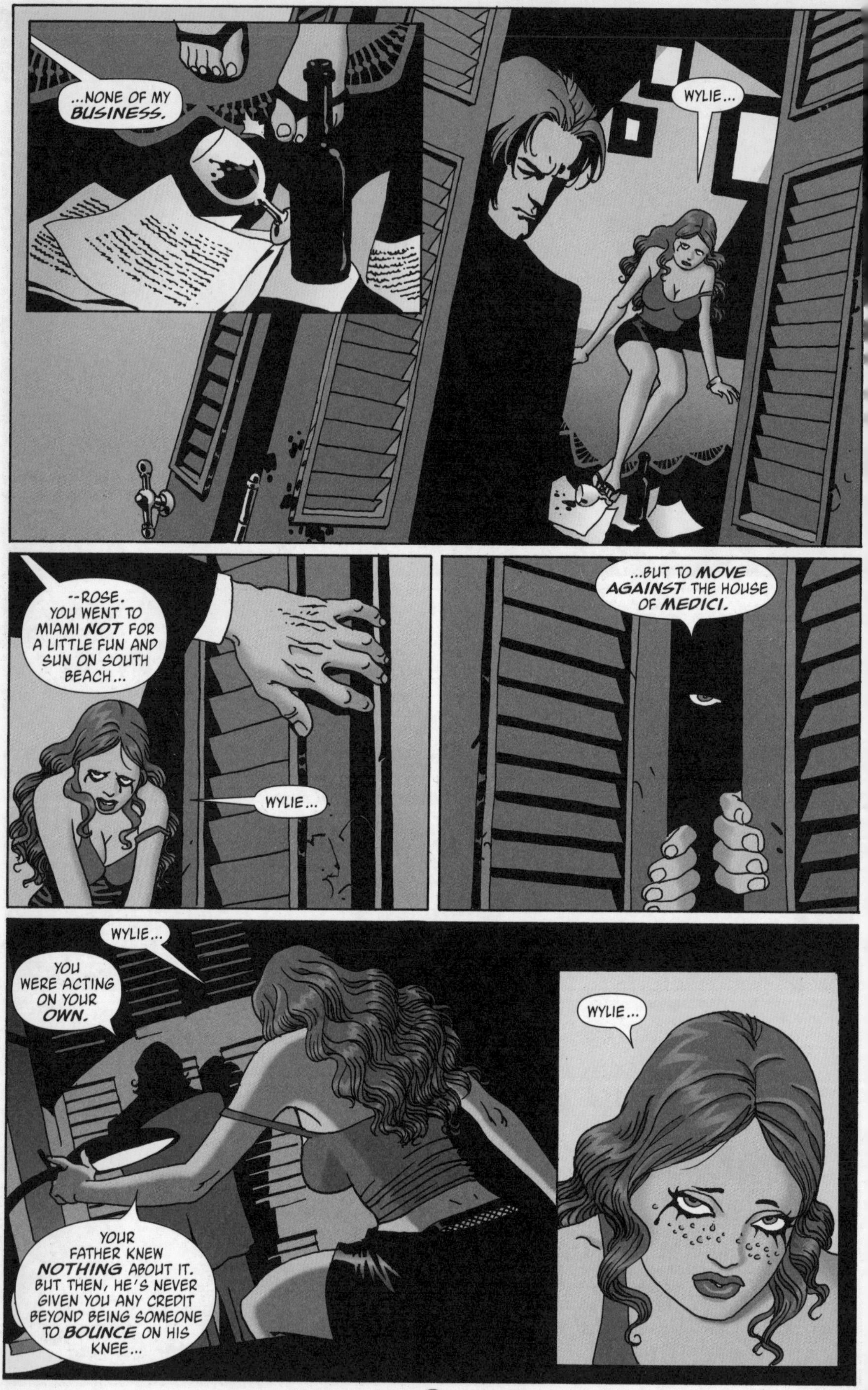
...NONE OF MY BUSINESS.
WYLIE...
--ROSE. YOU WENT TO MIAMI NOT FOR A LITTLE FUN AND SUN ON SOUTH BEACH...
WYLIE...
...BUT TO MOVE AGAINST THE HOUSE OF MEDICI.
WYLIE...
YOU WERE ACTING ON YOUR OWN.
YOUR FATHER KNEW NOTHING ABOUT IT. BUT THEN, HE'S NEVER GIVEN YOU ANY CREDIT BEYOND BEING SOMEONE TO BOUNCE ON HIS KNEE...
WYLIE...

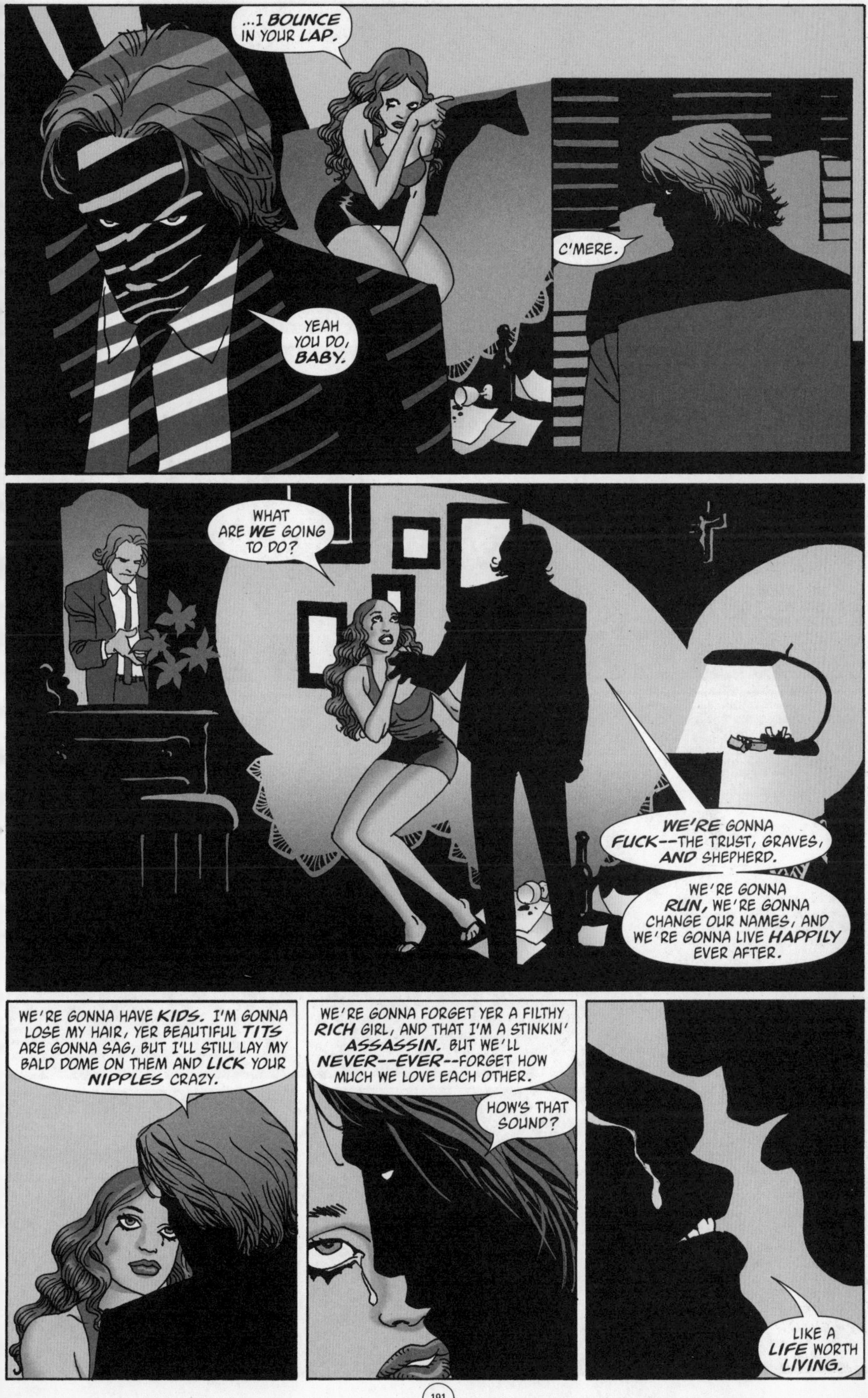
...I BOUNCE IN YOUR LAP.
YEAH YOU DO, BABY.
C'MERE.
WHAT ARE WE GOING TO DO?
WE'RE GONNA FUCK--THE TRUST, GRAVES, AND SHEPHERD.
WE'RE GONNA RUN, WE'RE GONNA CHANGE OUR NAMES, AND WE'RE GONNA LIVE HAPPILY EVER AFTER.
WE'RE GONNA HAVE KIDS. I'M GONNA LOSE MY HAIR, YER BEAUTIFUL TITS ARE GONNA SAG, BUT I'LL STILL LAY MY BALD DOME ON THEM AND LICK YOUR NIPPLES CRAZY.
WE'RE GONNA FORGET YER A FILTHY RICH GIRL, AND THAT I'M A STINKIN' ASSASSIN. BUT WE'LL NEVER--EVER--FORGET HOW MUCH WE LOVE EACH OTHER.
HOW'S THAT SOUND?
LIKE A LIFE WORTH LIVING.

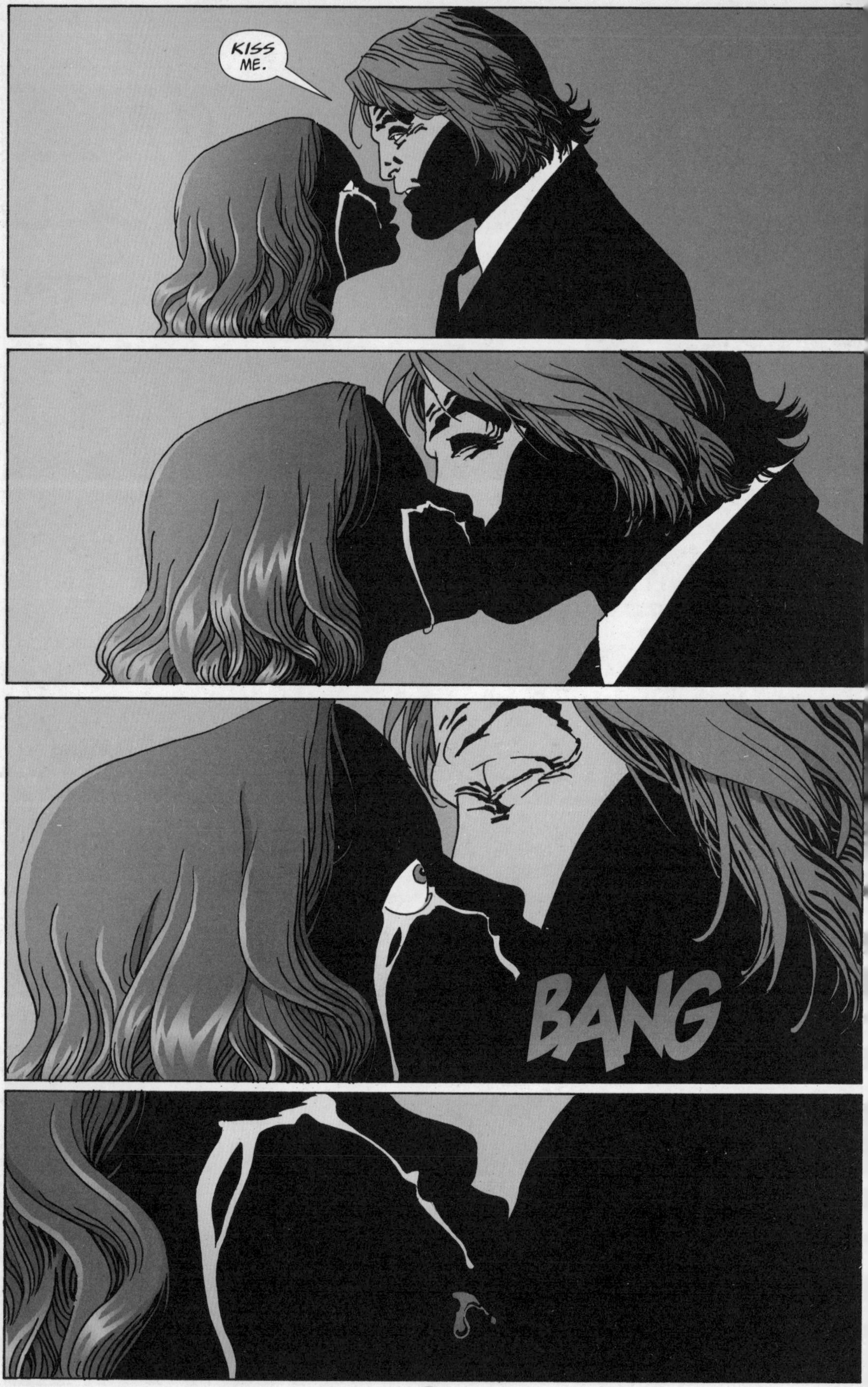
KISS ME.
BANG

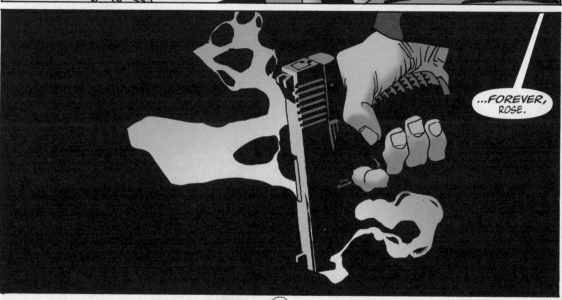

...FOREVER, ROSE.

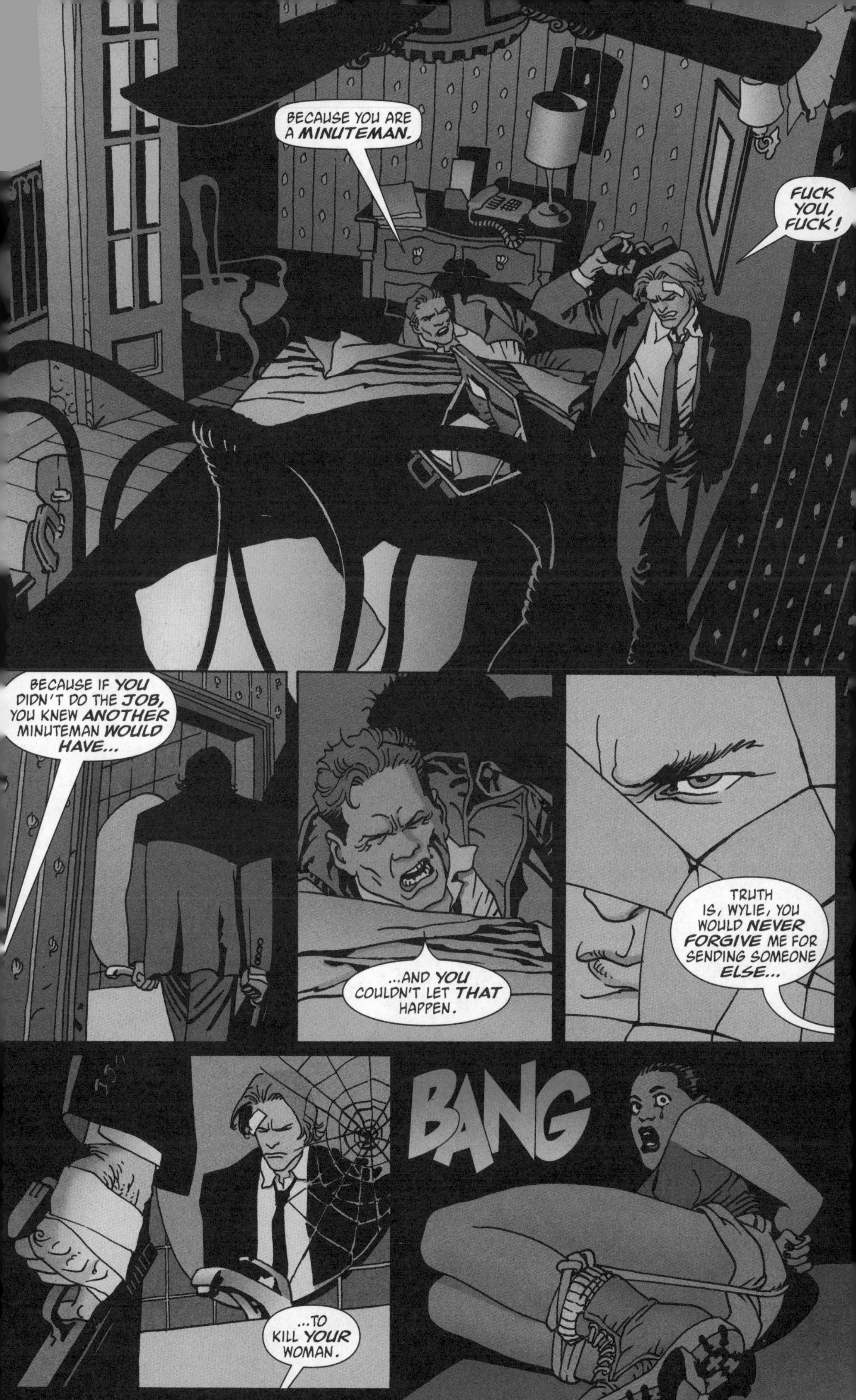
BECAUSE YOU ARE A MINUTEMAN.
FUCK YOU, FUCK!
BECAUSE IF YOU DIDN'T DO THE JOB, YOU KNEW ANOTHER MINUTEMAN WOULD HAVE...
...AND YOU COULDN'T LET THAT HAPPEN.
TRUTH IS, WYLIE, YOU WOULD NEVER FORGIVE ME FOR SENDING SOMEONE ELSE...
...TO KILL YOUR WOMAN.
BANG

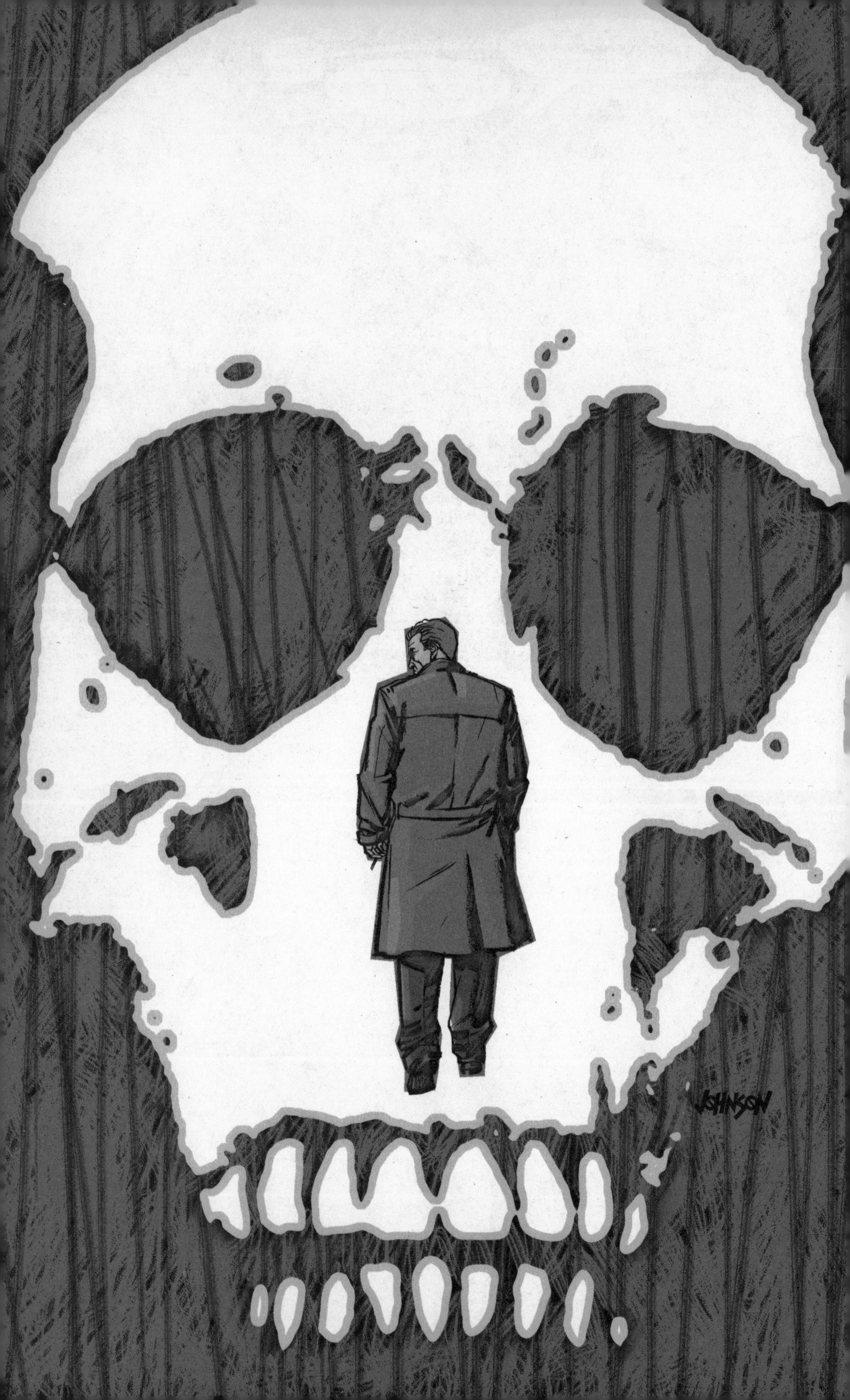
JOHNSON

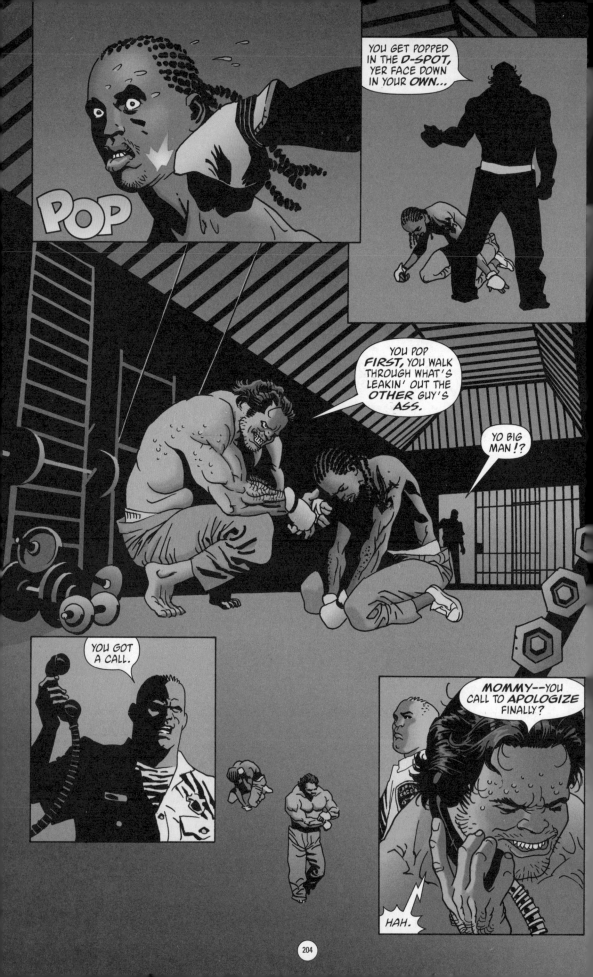

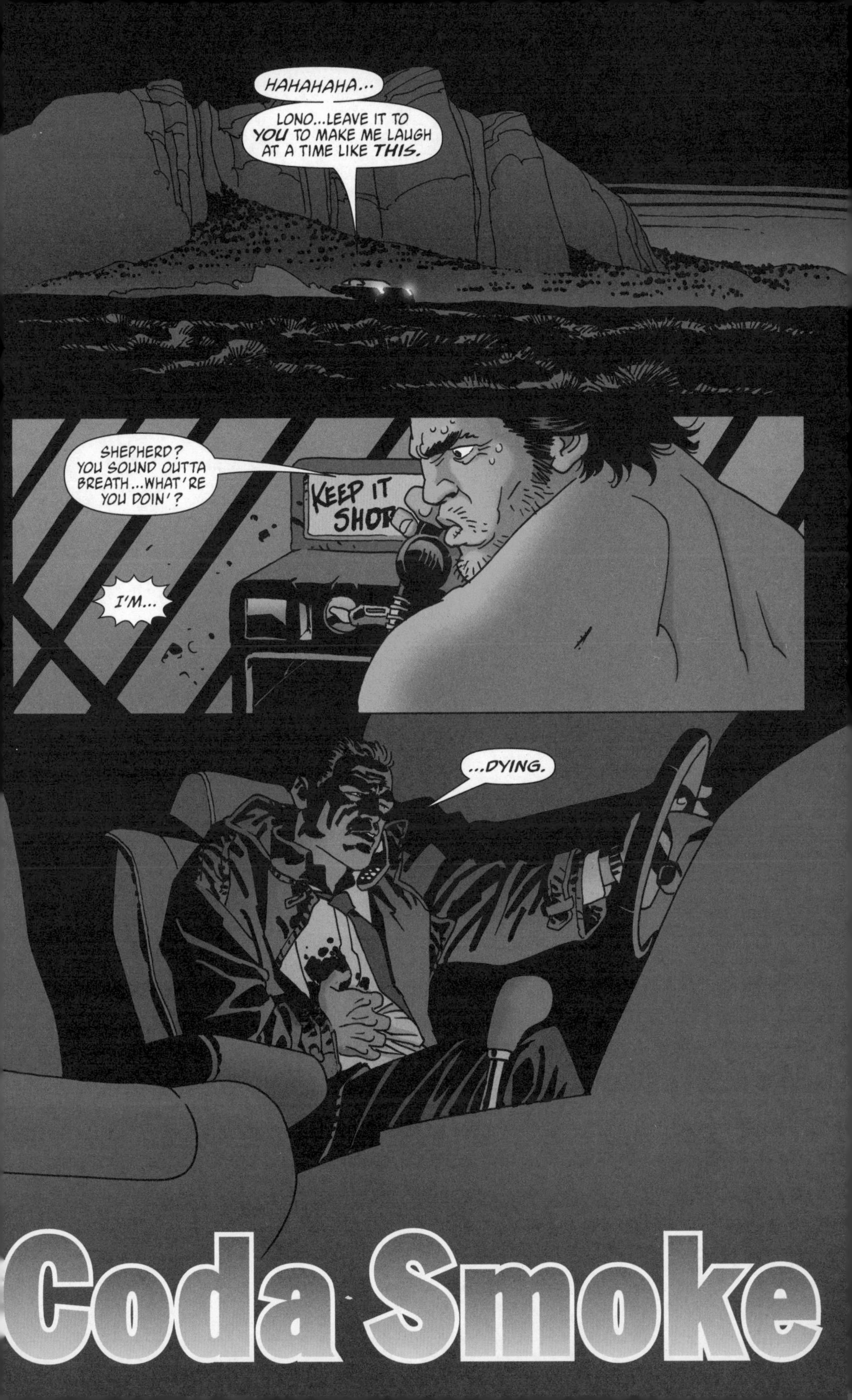
HAHAHAHA...
LONO...LEAVE IT TO YOU TO MAKE ME LAUGH AT A TIME LIKE THIS.
SHEPHERD? YOU SOUND OUTTA BREATH...WHAT'RE YOU DOIN'?
KEEP IT SHOR
I'M...
...DYING.
Coda Smoke

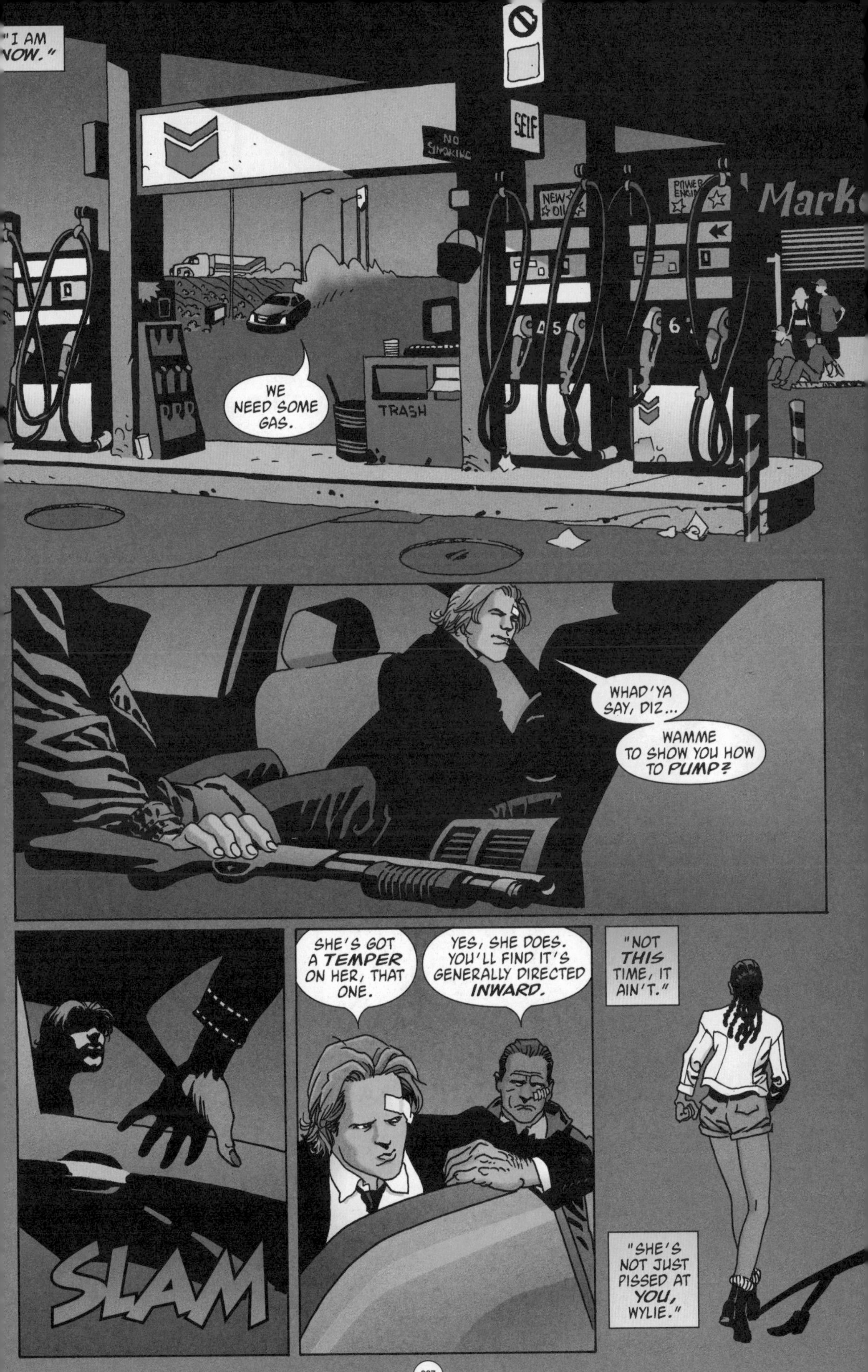
"I AM NOW."
SELF
NO SMOKING
NEW OIL
POWER ENGINE
Mark
TRASH
WE NEED SOME GAS.
WHAD'YA SAY, DIZ...
WAMME TO SHOW YOU HOW TO PUMP?
SLAM
SHE'S GOT A TEMPER ON HER, THAT ONE.
YES, SHE DOES. YOU'LL FIND IT'S GENERALLY DIRECTED INWARD.
"NOT THIS TIME, IT AIN'T."
"SHE'S NOT JUST PISSED AT YOU, WYLIE."

"WHEN I FIRST MET THAT GIRL, ALL SHE HAD WAS A **GUN** FROM GRAVES.

JUICE

BLUE DRINK

BOOK NEWS

lotto machine

XXXX....

SELECT YOUR LOTERY

DONE

23

4

07   15   5   10

32   18   8

22

Play here

SINCE THEN, I'VE TAUGHT HER A FEW TRICKS.

TV CLOSED

"IT WAS THE ONE THING THAT GAVE HER ANY **CONTROL** OF A LIFE SPINNING TRAGICALLY **OUT** OF IT."

I'LL BET.

SHE'S COME INTO HER OWN...BUT AFTER WHAT WENT DOWN IN NEW ORLEANS... SOME THINGS I SAID...

...SHE KNOWS **HER OWN** BELONGS TO SOMEONE **ELSE.**

AND SHE HAS **NO CONTROL** OVER IT.

SO YOU'RE NOT THE ONLY ONE WHO HAS TO **EARN** HER **TRUST** BACK.

NO SMOKING

SPEAKING OF THE **TRUST**...

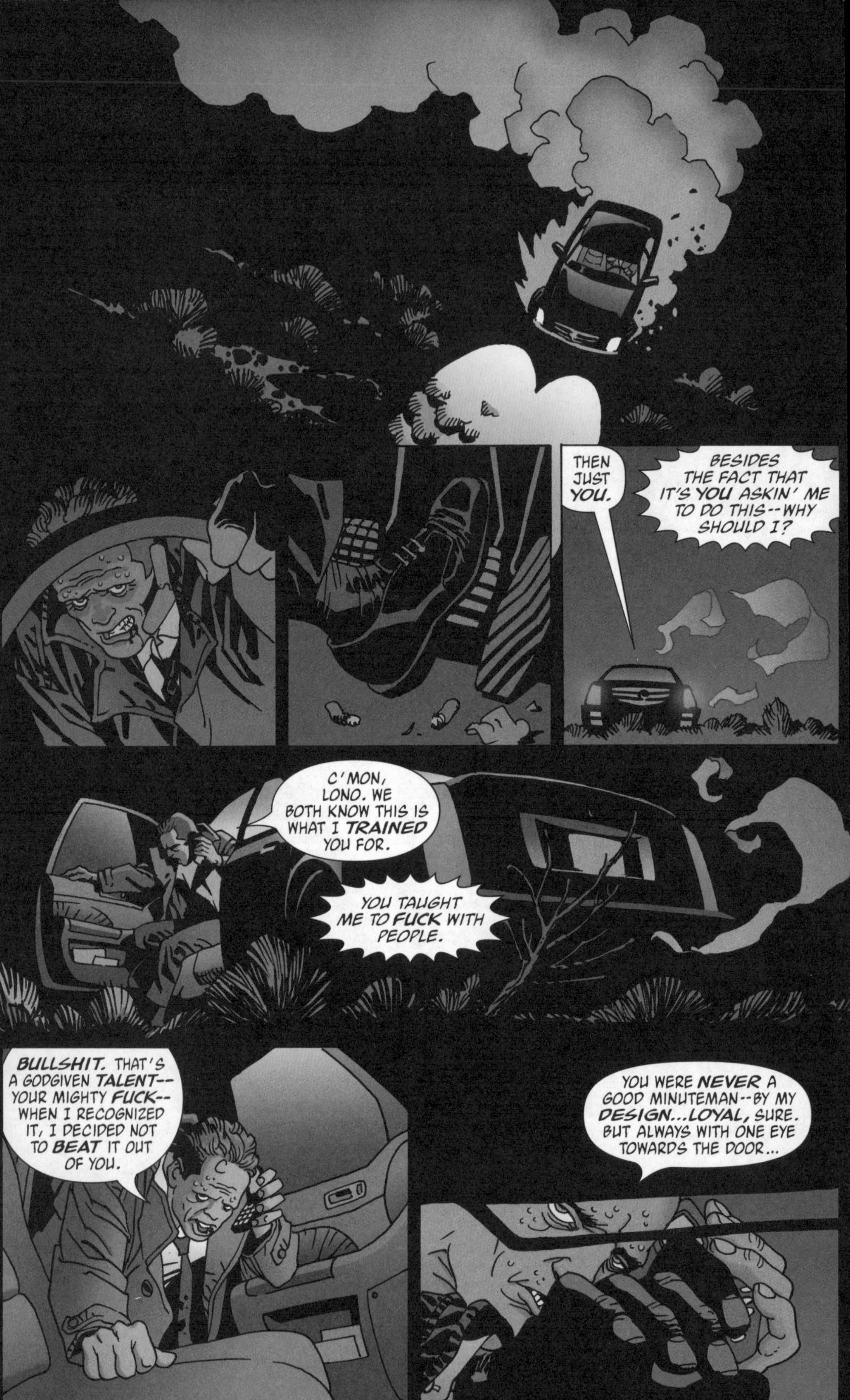
BESIDES THE FACT THAT IT'S YOU ASKIN' ME TO DO THIS--WHY SHOULD I?
THEN JUST YOU.
C'MON, LONO. WE BOTH KNOW THIS IS WHAT I TRAINED YOU FOR.
YOU TAUGHT ME TO FUCK WITH PEOPLE.
BULLSHIT. THAT'S A GODGIVEN TALENT--YOUR MIGHTY FUCK--WHEN I RECOGNIZED IT, I DECIDED NOT TO BEAT IT OUT OF YOU.
YOU WERE NEVER A GOOD MINUTEMAN--BY MY DESIGN...LOYAL, SURE. BUT ALWAYS WITH ONE EYE TOWARDS THE DOOR...

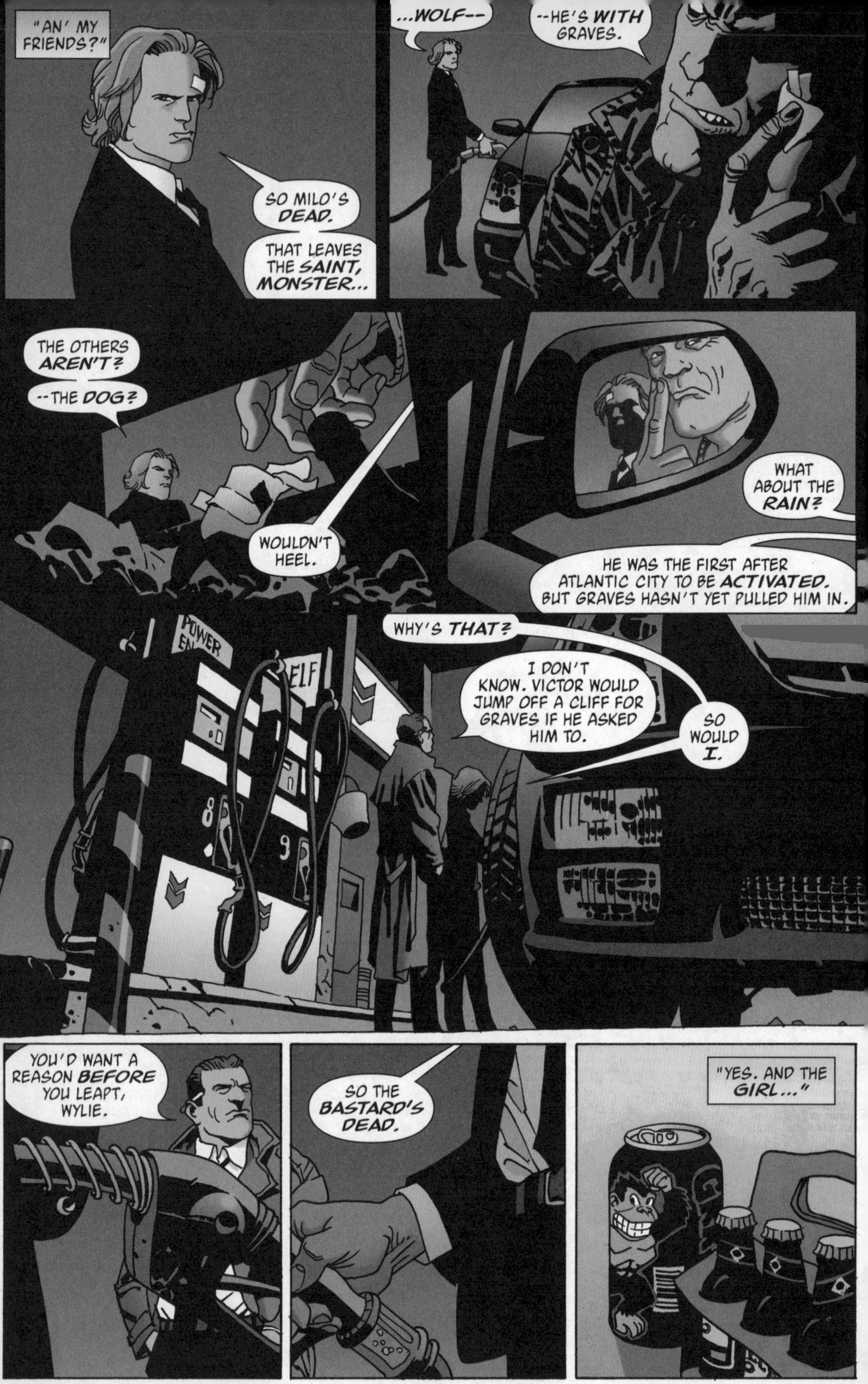
"AN' MY FRIENDS?"
SO MILO'S DEAD.
THAT LEAVES THE SAINT, MONSTER...
...WOLF--
--HE'S WITH GRAVES.
THE OTHERS AREN'T?
--THE DOG?
WOULDN'T HEEL.
WHAT ABOUT THE RAIN?
HE WAS THE FIRST AFTER ATLANTIC CITY TO BE ACTIVATED. BUT GRAVES HASN'T YET PULLED HIM IN.
WHY'S THAT?
I DON'T KNOW. VICTOR WOULD JUMP OFF A CLIFF FOR GRAVES IF HE ASKED HIM TO.
SO WOULD I.
YOU'D WANT A REASON BEFORE YOU LEAPT, WYLIE.
SO THE BASTARD'S DEAD.
"YES. AND THE GIRL..."

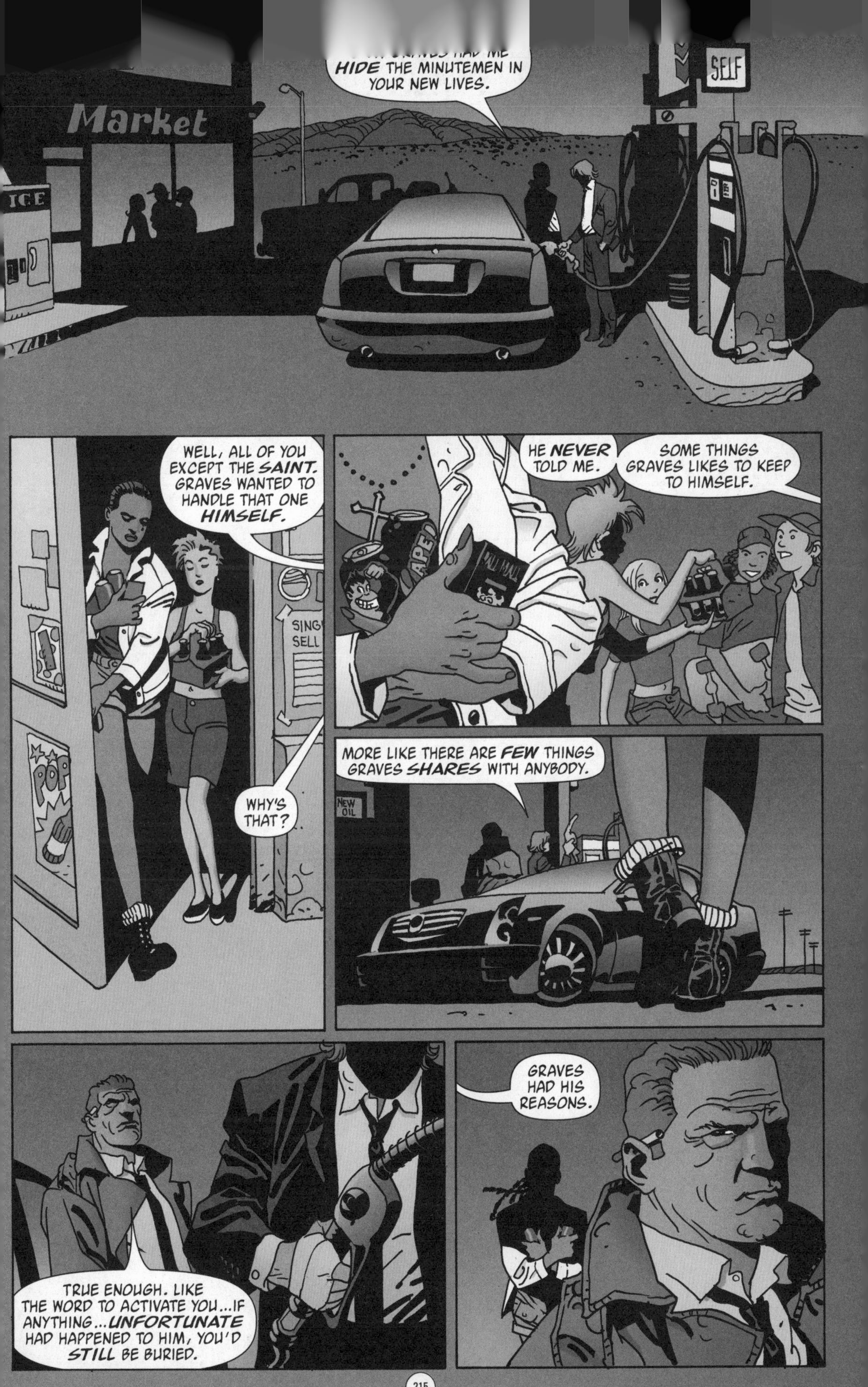
HIDE THE MINUTEMEN IN YOUR NEW LIVES.
Market
ICE
SELF
WELL, ALL OF YOU EXCEPT THE SAINT. GRAVES WANTED TO HANDLE THAT ONE HIMSELF.
WHY'S THAT?
HE NEVER TOLD ME.
SOME THINGS GRAVES LIKES TO KEEP TO HIMSELF.
MORE LIKE THERE ARE FEW THINGS GRAVES SHARES WITH ANYBODY.
NEW OIL
TRUE ENOUGH. LIKE THE WORD TO ACTIVATE YOU...IF ANYTHING...UNFORTUNATE HAD HAPPENED TO HIM, YOU'D STILL BE BURIED.
GRAVES HAD HIS REASONS.

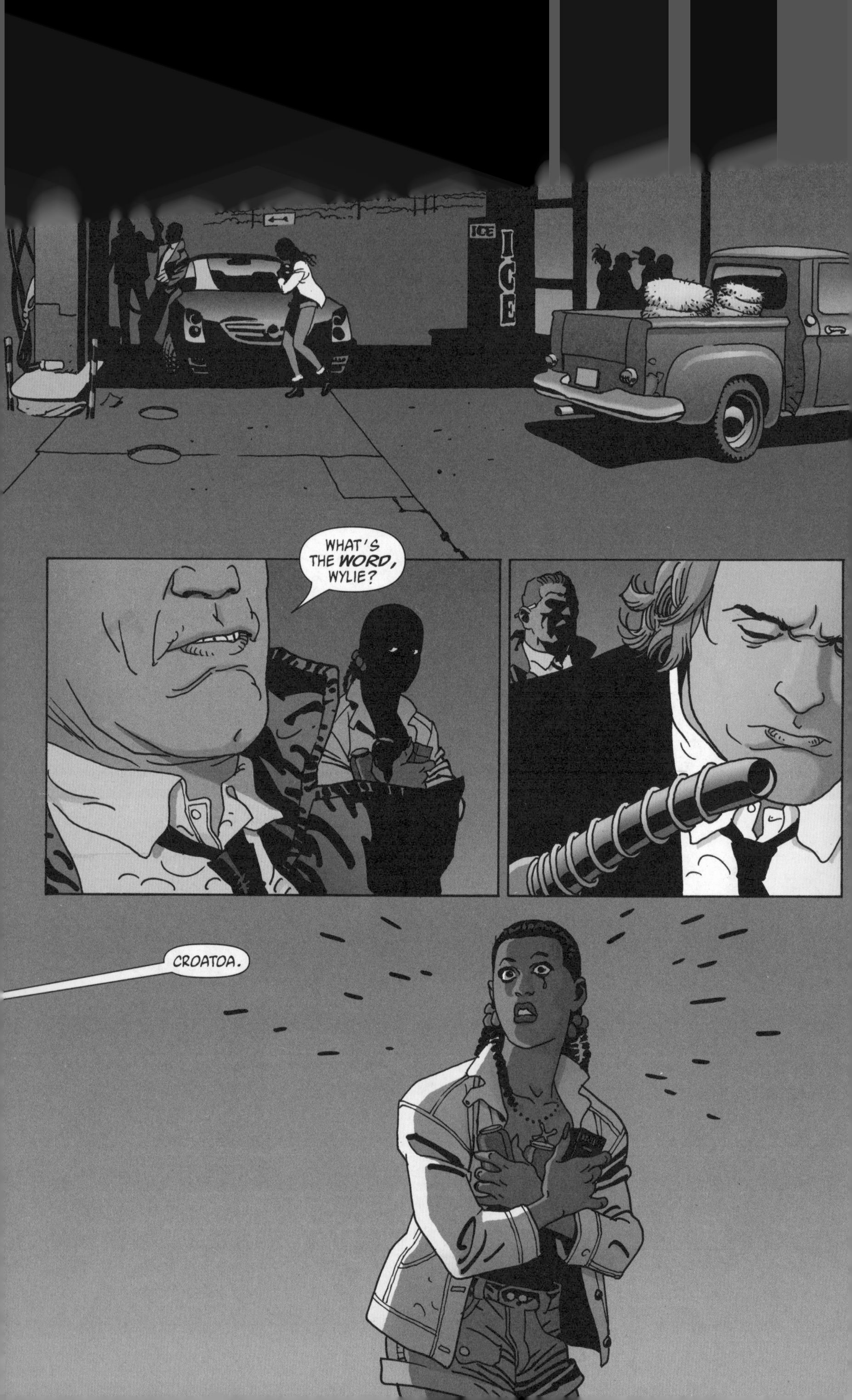
ICE
ICE
WHAT'S THE **WORD,** WYLIE?
CROATOA.

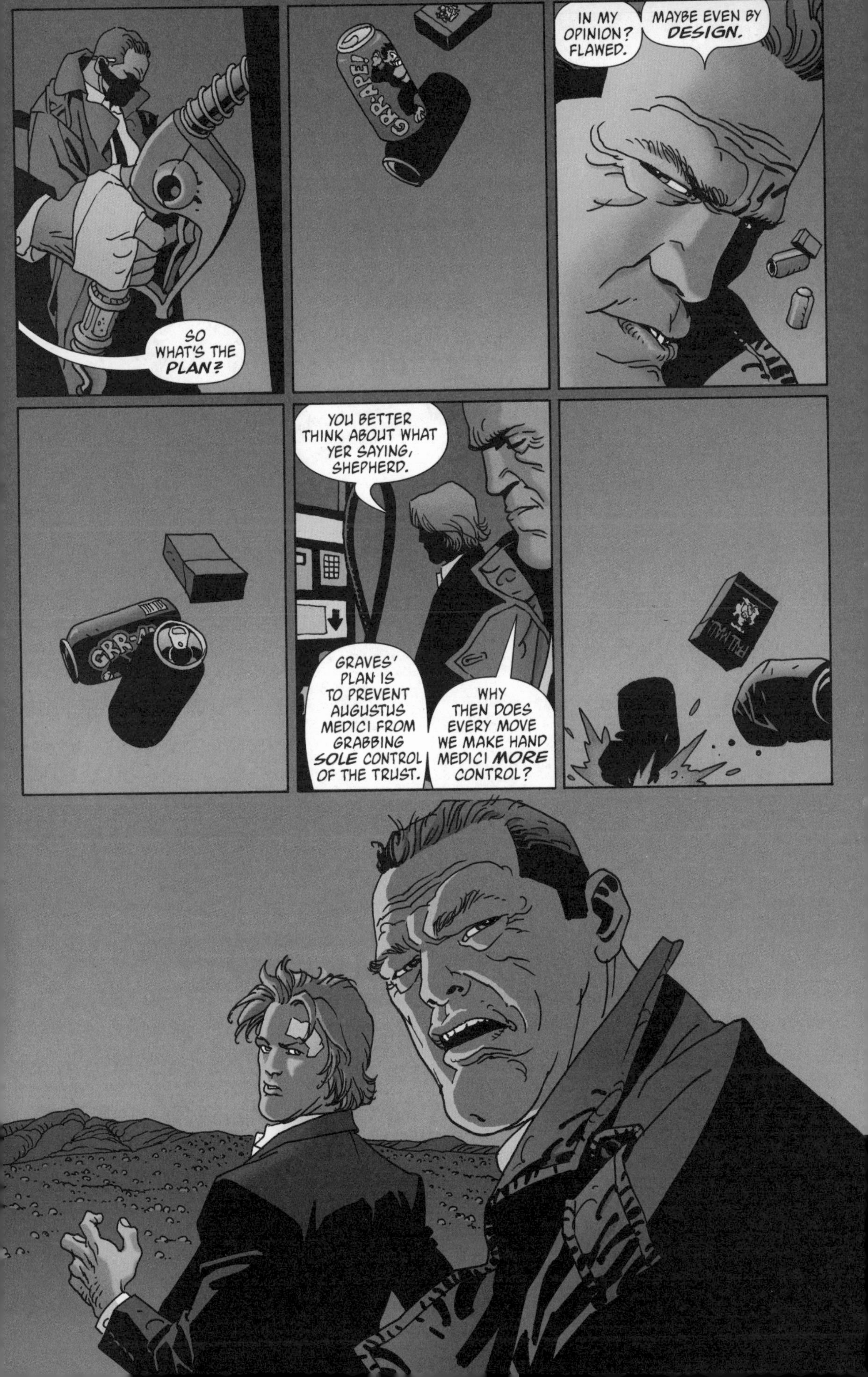
SO WHAT'S THE PLAN?
GRR-APE!
IN MY OPINION? FLAWED.
MAYBE EVEN BY DESIGN.
GRR-A
YOU BETTER THINK ABOUT WHAT YER SAYING, SHEPHERD.
GRAVES' PLAN IS TO PREVENT AUGUSTUS MEDICI FROM GRABBING SOLE CONTROL OF THE TRUST.
WHY THEN DOES EVERY MOVE WE MAKE HAND MEDICI MORE CONTROL?

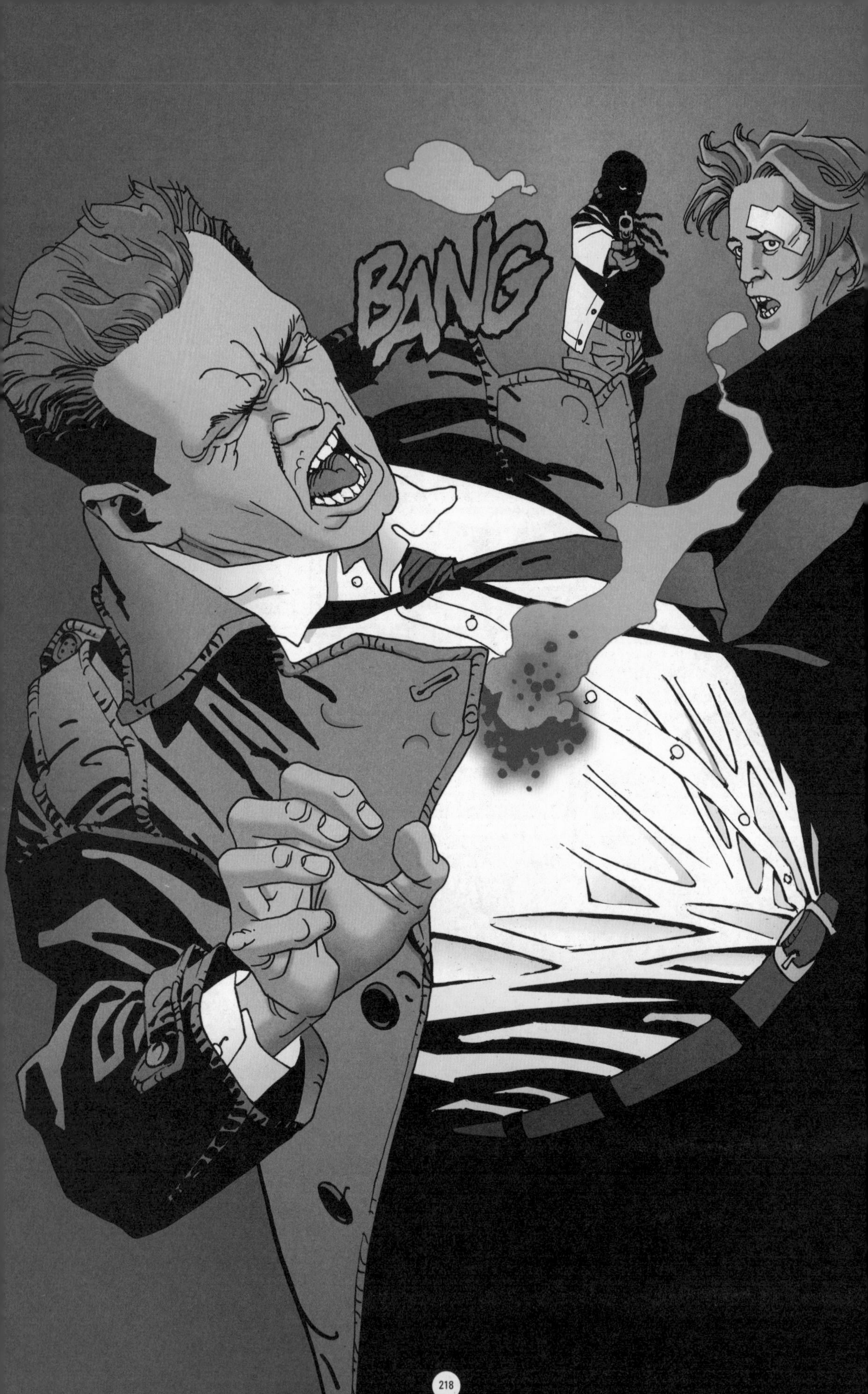
BANG

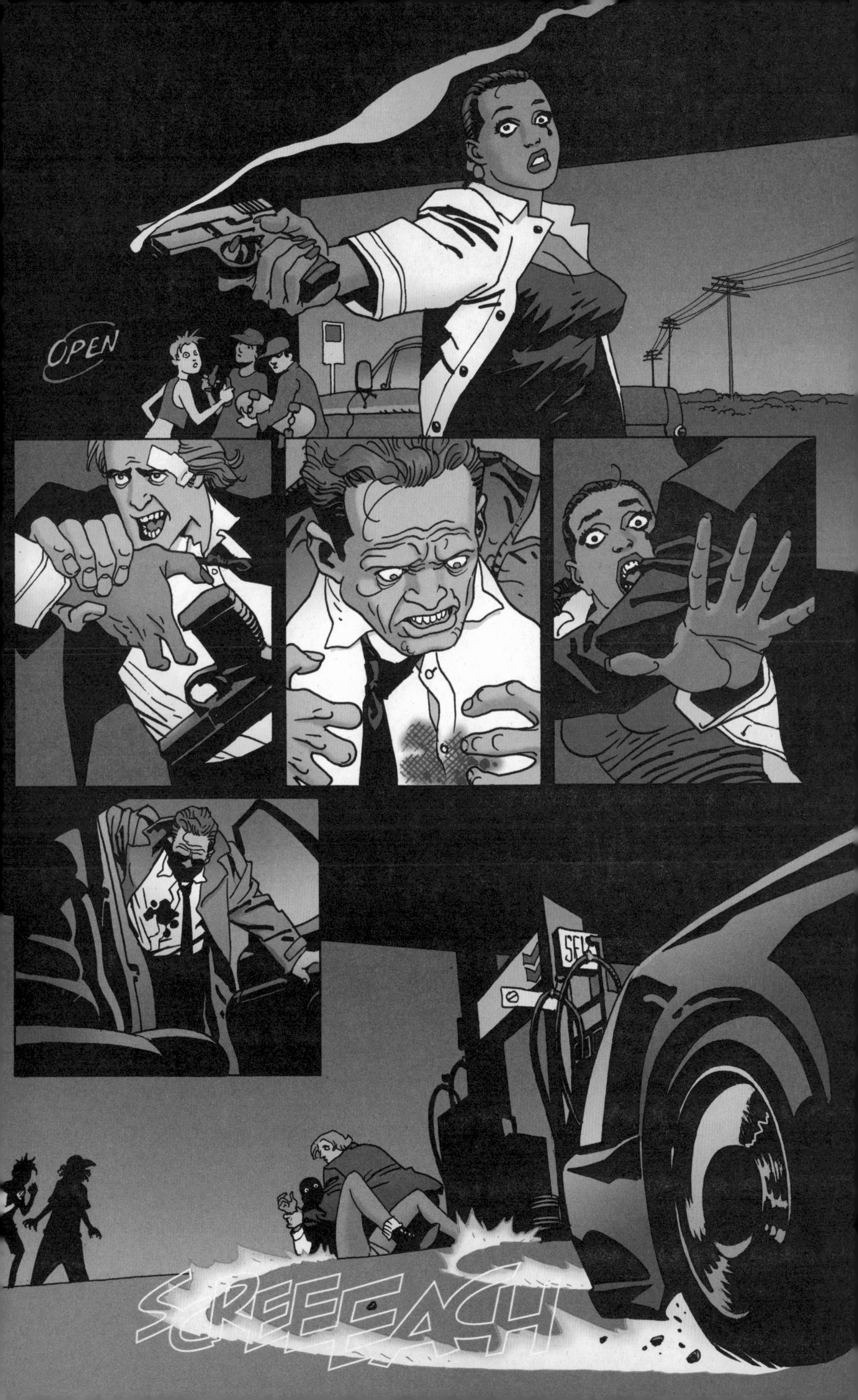
OPEN
SCREEEACH

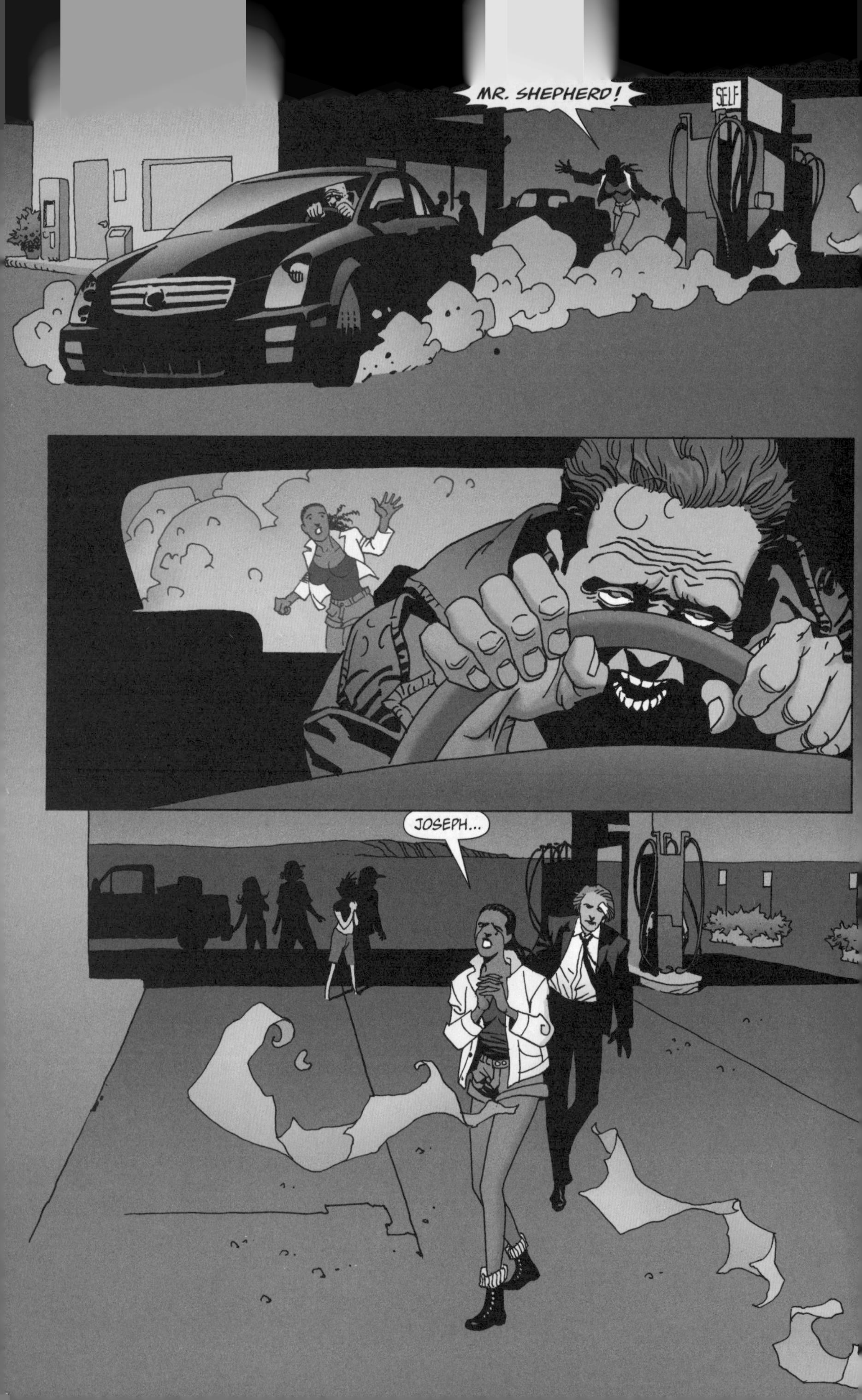
MR. SHEPHERD!
SELF
JOSEPH...

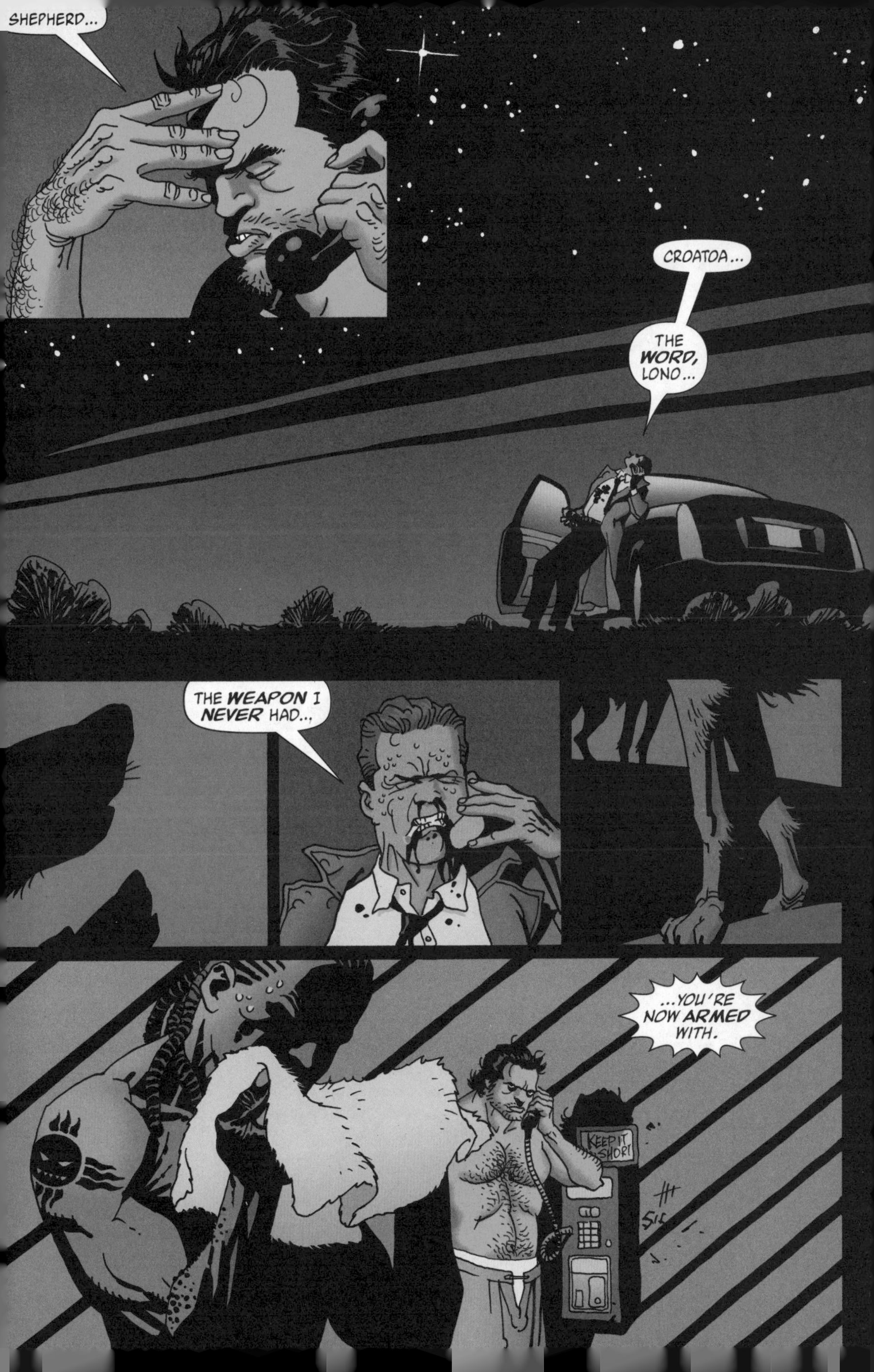
SHEPHERD...
CROATOA...
THE WORD, LONO...
THE WEAPON I NEVER HAD...,
...YOU'RE NOW ARMED WITH.
KEEP IT SHORT

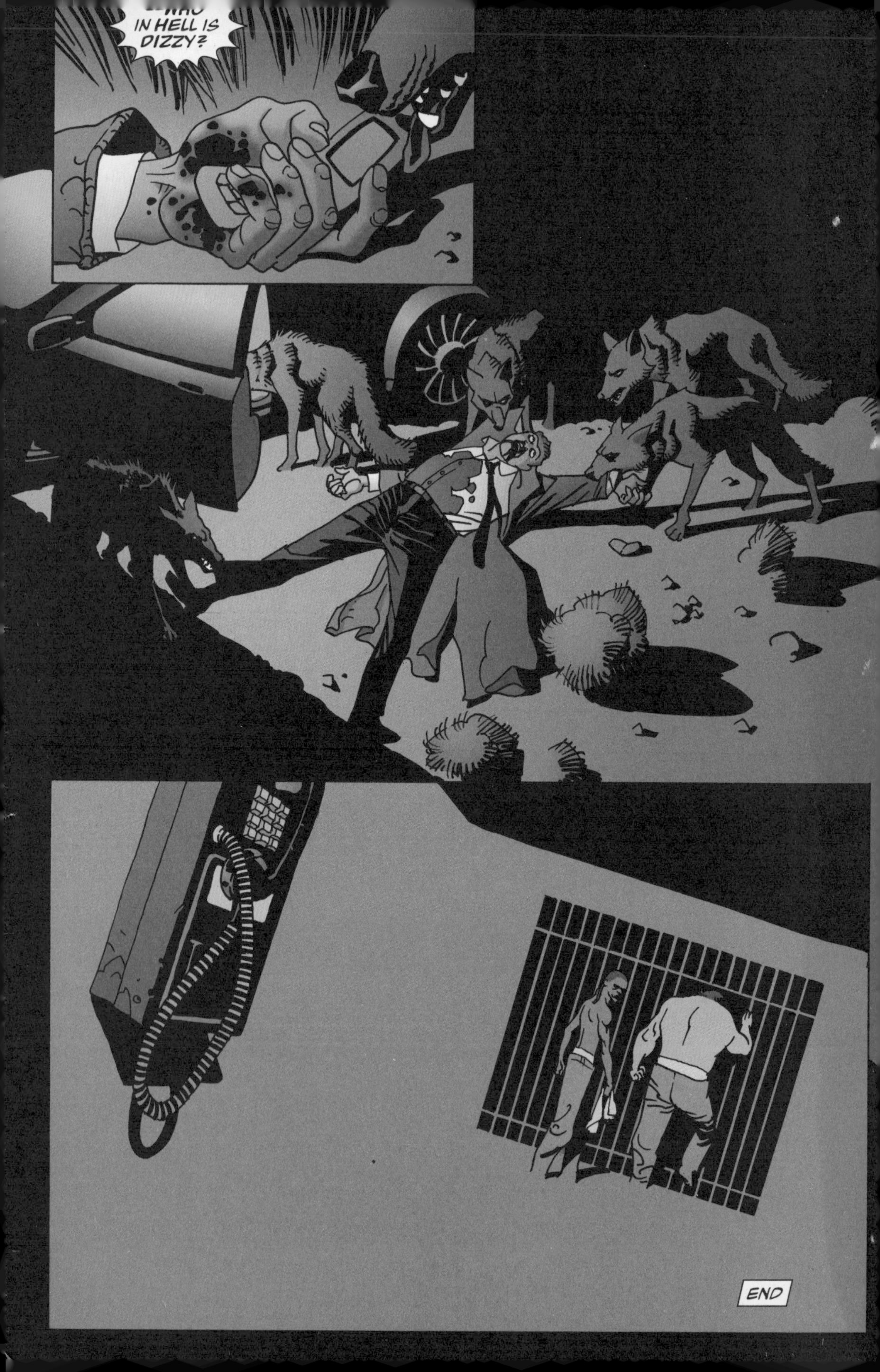
—WHO IN HELL IS DIZZY?
END